I0824555

FIRESPITTER

FIRESPITTER

THE COLLECTED POEMS OF JAYNE CORTEZ

EDITED BY MARGARET BUSBY

FOREWORD BY SAPPHIRE

NIGHTBOAT BOOKS

NEW YORK

Copyright © 2025 by the Estate of Jayne Cortez
Introduction Copyright © 2025 by Margaret Busby
Foreword Copyright © 2025 by Sapphire

All rights reserved
Printed in the United States
Second Printing, 2026

ISBN: 978-1-643-62232-3

Special thanks to Robert Hershon and the other editors of Hanging Loose Press.
Poems from *Jazz Fan Looks Back* are copyright © 2002 by Jayne Cortez.
Reprinted with the permission of Hanging Loose Press and the Estate of Jayne Cortez.
Poems from *On the Imperial Highway: New and Selected Poems* are copyright © 2009
by Jayne Coirtez. Reprinted with the permission of Hanging Loose Press and
the Estate of Jayne Cortez.

Cover Photograph of Jayne Cortez, 1986, by Melvin Edwards
Interior art by Melvin Edwards
Copyright © by Melvin Edwards
Reproduced with permission of the artist
Opening endpapers and the second image of the closing endpapers are
from Melvin Edwards's art for Jayne Cortez's *Mouth on Paper* (1977).
Artwork on title page, last page of the book, and the first image of the closing endpapers
are from Melvin Edwards's art for Jayne Cortez's *Firespitter* (1982)
All other artwork is by Melvin Edwards and appears opposite
the Jayne Cortez book in which it was originally published.
Design and composition by Kit Schluter
Typeset in Adobe Caslon Pro, Futura PT, and **Arbotek**

Cataloging-in-publication data is available
from the Library of Congress

Nightboat Books
New York
www.nightboat.org

CONTENTS

FIRESPITTER: FOREWORD

SAPPHIRE

It was 1982 and the brave, beauteous, Bronx-born #MeToo originator Tarana Burke was just nine years old. The hashtag #MeToo was thirty-five years in the future. My friends and I were talking about Michele Wallace's *Black Macho and the Myth of the Superwoman. Looking for Mr Goodbar*, a tale of brutal femicide that had been made into a Hollywood movie. I had never read anything like Jayne Cortez's rage-filled manifesto, "Rape," and neither had anyone else I knew.

RAPE

…And what was Joanne supposed to do for
the man who declared war on her life
Was she supposed to tongue his encrusted toilet stool lips
suck the numbers off his tin badge
…sing god bless america thank you for fucking my life away

This being wartime for Joanne
she did what a defense department will do in times of war
and when the piss drinking shit sniffing guard said
I'm gonna make you wish you were dead black bitch come here
Joanne came down with an ice pick in
the swat freak mother fucker's chest
yes in the fat neck of the racist policeman
Joanne did the dance of the ice picks and once again
coast to coast
house to house

we celebrated day of the dead rapist punk
and just what the fuck else were we supposed to do

Jayne Cortez stepped beyond exposing sexual abuse and/or asking to be believed. She went beyond asking her reader to look at what was happening to Black and brown women, low-income women, and incarcerated women. That was not the challenge the poem presented. There was nothing to prove, no plea to see our humanity. Our humanity was a given.

she did what a defense department will do...

What Cortez was talking about was ownership, agency, autonomy, the right to defend one's most intimate property—the self. The right to ownership and hence the right to defend that which we own—our bodies. We own our bodies. We do not exist to be human cows (wet nurses), organ donors, field hands, house servants, and/or sexual servants. Fine if we choose to do any of the aforementioned. But the choice is ours. Our milk, our labor, our kidneys, our sex—they belong to us.

During slavery we were considered property. Property had no right to defend itself. The wood can be chopped, the hog's throat slit, the bull's nose pierced, the stallion gelded, the mare artificially inseminated. One does with one's property what one wishes.

black bitch come here

Joanne Little responded with an action that said, I own myself. Even incarcerated, my body is *mine.*

Joanne came down with an ice pick in the swat freak motherfucker's chest
...
and just what the fuck else were we supposed to do

If women were a country with borders that could not be transgressed; if only the hands we wanted got past customs; if we controlled the exits, entrances, bridges, breasts, crossroads, tunnels, vaginas, then the poem "Rape" is telling us in no uncertain terms that we own our bodies. In the poem "Rape" Jayne Cortez was unraveling the very warp and woof of white male supremacy.

*

JAYNE CORTEZ

Who was she? She had taken her grandmother's maiden name, Cortez, an identification with her matriarchal lineage. In her mouth, a resisting woman morphs into the land, Africa, the Caribbean, the Carolinas. Unlike the white male Hernán Cortés, who brought the name from Spain to the Americas in the 16th century, who came to extract, plunder, pillage, and conquer, this Cortez, Jayne, set out to communicate, confront, and connect with a Black, brown, revolutionary and creative diasporic world. And in doing so she became a transnational intercontinental galactic chronicler and creator of Black experience. Gwendolyn Brooks called her a "Black Nation song."

I read her poems over and over, the incredible rhythms of the poems springing to life as I took the words off the page and spoke them aloud. She broke her lines as we were broken, separating subject from its object as we were separated from a continent, immersing us in a hallucinatory surrealism that told the truth of our existence.

A generation of spoken word artists who came after Jayne Cortez were influenced by her collaborations with avant-garde jazz musicians. And that generation who followed her and hit the stage and "took the mic" also noted that she had founded a publishing company, Bola Press, assuring that her "spoken words" didn't disappear when she stepped off the stage.

Store that
contaminated
fetus
of dioxin in
the womb
line those lungs
with the snowflakes
of asbestos

*

THE FIRESPITTER

I remember the first time I saw her, the Firespitter. I had read the work and was expecting a large imposing presence in "traditional" dress. I mean, what does a Black female warrior look like? This warrior, who cleaved and cracked language into surreal shards to deliver it more wholly, turned out to be a petite woman in a dark green silk dress with a Kente cloth belt and designer ballet flats.

I associate the early poems with the stages/microphones of West Village clubs where I first heard her. Where I heard McCoy Tyner, Ntozake Shange, Brian Jackson. And Gil Scott-Heron—"Say, what's the word? Johannesburg!" With minimal mainstream media coverage of revolutionary struggles, our poets were a kind of Twitter spreading the word faster than the powers that be could erase it. Black consciousness and female consciousness crackled through the air like lightning.

For Cortez, poetry was not about mastery of form. Poetry in the mouth of the Firespitter was the creation of form—the form necessary to hide behind a tree in a Louisiana swamp and watch a Black man's testicles severed as he swung from a tree. She created a form to cull language from the broken neck of the dead-speak of the evening news so that she could reveal to us the disturbed scintillations of fresh black blood glistening and dripping down the pant leg of our own annihilation. Cortez assaulted the line. She disallowed its being used as a vehicle for entertainment. The Firespitter took the language they had used to lynch us and gave us the tongue of the wolf, the pink penis of a howling lizard, and the liquid from a leopard's eyeball to take us beyond capitalism's rotting green testicles. She mirrored a deep Blackness that had little to do with color and everything to do with being a diasporic Black descendant of slaves brought to America in a nefarious and unsentimental transfer of flesh by one race to another, where she/we became Cortezes, Loftons, Pinkies, Beulahs, Bakers, Freemans, who left blue black skin, fufu, and an old slave status for a new slave status when we emerged from the belly of a filthy toilet-smelling ship that had started out in Liverpool.

This Middle Passage connected us and separated us—who we were, what we had endured, how we had succumbed, carried on in spite, despite, and because of it. She named us. She named the way Baby Laurence slid across the floor, the way the trumpet slit Fats Navarro's lips. "Take us to see Muddy Waters," the Beatles said when they arrived from the major slave port of Liverpool. The news reporters at the airport asked, "Where's that?" The white boys from Liverpool replied, "Don't you know who your own famous people are?"

Jayne knew who our own famous people were. They were us. The ones transported on slave ships from Liverpool and dropped off like UPS packages in Haiti, the Dominican Republic, Brazil, Panama, South Carolina, New York. They were the diamond embedded in the diasporic tooth that made men and women of the silenced drum beat and wail: A Love Supreme. A Love Supreme. Africa. Nagasaki. Cuba. Trench Town.

Fire is dangerous. Fire burns, destroys, cooks, transforms, illuminates. Firespitter does not play it safe. Firespitter says *Palestine*, thinks about

> *...the concentration camps full of sad*
> *Palestinians.*

She writes "For the Brave Young Students in Soweto." She tells them she sees them, that this will not last. She cracks apart the bones of apartheid with her lion's teeth, ferociously calling out apartheid and sliding like a razor into Israel. Firespitter is seeing the future rising up in 2024—in blood and recycled hate. Firespitter travels the vast lands of Africa, the Caribbean white beaches eaten by billionaires shitting black oil onto birds and blue water and people who were never more than things to be transferred to Bantustans, to Indian Reservations, to ghettos, to Gaza, to the hills, and then down from the hill when the sea starts to rise.

FOR THE BRAVE YOUNG STUDENTS IN SOWETO

Soweto
when i hear your name
I think about you
like the fifth ward in Houston Texas
one roof of crushed oil drums on the other
two black hunters in buckets of blood
walking into the fire of Sharpeville
into the sweat and stink of gold mines
into your children's eyes suffering from malnutrition
while pellets of uranium are loaded onto boats
headed for France for Israel for Japan
away from the river so full of skulls
...and Soweto
when i hear your name and look at you on the reservation
a Xhosa
in the humid wrinkles of Shreveport Louisiana
walking down fannin street
into the bottom hole in the wall of endurance
i smell the odor of our lives together made of tar paper
the memories opening up like stomachs in saw mills
...When i look at this ugliness

and think about the Native Americans pushed
into the famine of tribal reserves
think about the concentration camps of sad
Palestinians
and the slave quarters still existing in Miami
the diamond factories still operating in Amsterdam in Belgium
...our bodies exploding like whiskey bottles
as the land shrinks into the bones of ancestor
"Bushmen"
and i tell you Soweto
when i see you stand up in the middle of all this
stand up to exotic white racists
in their armored churches
stand up to these land stealers, infant killers, rapists and rats
...to see you stand up to this epidemic of expansion
and flame passbooks into ashes
fling stones into the mouths of computers
...to see you stand empty handed
your shoulders open to the world
each day young blood falling on the earth
to see you stand in the armed struggle
...when i see you standing up like this
i think about all the forces in the world
confronted by the terrifying rhythms of young students
by their sacrifices
and the revelation that it won't be long now
before everything
in this world changes

Jayne called, we came, and the Organization of Women Writers of Africa (OWWA) was born!

> Black women writers from around the globe have been struggling against poverty, racism, exploitation, gender oppression, censorship, and other human rights violations. What we want is to participate in global decisions
>
> .

We came for Jayne. Maya Angelou came. Maryse Condé came. Rashidah Ismaili came. Edwidge Danticat came. Nancy Morejón came. Rosamond S. King came. Set against each other for centuries by region, color, and academic affiliation, we came. We came against slavery, indenture, being hung out of a nineteenth floor window by our jailor, we came against being held down and having our clitoris, labia minora, and labia majora excised and our genital openings sewn together or closed with thorns. OWWA came together against mulatta-ism, quadroon-ism, octoroon-ism, one-sixteenth-troon-ism, one thirty-second-troon-ism. We came together to keep from being operated on without anesthesia by the father of gynecology, J. Marion Sims. We came together to keep Sally Hemings from being erased. We came to laud Carmen McRae and ask Big Mama Thornton to sing the blues and take the chains off Billie's hospital bed. We came together because we knew they were planning to end affirmative action and anything else we'd worked for.

I thought she was a genius. I asked her, "Why are you spending time organizing when you could be doing your own work." "I do it because I can," she said. "And because so many are not able to do it." She was refuting a Western individualism I had not yet come to question. Her actions were saying that collective effort and self-sacrifice outshone individualism any day of the week.

The next call I get is not from the Firespitter, it's *about* the Firespitter. It's urgent.

Al Loving wrapped his body in one hundred painted canvas strips &
set off for the egungun festival
John Hicks packed up his piano keys and
took the greyhound bus back to St. Louis
Hilton Ruiz entered the other world like a newborn baby
Alberto Chissano left Maputo wearing
...Alice Coltrane hurried off to reminisce with
John about ascensions
...Pedro Pietri put on his applejack cap
& tuxedo t-shirt
then sailed off in an antique telephone booth
to have an extended conversation

When I get to the hospital I say, "I'm here to see Jayne Cortez, fourth floor, room—"

"Fourth floor, are you sure?"
"Yes."
"Fourth floor is hospice."
Oh no! The Firespitter is flying home!

It is on us now. To rearrange and transform the trauma stuck in the amygdala. It is on us, cuffed in the back of a police cruiser; it is on us, kicked out of our parent's house; it is on us, intubated and falling into darkness through the invisible net at the safety net hospital; it is on us, bleeding out like Biko in a holding cell; it is on us, anonymous backroom girls with ice picks up our vaginas. It is on us to continue through the smashed glasses of our lost vision until

...everything
in this world changes

and we fly home ourselves to join her and the brave young students of Soweto.

INTRODUCTION

MARGARET BUSBY

Firespitter: The Collected Poems of Jayne Cortez emanates passion, rhythm, musicality, energy, authenticity, and surrealism. It could hardly be otherwise. From her earliest engagement with creativity, such were the dynamic hallmarks of her work as a poet, performer and activist. Indeed, the multi-faceted career of Jayne Cortez, spanning more than half a century, encompassed an ever-expanding inventiveness, shaped from the start by vibrant childhood experiences.

Born Sallie Jayne Richardson on an army base in Fort Huachuca, Arizona, in 1934, she and her family moved to Los Angeles, California, where she grew up in the Watts district. Enthralled by her parents' jazz, blues and Latin record collection, and inspired by musicians from the area, she played bass, as well as studying art and drama. She recalled:

> As a young girl, I saw drummer Chano Pozo with the Dizzy Gillespie big band in Los Angeles, California, at Wrigley Field, 1948. When a new Charlie Parker record came out, I had it before most people in my neighborhood. I took piano lessons and harmony, played bass in the orchestra in junior high, and hung out at the record shop after school. I knew who Fats Navarro was when he was alive. I was a serious Jazz fanatic. I met Charlie Parker, heard Billie Holiday and Clifford Brown in person, and had a conversation with Duke Ellington.

Early in her career she took the surname Cortez, the maiden name of her Filipino maternal grandmother. In 1954, she married avant-garde saxophonist Ornette Coleman (a track on his first album is entitled "Jayne"). Their son Denardo was born in 1956. He began drumming at the age of six, joined his father's band as a ten-year-old, and would go on to collaborate as an adult with both his parents in their separate careers.

In the early 1960s, Jayne Cortez began writing down "thoughts" that turned into poems, and she became involved in the civil rights movement. She spent the summers of 1963 and 1964 working with the Student Nonviolent Coordinating Committee (SNCC) on voter registration drives in Mississippi, an experience that profoundly impacted her life and art. "I wrote more political kinds of works, works that could be read at rallies. I became more active, not just in writing but as an organizer," she told Val Wilmer in a 1985 interview.

Divorcing Coleman in 1964 ("Poetry came back to search for me at the end of my first marriage," she later wrote), Cortez was a founder of the community-based Watts Repertory Theater Company, as well as its artistic director. She subsequently settled in New York and became a notable figure in the Black Arts Movement, founded in the mid-1960s by Amiri Baraka, and transformative through both activism and artistic practice, with cultural links to Black power and the Black liberation movement.

A charismatic visionary, ahead of her time as a spoken-word performer, she was praised by Amiri Baraka, Maya Angelou, Gwendolyn Brooks, Gloria Naylor and other contemporaries. Jayne began reading her poetry with music in 1964, and in 1980 formed the band The Firespitters. As she wrote, "The Firespitters are filled with initiations, wilderness, wild car chases, flying carpets & Eldorado."

At the beginning of the 1970s, ever a pragmatic innovator, she set up Bola Press, an independent imprint that would publish most of her works, allowing her to experiment and be free from censorship. Her subject matter, she decided, was "to talk about my inheritance, to discuss political issues, taking a stand against domination, exploitation, ecological devastation and to poetically probe those issues in poems..."

Between 1969 and 2012, she produced more than a dozen books of poetry, as well as nine recordings with music. The later productions revisited earlier works, occasionally with minor revisions. These invaluable books and recordings of Jayne Cortez are represented together in this volume for the first time. Some poems from her first publication were not included in later collections of selected works, because she felt she had moved on with her life—she certainly moved on from Ornette, whose name titles one of those poems. Where poems from the pre-computer years were reprinted, there were often slight changes that she felt were improvements—usually to punctuation, or spacing, with lines added or removed in different versions. Judgements have been made about whether such variations were intentional as opposed to being attributable to typographical constraints or whether they can be simply accounted proofreading errors. Yet some omissions may be deliberate reflections of Jayne's changing views. Balancing and bolstering that possibility is respect for her principles as a lifelong champion of truth.

Of her printed works, her 1969 debut offering, *Pissstained Stairs and the Monkey Man's Wares*, was an unpretentiously produced chapbook. Dedicated to members of the Watts Repertory Theater Company, it featured twenty-seven poems and a dozen graphics by Melvin Edwards, heralding the start of a collaboration of life and art, a partnership in every way. They got together at the end of 1969, were married in the mid-70s, and travelled to the African continent in 1970. As Melvin has recalled:

> From 1969 to 2013 relationships with universal African culture was an essential part to our approach to life and aesthetics in general. Collaboration is an important word here as we came to a lot of ideas together from our own experience.[1]

Anchoring their continuing connection with the African continent, they began to divide their time between living in Dakar and New York City.

Bola Press published Jayne's next four titles: *Festivals and Funerals* (1971), *Scarifications* (1973), *Mouth on Paper* (1977), and *Firespitter* (1982). In 1984, *Coagulations: New and Selected Poems* was published by Thunder's Mouth Press in the US and by Pluto in the UK. *Poetic Magnetic* in 1991 brought to the page poems from the Bola recordings *Maintain Control* (1986) and *Everywhere Drums* (1990). These were followed by *Fragments* in 1994 and *Somewhere in Advance of Nowhere* in 1996.

She dedicated her next book, *Jazz Fan Looks Back* (2002), to the memory of her mother, Ada Johns, and considered it a "poetic response to African and African American music, Blues, Jazz, Black Music, The Music and its environment." She noted that she had "met or heard most of the musicians mentioned in this collection, with the exceptions of Ma Rainey and Bessie Smith." The result is an extraordinary soundtrack on paper, filled with vivid first-hand encounters. She wrote two more full-length books during her lifetime: *The Beautiful Book*, published in 2007, and *On the Imperial Highway: New and Selected Poems*, published in 2009.

Reading tributes to Jayne Cortez, one notes the terms repeatedly used to characterize and describe her work: revolutionary, powerful, dangerous,

1. Brenson, Michael. "An Oral History with Melvin Edwards," *BOMB*. November 24, 2014.

imaginative, self-reliant, fearless, visceral, intersectional, interdisciplinary… Writing for *Black Renaissance Noire* (Spring/Summer 2013), historian Robin D.G. Kelley recalled, "her poetry was never 'protest' but a complete revolt, a clarion call for a new way of life."

Jayne Cortez practiced an outspoken activism at a time of institutional silences. Bolstered by African-American feminist perspectives, she presented her work and ideas at universities, museums, and festivals globally. In 1991, with Ghanaian writer Ama Ata Aidoo, she founded the Organization of Women Writers of Africa (OWWA), which convened two major international conferences in New York: 1997's *Yari Yari: Black Women Writers and the Future* (Jayne directed a film of the same name) and *Yari Yari Pamberi: Black Women Writers Dissecting Globalization* (2004). A third iteration of Yari Yari that she had been planning took place in Accra, Ghana, honoring her posthumously. She also participated in the films *Women in Jazz* and *Poetry in Motion* and directed *Slave Routes: Resistance, Abolition & Creative Progress* (2009).

She laid claim to the world with her output, and the world embraced her. Journals, magazines, and anthologies brought Jayne's poems to a global audience. To date, her poetry has been translated into twenty-eight languages. She appreciated poetry globally—admiring the likes of Nicolás Guillén, Federico García Lorca, Pablo Neruda, Aimé Césaire, and Jacques Roumain—but was an imitator of no one, true to her mantra: "Find your own voice & use it / use your own voice & find it." Her accolades were no-less farflung. They include the International African Festival Award, the Langston Hughes Medal, and the American Book Award.

In her 2002 address at the 27th Annual Sandhills Writers Conference, she reflects on writing's capacity to connect people across languages and histories:

> In an effort to have a better life and a better understanding we continue to exchange information, translate texts, and increase the speed of transmission into action, into different modes of communication. When we put all of our ideas, all of these centuries of marks together it's pretty spectacular.

She concludes by recognizing the unique forms of community that poetic practice and literary production create:

> Why do we have poetry festivals, why do we have the congress of writers? We have these gatherings because we need the feeling of solidarity, the feeling of togetherness. We need to talk about writing, publishing, excellence, mediocrity, consumers and the marketplace. We need to speak of the

> sun, the moon, relationships and the animal world. It's important to discuss crucial problems such as the protection of the environment, the rational use of natural resources, human rights, disarmament and peace. This is where we come to discuss all topics, listen to all the different viewpoints and be updated on current literary developments. We make ourselves think, and we make others think and we write. . . . [W]hoever put together the idea that you could somehow communicate by taking your fingertip and making some marks and another person could see the marks you made and respond, then doing something about life based on the fact that they saw the mark you made. That's a great deal of potential power and it's a wonderful miracle to be a writer.

This volume offers readers the unique opportunity to reappraise her work, highlighting how critical her melding of poetry, jazz, and politics remains in the present day. Jayne Cortez set an example of how to champion independent cultural production, whether recording or publishing, always with community at the heart, tirelessly serving to support and encourage others.

Jayne Cortez's death on December 28, 2012, prompted an outpouring of appreciation for her life and her poetry. Writing for the *New York Times*, Margalit Fox praised her work's "visceral power, its political outrage and above all its sheer, propulsive musicality," saying it "was beyond category by virtue of embodying so many categories simultaneously: written verse, African and African-American oral tradition, the discourse of political protest, and jazz and blues. Meant for the ear even more than for the eye, her words combine a hurtling immediacy with an incantatory orality."[2]

In an obituary I wrote for *The Guardian*, I quoted Jayne's unambiguous understanding of her craft: "Words are musical—there's nothing more to say about it. That's it . . . there is the sound of the voice . . . and your attitude you put on top of it." The conviction with which she imbued her work revealed her as a passionate cultural activist, both on page and stage, transforming elements of her personal history and that of the African diaspora into cutting-edge blues poetry. As Maya Angelou had recognized upon the publication of *Coagulations*, "No ravine is too perilous, no abyss too threatening for Jayne Cortez."

In her music, as in her poetry, she spoke compellingly of social and environmental issues in a global context, fought injustice wherever she found it manifested, was in the frontline struggle for racial and gender equality, and celebrated the all-pervading power of music. Her band The Firespitters—

2. Fox, Margalit. "Jayne Cortez, Jazz Poet, Dies at 78," *The New York Times*. January 3, 2013.

featuring Denardo Coleman on drums, of whom Jayne said, "he is bold, knows no boundaries, and spits in all directions," alongside reed player T.K. Blue, saxophonist Alex Harding, guitarist Bern Nix, bassist Al MacDowell—provided a jazz-funk-blues response to her often mantric delivery.

Something of what she stood for is embodied in the closing lines of her poem "There It Is:"

> And if we don't fight
> if we don't resist
> if we don't organize and unify and
> get the power to control our own lives
> then we will wear
> the exaggerated look of captivity
> the stylized look of submission
> the bizarre look of suicide
> the dehumanized look of fear
> and the decomposed look of repression
> forever and ever and ever
> And there it is

Gathered within these pages are not only countless iconic poems, linguistic joy, and wisdom aplenty, but above all a timeless reminder of the principled and uplifting spirit that is the legacy of Jayne Cortez.

ACCRA, GHANA/LONDON, UK
JANUARY 2024

FIRESPITTER

PISSSTAINED STAIRS AND THE MONKEY MAN'S WARES

(1969)

THE ROAD

Blue Stone in Memphis
Stony blue cries
in honky-tonk taverns
        on the road
        from K town
        to K town
                      the road
the same road that downed
Bessie in the ground
and amputated round-way over in London Town
where another Hank moans

Stony Lonesome
Bessie's arm was torn
when the Blues come down mean

Them Low Down Dirty Blues
    Dancing Round
    Whining in Bessie
"Get Back Blues"

LEAD

They were like fish meal
poppin in a greasy skillet
cracklin hot at sunrise

Watching for the leed
that turned Lead
a belly eye bucking
outhouses to chase
the hurt from mud
and put the knife
to the other woman's
cool poppa please can I rub your thigh man
and ran like beans
through swamps & screams
up north
where the El broke off
and the urban nigguhs blues
was stomped
right through the piss stain stairs
of the monkey man's wares

When festered coons wrapped
a soulful purple meat grin
round a heart full
of black pride
comin out pork chops
on the depression line
that'd make any nigguh
bite back dust
eating black earth Delta
to hear Lead Belly
spit the Blues out

BEADS

With death
smelling so clear
so near
The composition of my life now here
Can't you see I ate fire in alcoholic grief
Cowered under the power of them good R.D.s
shooting smack from the spines of a cactus weed
Incense was the vomit
covering my beads
I was the fumes
& Harlem hid me

SUITE

"It's hard to learn
how tears can burn
one's heart
but that's the thing that
I found out
too late I guess
I'm in a mess"

That was a suite
Yardbird Suite
so says Earl
who fell in dark shadows
under the wings of the winged Bird
tripletted man—distorted man
Man you were distorted
by the stealer
the same stealer that stole you from K.C. to
use misuse reuse use use use
Jew historians turned black
doo-doo dues
thieves of Perfect Blackness
transform to waxes
for extra kill

Yeah Bird you dead
and greens are bestowed
upon your inheritor's head
Not mama—not children—not Black People not
nobody but Goldberg
A memorial—in memory of—dedicated to
Goldberg Greenberg—Burger
from Charlie C. Parker
exploited from birth to death & after death

forever
long as the White Man is:
from beginning to end—they live—you dead—Yard
Black Grave Yard—Yard
where women fought—forgotten women
whose only claim to fame lay slumped beneath feathers
Bird Feathers,   C. P.
you there—way in K. C.
where you slept on pool tables
took a box car to scrapple in the apple
the same box what brought you back
to sink in six feet and
sell for yards—mmmm hmmm uh huh mmm hmmm
"Oh Lord I Need Two Wings To Fly Away"

SAME WORDS SAME SONG

So high reached my sadness today
that but for your face
I would have shuddered out
in disgrace
                Hold me
                Hold me to you
                whom I love today
                & tomorrow will love more than words can say
  What cry of distance is this shit
& why should it be king of kings
to make me play in a hell hole of fantasies
blessing myself with dreams

    What is this version of a vision
    keeping death's head from sunken shrinkage beneath
    the salted tears of despair
& how much blood from sorrow will my memory stir up
as I rise & lick the air where the smell of my man be's
      My grieving tongue blabbing prayers
      when I should be pissing down the throat of god
      making my body a trampoline instead of pity's flesh on fire

Who robbed me of my savage scent
my rhythmic bone that shook with music inside my fine brown skinned thigh
as now I lynch the eye with a million wrinkles of sadness
my whole self an ugly stroke of sorrow e-t-c.

ORNETTE

ORNETTE ORNETTE
Go listen to Ornette
Rambling Blessings
with Cherry Higgins Haden
O. D. C. B. holding church
at the five spot in
N. Y. C.

Listen to the shrill voice
Vibrating with
Love & Agony

The great drops of water
spilling from
tears inside

Hear the womb of spontaneity
A Quivering fever
rising
Rising rapidly from
Bitter broken rhythms
stomping
crying out
Fierce Freedom Screams

heard in the beating heart
of R & B
Revolution & Blood
Revolution & Blood

Liquid blood
foaming passionate
Violent blood
gushing from the life of
Ornette Coleman O. C.

O. C. Spitting black milk
blood milk
splattering
the bleached looters mask
with
a million strokes
of Naked Unashamed
Blackness
Walking Proud

NOIR MARTYREE

Today
today your cries
are forbidden
      by
the artificial
manna sucking
plotters

as your sadness
heaps laughter on
the heads of
the tearless
beast
who flood alcohol
into the veins of
the Liver Lipped
Nigguhs

the pangs
of delicate moans
bleeding a monument
to
Noir Martyree
Black Martyrdom

Invisible rays of Blackness
throbbing softly
in a silence of unity

Noir Martyree
Black Martyrdom

Trembling voice shuddering rocks
in reply to
the enemies of liberation

whose uncalled for repetition
swishes down the ramps of backs
baptizing blacks with
manhood propositions

Noir Martyree
Black Martyrdom

  Yes
we are prepared
for the R & B
(revolution & blood)
you sang about
        Now
before the monsters
fuck black music
in the ass again to
create another mulatto
We too will join
Noir Martyree
Black Martyrdom

SUPPRESSION

I lay paralyzed
with moorish fingers pressed firmly against my head
hypnotizing my temples as I attempt to scream
but cannot move
Held firm
firm as a baby's head pulled from darkness
a thin hair between giant tweezers

I left my body
I left the cry in the air to become spectator to my dream
The cry in the air was my body
The great pussy pinching throb between my thighs in the nest of pleasure
was my body
the pregnant volcano pressing my belly near eruption
was my body

I rose from this my body to see me on fire
and the fire burnt my eyes & I could not see
The fire cracked my eardrums & I could not hear
The fire charred my tongue & I could not speak
The fire consumed my brain and I could not think
The fire brushed ashes onto my forehead so I could not be blessed
as I threw myself upon me to purify me with myself by fire

In this heated passion
I wanted to wrap myself in the calling tunnel of darkness
to produce the flood that flashed from your rod
through quivering succulent lips
and at that moment
my body merged with myself
transferring the cry in the night to where you lay listening

RACE

Black Man
breeder of the great race
of black faces

Your son's tongue hangs low
with loose diseased pink
pale dying flesh
between his gums
suffocating in farts
& howling like a coyote in the wind
his bent-over dedication to
the grunting demons that madly
ride upon his back
flying high his ass tonight
swallowing sperms of fantasy
in this the great Age of Reality

Your son black man
becoming a piece of
the long-lipped whip
that ripped you apart
leaving your whelped woman beat
with this bubble-eyed boy
who blames now his mother
who fed him from the gutter of loneliness
from long titties filled with tears
her bitter love sorrows
all she had to give

Not knowing black man
not knowing
that your son's eyes would protrude
mouth pulled down with bulldog stares of hate
Hate for her whom you left dead

Daring not to look
to see
and know this guilt
she spilt upon your son's head
who thinks himself another
Another like the other image
of the master-taker

Your son strutting in
red plastic high heel shoes
twisting down the street of despair

Is there
a place to cure
this strange illusion
this prancing agony
this cocked-head arrogant-neck eye-lash-batting Tragedy

Is there a place
A point of return
for this lost tribe of whimpering sons
whose only desire now be revenge
who throw heads back & laugh
eyes rolling cast upward
lusting after God
cause they know he goes

So what?

Men do not lay with men
to claim god-hood
Dreaming that one day a child would call you daddy
and what will you tell him when he calls you
Faggot Queer Punk Sissy
will you then admit
the illegitimate passion of a so-called love affair
meant only a smack-dab in a greased ass
from the holders hard-rod

Will you admit your faggotry
to hear him say "then what am I your son"

Is there a place black man
for sons unloved confused
screaming "I can't help myself"
Unable to come back
Unable to grasp the fact
and responsibility
of manhood black

Is there a place
other than the streets
offering open coffins
for humped bodies
raw flesh dangling on wish-bones
wishing to be Aretha
wishing to be Streisand
Bleeding
as we must slaughter these
our sons to bring a revolution on

For what good will he be
when the time is here
a non-functioning product
used openly against We
as he pleads his creative ability
Ability to create what?
A Race called Faggot

He chosen enemy of young boys & girls
must not be left as an example of our lives
Betrayers of the future
Yelping love for the devil
in African robes to attract more beastly trade
proud of Blackness—Yes
Black men fucking Black men Now
lapping chocolate shit sticks Now
Parading in white gay bars Still

soon to be like rabid dogs
foaming—aging in jacked off old faggots homes
Bowels caked with blood pleading to be fucked
in the dry raisin hole that will not cry
sinking in gin
peeing the songs of Leontyne
who he thinks he is

Oh black man quick please the laxative
so our sons can shit the White Shit of Fear out and Live

LONELY WOMAN

A wasted flow of water hiding
   Sliding
down the face
of a lone-ly one

This black woman's
oblong tears
renders
softly felt wetness
warm like sperms
to melt
the calling—calling
flesh
        Is there any reason
        for this not so
        dry—Dry season

Cutting tongue of fear
please
won't you hear
the stretch marks
of Loneliness
bent—in this
cold woman's tear
Night Raining
in
The Woman's Quarters
Listening to
Crickets
small—weak
dark like me
—sit—
Stripped——nude
from the trembling cadence of fire
Lit——

in Ornette's horn
                                        Crickets that cry

Come—weep—with—us
come—weep—with us
come weep with us
Lone-ly wo-man

Lonely Woman
come weep with us

DINAH'S BACK IN TOWN

I wanna be bitchy
I said I wanna be a bitch
cause when you nice
true love don't come
into your life

You get mistreated
Mistreated & abused
by a no good man
who don't care nothing
'bout no blues

Throw a kiss to a
lonely bitch
crying on your
back porch

gambling man

Money man
don't you wanna
take a chance
with the blues

Well if you find
a dreamer
Let him know
about the schemer
just tell him
Dinah's back in town

I'll put on my pretty face
just in case he decides to drop
around
You tell him

you know a bitch
who only does
what a good man
wants her to

Tell him
Say
she put
her helpless case
of the blues
out on the Street of Regret
buried in this
Bitter Earth
and now
she's not bothered, confused
and all tied up with
Mr. Blues

Tell him
Miss Dinah's back in town
and she's waiting
just for you

WE THE REVELATION OF THE SHOE SHINE BOYS REINCARNATION

Inherited bayous of sadness

SHUFFLIN THROUGH FIELDS OF HOT SALIVA

Eatin artificial sugar at string up time

FACE WEEPING IN A ROCKET OF PAIN

Tears . . Blessed . . Preserved . . The Covenant of Salt

THE BLUES WENT RACY

        Lard became oleo

        & EGGS POURED FORTH THEIR

        ROTTEN YOKES

                        HA HA

RAIN

You are the rain
beating back time
to the good days
when we turned on each other
in defense of our hearts
which were destined
to live break & live again
Our love being strong
living beyond what we were
what we are
You rain Love rain
piss down on this animal cocky
whose smell contaminate brains
leaving dung-tongues dribbling out shit to
pacify, classify & erectify a thing called life
Look rain
I walk naked pulling out my guts to you
Pour down & anoint my body
purify me for the on coming slaughter of loneliness
Put your healing hand upon my pulsing pussy & feel the
heated pleasure bone
reigning king
whose babies will kiss my soul
whose gentle fingers
stroke out the meanness livid in me
beating down all that is hard
dripping sweat like beads from a rosary
blessing my long drawn breast in love currents of contentment
as the rhythm of my thighs whisper praises in your ears
my buttocks shake prayers between your fingers & cry
come Rain come

THEODORE

Heading for
the Low Lands
down 52nd Street
Heard tell of
a fat man
that would make us
pray at his feet

His name was
T. Navarro
but they called him
Fats for short

They say
he had a scream
so mean
it make a
dead man cream
with a hum
from the slum
to make a
numb sister
come

He was
T. Navarro
they called him
Fats for short
Said
he wailed through
the Wailing Wall
Bounced with Bud
beyond the Infidels
to let Ice
Freeze Red and

Moved it on out with Max
to clean E.C.'s Guilt
and shout
"You must remember this
I lived
and played my horn
the best that I
knew how
and all I got
from those who said
they dug the music cats
was:
        You should do this
        You shouldn't do that
        cause I'd do thus & so
        if I was you Fats."

Let me tell you one thing
he didn't need nothin
to make him play that way
but he took a whole lot
of somethin
                to keep them
                bats & flies away

Fats
no longer fat in size
Gone from XXL
                        to ssz
            Died inside that
            not-so-shy
            but lonely Hag
            friend of the devils
            known as Mrs. Scag

Yes remember
the name was
T. Navarro
they called him

Fats for short
and his life
was snuffed by
inadequate people
whose minds was
dry as chicken-shit-slime

SONG

Don't let the fangs pull you south
poison drinking from twisted chains
coiling ignorant pain
stuck in the sad machinist mouth
way down deep crying
in the rawness of you
Life   Life   Is Living Worth It
Coon Man
Mosquito Bush
Mounting fever lava roiling
beneath a strange strange land
Be
Bitter   Bitter   Bitter
ripe moving bite of reason . . . ready . . . bitter
Life   Life   Is Living Worth It
Oh Jewel Of The Sun Blacken Son
Of a Black Man's Sun
Shine through wasted sockets
Shimmering diamond studs in a blindman's pit

Heart Murmur of Sweet Black

Sweet Life

Oh Sing Your Nigguh Song

BRIGHT BROWN SUMMER

Lord Nelson
Star dusted
on Barbara
in Max's free-town

You and Lord
preacher Brown
stroking prayer bells
as you ate the horn up
you did

Moist fleshy lips
weeping willows
under a blue moon
on a new day

Kissing the foot of
Oh Woo Wee Doo
smacking Blackies
heart in a
flashy mass spittle
of fire
stompin pride
from muted cries
on the truth hunt

Some of us heard
the delivered word—Clifford

Keeper of the horn
Young sputtering deacon
in the spiritual choir
singing with Fats & Freddy

Untouched by bets
and other Chets
even full-fledged taps
wouldn’t begin to cut
the tone-blown love
flung from
the mack-man’s bad tongue

FLOSSIE

In smoke-filled joints
where syncopation
shakes a mean dance
and body thunder
gets down fonky
there—skunky ho's rub
their titties in destitution
as little Babs scuba doos
Round Midnight and
Flossie screams Pee Boy Pee
screeching saxophones
cum shooters blinding the eyes
of W. W. W. White women watching:
spellbound leeches . . . foaming fumming squirming itching:
mash-mouths leaning beneath the peeled penis purring
and black Flossie yells . . Blow . . Blow Baby
Yes Dex
"I smoke Greefa, you smoke greefa
lets get high—yeah
I sniff coke & you snort H
so let's get high tonight"

PEEEEEEEEE EE E Boy
Flossie's workin on it.

At that—Your cue
your eyes tight
to shut from sight
night riding
desperadoes . . white . . and
let go streams of loneliness
Flossie says play it purdy baby
A strange change . . silence
and you're on your own
zero . . crazy

but you didn't know
till your eyes screamed open
was a 12-bar death
with you . . the only one left:
Serenade to a dead corpse
in a dead hall
in a world full of dead people
who don't hear
don't know
don't care
and you remember Flossie
tricked—baited in by death
funky butt ho in gold tooth zest—dead
and the horn begins to weep
the resurrection suite
as you pee just for Flossie

HUNGRY LOVE

Warm night of flesh pimples
Alone
Fear pressing between my eyes the mark of despair
& my thighs once a sanctuary guarding your precious cage of ribs
have shivered to invisibility
and do not exist
Forget the ocean
Love water falling from the gate of my soul
for the sea wiped its eyes sometimes ago
and all is dry
Madness
What is this madness
Hungry love bathed in hot cinders
waiting to be drenched in rain crying from your open pores
Love the mystery of life
The seed
The Master Seed you said
Lives
and like a bleeding locust
feeding from this tree
the ripe plum of everlasting love
I kneel
humbling myself before perfection
My quick tears sagging the earth
as I eat mud to touch the root of you

[HARSH CRIES FROM]

Harsh Cries From
The Tomb Of
Little Rock
Blown In The Soul
Of The Pyramids
Where The Sphinx
Keep Watch
Over Pharoah
Whose Ferocious Whip
Bleeds Fire & Stone
Burning The Priestess
As The Final Course
Of Pain
Before Freeing
Money Torn People
In The Bethel City
Known As
LITTLE BLACK EGYPT LAND

A GATHERING OF FISHES DRIED WITH SALT WAITING TO WIGGLE IN THE NET OF LIFE

Dead hair
slithering through
greased strings
oil dripping on lips
hung with evilness
rolling eyes to match
her pooch mouth gait

An old woman at sixteen
slipping sliding
scraping across the floor
in bent shoes
turned up toes pointing at the sagging bag
beneath two pouches
limp like wet rags
slouching between
the baby's thighs
who rides
the heavy air of hatred
Sits
eyes fastened on the door
swinging through drunk
smelling of scotch & skunk
from the grinning eagle stolen at day break
he must come
Wait
ain't gone have
no wrong doing man
treatin her like dust
Drink
stealin the welfare check
for good time clothes
& shakin more babies up
"Say it loud I'm black & proud
I said say it loud I'm black & proud"

Down
Stone blind gin mama
rubbing the air with salt tears
thinkin bout her man
pinchin her legs together
dancing to the music
between her thighs
that cries out for her
sweet married-lookin man
lying next to his other woman
as she wishes he were here
to scrub bellies
tongue cuss
dry fuck
so she could get down nasty

HURTIN BLUES

Sad eyes
        Is there any way to send you to me
to hold
        to keep
to reap goodness dripping from
        your form

The way I would love
& feast upon your life tonight
Blues around my body tight
blues turning churning
Oh baby I love you
you do's right
Oh baby I wanna hold you
love you every night
cause you a good good man
who do's it out of sight

Now the other blues done moved in
chasing good daddy blues away
        I'm gonna cry tonight
        I'm gonna stay dry tonight
        I'm gonna say nobody really cares
        and get high all right

I'll pray baby boy
Nigguh Man
        I wanta give you all my love now
        so please come tonight
        please come tonight
        and say that you will never
        never leave me

SUN

The Fluid Flow
Of Ochre Rays
Spontaneously Engulfs
A Soaring Unpure
Thing

Aspiring Cosmobrating Men
Must Open Wide
Their Veins
To Gather
Shuddering Brilliance
From The Astrological Jolts
Thrown Out From
The Aged Sage
In Metallic Gesticulation
Pointing Finger
Of Tantalizing Visions
Copping No Z's
In This World Of Ra
Sun Ra
  The Giver Ra

IF YOU WERE MINE

for Billie Holiday

Fear fell
in a mellow spell
under the reign
of the Gardenia Goddess
Royal Throated Queen
Majestic Earth Mother
Of All Edens
Life—Death—Paradise
    Black Woman
Bruised Woman Moaning
Notes of Sadness
Wrapped in Pure Black Madness

It's my man
my man don't love me
my beautiful Black Man
    Love God
    Black God
Giver of Life
To The Source Of
Lifes Force

fonky fonky Black Man
with your cries of passion
and your monologue of sorrow
to you I sing the Blues
    You who made me
    Me on bended knees
    Knees of a beggar
    A begging beggar
Begging to you Blackman
    Kinglet
for matted white pussies
    Kinglet
to the masters ass hole

  Kinglet
slobbering in slime
till its time to whine
inside the Blues
of turpentine
me—

I Am The House Of Turpentine
Queen Of Spades
on the installment plan
low down—bent—and
most dissatisfied

I cried on
how I come to be
bout my Easy Rider
in his ragged B.V.D.s
    (God Bless the Child
     Who's Got His Own)

Blues Daddy

I wished on the moon for you
If you were mine
I would live for you
and you alone

If you were mine
You would be the King of Kings
With me at your side
No Detour Ahead

If You Were Mine
If You Were Mine
if you were mine

PAYMENT IN ADVANCE

Number playing dues paying members praying
through the monkey thought saloon
            Blood of my blood & our peoples blood of
          their peoples peoples blood in wombs of seeds
in birth of death Flies
        Steppin harlem flies
        Frozen flies
Amplified astringifying flies in tarpaper hives
     no teeth purple heart wearing lynch meat tree
can't you see
            one hole one hole
            never wide never wide
Fly through fly
              Understand the dream unchanging
              Understand the dream gesticulating
              Understand the mainstream articulating
third stream innovating time scheme of timeschemes time
   Terrifying Identifying
   Tribes crying uniting within our soul souls time
        Long live time
        Long live the tribes
From the fields
From the mines
From the cities
          obsolete machines in flames on fire
Fire faces in mirrors burnt on every mirror of everything
black Eternal Blackness
              The Goodness—all that is good
              The Truth——all that is true
              The Immediate—right now
Future violence in our minds uh uhmm
   Taker of blood
   Giver of light
Blues blowing revolution its you we paid for you South Africa

HOW LONG HAS TRANE BEEN GONE

Tell me about the good things
you clappin & laughin

Will you remember
or will you forget

Forget about the good things
like Blues & Jazz being black
Yeah Black Music
all about you

And the musicians that
write & play about you
a black brother groanin
a black sister moanin
& beautiful black children
ragged . . underfed laughin
not knowin

Will you remember their names
or do they have no names
no lives—only products
to be used when you wanna
dance fuck & cry

You takin—they givin
You livin—they
creating starving dying
trying to make a better tomorrow
Giving you & your children a history
But what do you care about
history—Black History
and John Coltrane
No
All you wanna do

is pat your foot
sip a drink & pretend
with your head bobbin up & down

What do you care about acoustics
bad microphones or out-of-tune pianos
& noise
You the club owners & disc jockeys
made a deal didn't you
a deal about Black Music
& you really don't give
a shit long as you take

        There was a time
when KGFJ played all black music
from Bird to Johnny Ace
on show after show
but what happened
I'll tell you what happened
they divided black music
doubled the money
& left us split again
is what happened

John Coltrane's dead & some
of you
have yet to hear him play
How long how long has that Trane been gone

and how many more Tranes will go
before you understand your life
John Coltrane who had the whole of
life wrapped up in B flat
John Coltrane like Malcolm
True image of Black Masculinity

Now tell me about the good things
I'm telling you about

John Coltrane
A name that should ring
throughout the projects mothers
Mothers with sons
who need John Coltrane
Need the warm arm of his music
like words from a Father
words of Comfort
words of Africa
words of Welcome

How long how long has that Trane been gone

John palpitating love notes
in a lost-found nation
within a nation
His music resounding discovery
signed Always
John Coltrane

Rip those dead white people off
your walls Black People
black people whose walls
should be a hall
A Black Hall Of Fame
so our children will know
will know & be proud
Proud to say I'm from Parker City—Coltrane City—Ornette City
Pharoah City living on Holiday street next to
James Brown park in the State of Malcolm

How Long
how long
will it take for you to understand
that Trane's been gone
riding in a portable radio
next to your son whose lonely

Who walks walks walks into nothing
no city no state no home no Nothing
how long
How long
Have black people been gone

LOVE

Love I want you love
upon love after love
upon love seated in the seed
the fine tool carving melodies of dust rasping love in ears
tickled wet with love dripping deep in caves of desire
to pour weeping through the veins of pleasure love cries wide in nights
of plunging bodies hard in soften rise
upon the stone of love
above the scars & wounds
tender strokes of passion caught between lungs breathing out the gate of
moans on those days when sadness cracked & suffocated
stinking slow death flew from blows impregnated with sperms of love
sang in the arched back falling on loves lips
sensitive tips of nerves twitching on the way to glory
and Oh I need you Love
after love upon love supreme
A midnight piece rammed tight in loose warm wetness anointing the spit head
brawling love tears
sobbing rain
dark in sweeten meat
the love quilt twine-kissing in a twist of quivers that love so lassoed
in this loop would look through minds
mirror distance
& measure time
dying no
would swoop down
a punting belly bouncing in a birth of flames
trembling womb moving in a mass of tears
fasting fear
ashes in the wind
as king love—joy so appears
to wipe on love in night
on day upon love
after love upon love

FORREAL

Holes in my arms
Gone Gangrene

Roaches spilling from my ears
on rats chewing the remains
of a bastard
I killed with
a hair pin up my womb

Purplemouth
Bubblemouth
    Death
You are ugly
You are white
Death you are Death
no more Uh Uhnnn
Don't touch me

I'm on my way to Mecca
Elijah in my head
a panther in my eye
    Love Lives
& I wanna taste myself inside
Mmmmm that pure nigguh pain
I don't feel strange
I hate the welfare line

Call me fool
Call me negro
Call me any old goddamn thing you want
    Assassinating mouth
    trying to assassinate me
But I'll survive the night
My gold tooth a lighthouse keeping death away

I'll sink shame
& beat my wings
I've killed fear
& my souls on fire

I confess
I am armed & prepared
to reproduce the love that
made me live

I confess
that this beautiful beautiful nigguh is ready

RIDIN HOME BLUES

Like a coon
        Smelling God on the storefront tongue in your open mouth singing
Do you love me baby do you love me
    Sipping in the slippery ear of all the goodness badness
                        of your mean sweet nigguh ways
Loving me   Loving you
        Beyond the stalk of the moon that is long like the long path of death &
short like the short stump of life
                        Isn't it sweet pretty man
Isn't it sweet
So sweet to moan to move to scream & holla groveling at your feet
            Oh Baby Ride Me Home
I'm so alone
      & I can't throw no more bones
            In the voodoo of my head
Moving out
        Moving in
            Moving behind the throne of your smile
Just blowing hot air on the devil
                        Get on out
                                Get on out of this
                                        our African haunt
Say now baby
            Please Please
                        Ride Me On Home

FESTIVALS AND FUNERALS

(1971)

INITIATION

for Denardo (to whom this book is dedicated)

During the season of cut organs we
shot forward like teeth spokes from runaways
a lost cargo of part flesh part ash part
copper and zinc
sucking in names like katanga
like congo
we dissolved our chains
celebrated the slit nose reality of
our severed hands and
at the base of a fifty million skull pyramid
we rehearse life
second headed face circles of
one handed life calling:
blood   blood   blood
and once again blood
where is the land for our blood that drips drips
blood
an arm for the rapist?
a leg for the servant?
No
take us to the place for the new birth blood

TODAY ON THIS DAY

Today on this day
I would like to push forward from
my shadow of rags
and offer this pop bottle of tears
I baptized in

good luck to you
from my torn suede shoes on
this same day of my daughters eyes
putrified
in donkey heat

Hooray for the health department

I feel damp before such an audience of
mascara and white coats waving
their bye bye's
to the Friday crowd of occupied stretchers
bye bye
today on this day of jaws
in the fifth month of resemblance at
the end of a pretzel on the heart of
my son's remembrance
thump   thump   thump

Hands off my vomit number three recruiting
number four turning the exit to
enter my torn shoes in numbers
Warning
I take back my tears
my luck
my daughters eyes
today on this day of
No admittance   No return   Keep out
Cash only day of Shit

PEARL SHEBA

To the northern pearl
sheba woman
that is i
my thighs whispered
back to memory calling
from inside glossy beads of
a past love
    is that you
shook my heavy loaded breasts
as ear to my belly tuned up its drums
and felt the ripple of a voice echo in its womb
overdue promises from slavery that
had stuffed our minds &
shuffled our feet
squeezing eternity from the darkened meat of
our frozen emotions and wet like
    decomposed bodies of salt
I turned slowly on the face of this memory as
song cries of flaming tissues listened
I chanted low magic slopes of
enchained sorrows
fucking me   fucking us
far beyond the promised feelings of god &
like a kilo of shit that couldn't be sold
I took the arc of midnight blood &
greased my flesh to the stones
closing off water as i let flash the
encrustment on my hairs to those who would perish
from the suneyes of a peacock

PRAY FOR THE LOVERS

Pray for the lovers
for those who are suspicious
for those who are jealous
for those who are revengeful
Pray for the lovers
for those who are unsatisfied for
those who are frightened for
those who are disappointed
pray for those who are lonely lazy & limited
Pray for the lovers
for those unwilling to reveal & unable to revolt
for those who are helpless
those who are hostile
for those whose flesh goes dead upon touching
the frigid
the passive
the latent
the soft
have mercy on the lovers in heat
pray for those with pain in their bodies
pain in their minds
for sorrow
for fear &
the spell of madness after love says goodbye
Pray for the lovers in the name of love
in the name of god &
the mirror of death
love in the name of some rollin hips
those churning lips & the blood
that drips incest to
incest
all power to the lovers in the name of love
all power to the lovers in the name of love
all power to the lovers in the name of love

IF I WERE THERE

I would sunday cry on
white sheets of a wedding
holding hands with laina and fred
if i were there against
ancient shadows
flames and wax flames of
hot tears torching throats into gin rolls of
dundun blessings
dubaa dubaa
from the sweet neck of my yoruba dream
invisible with denardo
with denardo
I would cry beer sundaes on
wedding circles like
funeral psalms splashing
worlds between fish if
I were there wrapped
in royal blue net
barefoot & warm as a
february cry in a yoruba drum

They winged his spirit &
wounded his tongue
but death was slow coming

They winged his spirit
& wounded his tongue
but death was slow coming?

Flash:

I lost a good friend & i
loved him
I lost a good friend & i loved
him

C.O.D.

collect on death
collect on death
collect on death

thorns on his casket
thorns on his casket

Roses red as my eyes
red red red?

Red as the blackman's blood consumed by vultures
red red red?

Red like the open head of a panther
red red red red red

Who killed Lumumba
What killed Malcolm

Who killed Lumumba
What killed Malcolm

There are no tears
we have no friends
this is the word

There are no tears
we have no friends
this is the word

before creation & after destruction
the word
winding through poverty and
bleeding into lips of the blues
screaming under oil fields
stretching across swamp fields &
laughing outside minefields
the word
murmuring through veins of gold
crying inside the crumbled crushed bones of
Chaney
against navels of beaten flesh
walking the streets of Harlem on
the rusty rims of a needle
the word
coming through like axes
a million year lesson book on solitude
we are alone

There are no tears
we have no friends
this is the word

Who killed Lumumba
What killed Malcolm

There are no tears
we have no friends

that is the word

festivals & funerals
festivals & funerals
festivals & funerals & festivals & funerals

In bebop livers of love
so hurt in wailing hearts of fear so sad
the word
back when burgundy tongues of oppression
became creators of masculinity & legends of
love sitting on milk crates
the word
back when poets screamed
"kill run kill walk kill crawl nigguhs
give me your money anything" shame
the word shame
enemy to revolutions that lesbian conspiracy
back when cultural vaginas rushed through
streets urging men to die for shame
dashikis in the wind
we knew the novelty of death
cadillacs & cocaine in every hole stuffed in
our heads pain
the word was
Love offerings from night time men to
bleed time women reeking
factories of blood time steel cut fingers
weeping our skills cannot laugh but
our flesh is united
Flesh
Our flesh of a flesh
in our mouths on the head of our souls
from the skin on his eyes up
the breath in our lungs
backing the beat of our brains was the
speech of his thoughts & the death of
our fear through the dark of his meat

sits the flesh of Patrice
our flesh of a flesh is Lumumba our flesh Lumumba
flesh

There are no tears
we have no friends
that is the word

the vanguard of precision
the virgin of communications
the erotic improvisation of uprooted
perfection the Blues

RHYTHM & BLUES

Bloomdido feathers of barbwire cries
birds alone
sip the night of the Blues
the first drops of music you ever heard

My man's touch is as tender as
rain on drums
African drums
he's Chano Pozo of the drums
so black so fine
so mine so black
so fine is mine
Zanzibar love comes the Congo

I'M A WORKER

to all of my sisters in the garment industry

My legs swollen from pressing pedals
my hands stiff from pushing cloth
I have a craving for food
that's why i have to piece work my ass off

You want some honey
you want some gunnie
I'm looking for that thing called
survival money

Yes in the mornings on the buses
and in the evenings coming home
you'll hear me talk about the foreman the
floorlady the bossman & the bossman's ho
cause they all gettin rich off me and my veins
varicose
and believe me that's all i've got to show

If I had some honey
If I had some gunnie
think i'd have that thing called survival
money

I'm so tired of this 8 to 4
sittin   standin   waitin for the bell to ring
daytime   nighttime   sometime shit with
these broken needles   broken threads & taxes
I don't know what to do

Why don't i collect unemployment?

that's right i paid 20 years worth of dues
but get this
if i quit?

the mothafuckin social security truant officer nazi's
don't wanna get up off my long earned fufu

I got some honey
I got some gunnie
but got dammit i can't find no
survival money

I think i'll kill me a machine and
see if i can't get a raise that way
cause this minute to minute agony
just ain't gon' bring in no sufficient pay

I got the landlord   gas   lights
the union   telephone   department store
subways   buses & 4 human beings
to feed
so tell me   tell me   tell me
do you think a revolution is what i need

THE PROMISE

Our sweat drops bit the land with urgency
as sixteen footprints engulfed the
presence of ourselves from the americas
to africa
that night at mama peters
in nigeria where little brother benin
gave up his prayer beads when
love declared love &
the tasty visions of our eight smelly bodies
rose to the sound of dogonyaru dogonyaru
the blood root of prophecy sucking power
within our skins beneath our skulls
new fumes of blackness

& we knew as we ate fufu sopped in red pepper
under the delicate blessings of lindsay's flute
that this was the future & nothing
nothing could take away this truth
even
while on the beach
when peter was knocked on his ass by another
brother & came up holding two clean teeth in
his hands crying revenge
even
this we knew would not halt the survival of
orphans from a sea of dead ancestors in
promise of nationhood

LYNCH FRAGMENT

My tongue whips blood through the
ribs of a cobra
I am a serpent
a parched cavity for lynched reptiles
iron rust of my musty scales sucking up the
secret strength of bad smells from two curved horns
clipped horns of a ram under the
bent pipe of my passionate sloping bone which
is the beauty mask that god wears like
the four part sun rising redly to the tip of
frozen nerves heard
beyond the muted cries of
mutilated flesh in a hole
a fox hole
a fixed hole where spirits erect themselves &
urinate inside my nostrils

COLLAGE FOR ROMARE BEARDEN

From white lightnin to
bowed heads in red
rooms of pregnancy
under blackness
spread out   closed in
how do you do
oval cries from target eyes
possessed by spirits
temple spirits of indefinite feelings
two jagged teeth
chapped lips peeling into
a conjur woman's towel at the insistence of
an imposing bull
the holy ghost
a sign of remembrance
the signal for new leaves of
spring tidings
to a lonely woman blemished against
G string banjos as she gumbos into
the wake of steel knives and
we molass rum spoiled omens on detached birth
truckin fuckin over to the sunrise baptist
church of the flying eagles church of
smelly garbage church of angel rats flying in
teeth formation toward
cheeks of churches tribal
marking the blues
stand up
for this slow drag of a slow death from
a fast world outside of choir books
dream books
comic books
junkie books &
bookies booking book
next to brick buildings

purple leaking roofs
next to lady's gardenia spray
magenta curtained hearse
next to life gone back
separated from the beautiful times
downhearted times
magic times   separated from
the time of melons gone from
evening meals in
front of potbellied stoves and
red checkered tablecloths
gone up in flames where we
used to love hard breathing fast against
the sound of hide & go seek voices
gone
the floors where we stomped all night to
drum boogies of duprees high
tight skirts of jelly shakes
fishtail fuchsia dark elderberry wine
"who's gonna hit on who tonight"
gone into saxophone obituaries like
a seventeen piece casket sailing to the tombs
we donated to the welfare office
in african masks & head rags
volunteers
cracking toes from tin tubs with
ashy legs from chicken shacks we came
covered in newspapers & blood
from barbershop mirrors
and beauty parlor smoke
we came like stripes from the sun in
defense of our numb stomachs
our out flung arms
withered hands
swelling feet
like stilts
we came to the rhythm of
embalming fluid

turned down
turned around
turned back
we came
& came & came
but there was no help coming
on blue monday
box car tuesday
step sitting wednesday
pawn shop thursday
liquor store friday
big lip saturday or
swollen jaw sunday
nothing
but the merciful revelation of our roped
ankles & sculpted profiles
understanding these disjointed faces &
nail covered bodies burning
and stinging with life force of
a powerful   juju
insideout
deuce by deuce
who owns the grey green roach infested
funk holes we pee pee on
who owns the handkerchiefs fanning
our doo doo butt riffs
who owns the jook joints we buy morphine in
who owns our hepatitis souls we
bend needles for
who owns the black bitch amazons &
their put on wigs
who owns those rejection slips computing
from a blackman's balls
who owns the teardrops on our fathermother's bed
who owns the back yards where
the old people rest
who owns these blue interior orange mornings on
fire escapes and wooden carved doors

this terror in our throats
who owns our sufferings if not our own
torn bodies the tremor & the quiver in
our left over bowels
who but we know the size
and the structure of
this patchwork quilt

I WOULD LIKE TO BE SERENE

I would like to be serene
to know pleasure & worship a sniper
be elastic with revenge
melancholy but deathless
I would like to know more than just fish smells &
part time love
I'm a woman
I eat food
I drink water
I confess my feelings
I cry
I up my dress & down my pants
part my thighs & fuck
I know relief
I'm on relief
It's good but he's gone
he's gone
he's gone
he's gone

WATCH OUT

Watch out for the woman
whose body is bloated with tears
watch out for this woman
whose brain reacts like foam from
the inflamed bowels of a whale
bitter
that bitter bitter woman
whose eyes have become the guardian
of men's fly's
her tongue working out like a machete
hacking up a taxi driver in kumasi
his pride blood in her mouth
the fatty tissues of her existence pain
his pain our pain
Watch out for the walrus face pain eater
with flesh under her fingernails
for this woman looking elephantiasis
looking woman is dying of neglect
Watch out for the neglected

TO THE ARTIST WHO JUST HAPPENS TO BE BLACK

Listen

why is your grandaddy's chopped up penis the
magic mallets of truth you hide from
your grandmama's vagina torn by mangy dogs
her hemorrhaging womb the blood mouth of
the blues you deny

Listen to us our own

You are artist so called by vultures who
would hark white pussy on the slimy tongues of
swines selling it to us as a meat called freedom
these are the same vultures who eat holes
through hot shit just to suck scabs off a
junkie's ass & call it jazz rock

and you my brother
my sister
my strength
my power
my god of vision
why do you reject us
twin of blackness oppressed by the same oppressor
whom in unity we must kill
why
oh why are you forsaking us

LATE ON TOMORROW

Late on tomorrow in my love softness
under the thrill of fallopian tubes
between drinkers
immune to fallen faces
on my lap i will
set fire to this seat of experience
above contortionated prisons where
we kill at each other in
slow time   no time
look out
here come my stubborn whimpers
on yesterday's deformation
through my red light district head
beat of a lover's nod
unflamed
wind   rain   snow
everything gone
my waiting arch
under arm mole
the sluefoot imitation of life
torso
torso i have pointed myself out
below this back bone of knives
tip of fingers
rust of elbows
again picks shovels pipes of workers
again in the gut milk of my plant
snake eyes
church uniforms and seven star visions of
child molesters
emblems to the moon
barges
old time queens of new orleans
torch shadows

crusted heels
masses pearls and women
on the last X smiling
cactus fire
at four in the morning of our repression

A BLUES

Give me some star beer and a bottle of gin
cause forty heads have rolled and
I'm celebrating the end

Blues drying in my eyes like salt

I'm talkin to the shaven head beauties
wrapped in orange and black
black and orange funeral wrapped sisters lookin
just like bessie
those bessie smith lookin women in
the ashanti tribe

Let me speak with the ancestor of this clan

Empress baby sister
no we didn't try to understand you so
chances are we'll never understand them

trouble trouble trouble everywhere

I'm on my way
going to a festival
a festival where the umbrella gods will
shade my tongue with an oath so powerful
I could become the link to paradise
but who would mock my breath
who would steal my soul who
would tell the people what
the blues is really without my being dead

Hot pepper on my flesh

Give me some star beer and a bottle of gin cause
more heads are gonna roll and i
wanna celebrate the end

ILLUSIONS OF VISIONS

Preaching from the bigness of his skull
bowing to flowers between butts
during the masquerade of our chained feet
this blistered mouth of a midget popping to
the arrogance of applauding cocks
(they laughed at his fist & drank to the spit of
his flight)
only he knew falsification sources of his pitch
as we watched each others wounds bleeding into
sounds of flesh
    Should we appeal to the gentleness of their
    faces from the beans of our sorrow
    to the air in their eyes
    this firing squad kissed by revolutionaries?
The music scalding the sun had refused his body
refused her body
clowns to each others bodies
bandaged in a wheel of imitation
they cried & sang
to the boils on their knees
She a woman only among rocks with
arms like thigh wings
her dress between her gums
    on wrinkled lips
    next to darkness scream
    a poot through the ear
    next to wars of leaning bones
    in the presence of rape
    cream shyly against the stance of
    a buck tooth
    oh oh oh
Our skins would not close during falls of
trapeze artists
when we were told
the music is a balcony of blood a circle of smoke

forget the music and accept the wisdom of asses
this man this woman this soul this
fire hose of distortion
whom the music had refused to enter
    a dog barked and independence was declared
Love from the heart of a dollar bill
They made us hum until we became demons praying
to flames under our spoons killing how we grieve
because of emptiness
because the hand clasp was not the experience
was not the realness of being
no no no
was not the music
the substance of loneliness
the georgia grind or
the resting buttocks of old age

And at night full of cemetery feelings of
gravel and tears and dirty words
a people sentenced to silence among coffins
empty empty empty
knows and releases the fat back odors of madness
onto the dark glasses of sorrow
disguised as a last respect

SHOOTING STAR

Crying against the money
of dead bodies
my shoulders ripped by puppets coming
at me like bats as i strum a guitar with
my lash and wait near the wall of suspicion
    Shooting star from a sacred people
menace to sorrow
speaking the language of bitter dwarfs i
saluted the mustache madonnas and
danced with mirrors of myself
    waving to the crowds with
a hole through my hand
a skull on my hip
your coffin on my head
a rug on my back
my torn flesh an offering
my bent neck crying
    me hanging on a log
the smell of my clitoris on their faces as
they try clubbing death with
the breakage of my tits

KNOW YOURSELF

When i met your ass in the air amplified
gold and black checkered inflammation
I knew that many thin legs outside of
begging
were exploited by your swollen hemorrhoids
choir boy
are we being conditioned to your infection?
pass me by tomorrow in this cycle of heads
outcry
who are we to these televised flare bottomed
rivals of death?
better know yourself in the ball of their
hands
economic inmates of sorrow

HERE I AM

Here I am
dispossessed moro
an incarcerated episode of gloom they say
and what is ate the bottom of this
compulsion in distress
is it really the revenue of my tin cup
that contaminates
or the constant duplication of rotating marble
this spectacle of eyes re-entering sockets
without matter
without help from anyone
I mean in the crust of this struggle of
my enlargement
god will try to intervene
& i will be aroused to shout from
the revenge of my hygienic membranes
demanding no filth
no pus
no doo nasty conception in
no immaculate form or
disguise

THE RISING

Horns protruded from the
holes of a skeleton
gripping my bed as I
closed my eyes to the men
falling naked from heaven
my teeth waxed with candles
the stars burning my lips
a metronome conducting
orchestras of bone people
parades
skeletons fighting skeletons
against my body sweet among skulls
I ran through ribs & my
legs were sawed off I
spat between rotted out seed pits &
my own seeds became knots on my forehead
I shot without looking & the moon
stuck out its tongue as I sucked
peyote & knelt for the wedding between
fire & the fluid of my sorrow
in combat with myself
a refugee without feet
a virgin in a cathedral of hanging flesh
I the new flag to a revolution
the failure of death
blackly tuning the sun for the reign of
the rising sphinx

AFRICAN NIGHT SUITE

Africa
take my hands from the newspaper shacks of
rotten existence and let my cataracts
flow into the red clay of your loyalty

keep me in the mud of your belly
fed from the forest of your resistance
far from these mercenaries of illusion

I tell you i have to
live with my throat open to
the buzzards

my neck of four lines
my nose of gold studs
my lip ring flashing signals
to the moon against mount Kenya
greeting myself
    welcome
    perdido of the mambo sun
    afro star
    afro light
    afro suite of crickets in
    the african blues tribe
    greetings
from myself
hated by lies
by deceptions
by distortions
by the devastating experience of
disaster and the truth of our children
adjusted without ears
without arms
without the miracle of a face
No

I will not weep over slavery
or die inside wrinkled fleshes of shame
with feathers in my womb
in my love
I have surrendered my shadow of sorrow
and i sit next to the fetish woman heart to heart
eating the dead man's explosives
our bodies together
flying
raging
avenging
at the moment of invasion
transcending

All of these things speak from me to Africa

In cape coast
in Kumasi
in Ibadan
oyo oyo
I am a ife woman
biriwa fish woman of the sea
night queen of night cities in nights
I remember
hashish nights of murmuring glands
rainy nights in Tunisia
in front of the club tangerine
the house
the man
the night eggs sticky in Congo bongo beep moods of
devotion
carving up the dues nights when
we were sperms in a memorial of things
a homage to yokes of what we were & the nudeness
of what we wanted to be

and the river knew
the ocean knew
the white foam of madness knew

& before we recaptured life
with the unity of our breasts
when at night our tears flooded streets
we knew
our condition and
the weapon of our approach
No
we didn't beg to the suffering of
their butts
like strange horses
for a coin
for crumbs
for god
for the deceased eyes of a miscarriage
we didn't present the
sadness of our knees and
the callouses upon our lips
to such wide leg madness as theirs
against our ovaries
against the personality of our blood and
the dance of shrunken skulls deaf
to our navels
our fists
our dedications
our chest pulsing against
the bayonets of their existence
in that hour of our fingers
our giant fingers
in that hour of attack
we were spitting on their knives their guns
their crosses on their dead bodies
a portrait of spit on blood

Listen
from the lungs of a shark
comes the gauntness of our agony

the miracle of erections

who were the peasants
where are the bones

my hat is off to the two toned
double breasted birds of no hesitation

who were the peasants
where are the bones

my hat is off to the two toned
double breasted birds of no hesitation

SOLO

A solo full of quivering flesh flying
like black crows from the bottom of nothing to
the top of nowhere in a hall of suicide
suicide hall of consciousness trying to
suicide us in yellow flames of awareness order &
whiteness
in the name of god and leprosy
wild pimps of desperation
wet dogs & pigs
frighten by the genius of pure black rage
the demise of death and the suicide birth of Shango
of Ogun iron magic and the mistress of moisture
Corina Corina
love goddess arched in the nostrils of Damballa
rising from the holes of Malcolm into the
massacred sharpeville gods of flesh
spirit nipples of unity
the music
protector of the delta
collector of sweet juices and paradise
sperm brother   blood sister
Oshun goddess of honey hot vinegar mangos and
castor oil
queen of fire at the crossroads eating in the
belly of Legba
the honk man honk
god of sound god of war god of repetition
kidney tears and liver drops
the word
holder of the past
creator of the future
and lover to the black birds building a
new world supreme
Welcome

I FORGOT TO REMEMBER

And one night in my
tennis shoe smell
I was no longer influenced by
invisible crimes
no longer available to erotic dreams &
revelations of emaciated flesh
I was desolate to memory
not yet born to
the state of myself inside the
whiff of a smell intimate to feelings i
no longer contradict
no longer desert
no longer need to forget to remember to
recognize
heart beat

SCARIFICATIONS

(1973)

I AM NEW YORK CITY

i am new york city
here is my brain of hot sauce
my tobacco teeth my
   mattress of bedbug tongue
legs apart   hand on chin
   war on the roof   insults
pointed fingers   pushcarts
my contraceptives all

look at my pelvis blushing

i am new york city of blood
police and fried pies
i rub my docks red with grenadine
and jelly madness in a flow of tokay
my huge skull of pigeons
my seance of peeping toms
my plaited ovaries excuse me
this is my grime my thigh of
steelspoons and toothpicks
   i imitate no one

i am new york city
of the brown spit and soft tomatoes
give me my confetti of flesh
   my marquee of false nipples
my sideshow of open beaks
   in my nose of soot
in my ox bled eyes
in my ear of saturday night specials

i eat ha ha hee hee and ho ho
i am new york city
never-change-never-sleep-never-melt
   my shoes are incognito

cadavers grow from my goatee
look i sparkle with shit with wishbones
my nickname is glue-me

Take my face of stink bombs
my star spangled banner of hot dogs
take my beer can junta
my reptilian ass of footprints
and approach me through life
approach me through death
approach me through my widow's peak
through my split ends my
asthmatic laugh   approach me
through my wash rag
half ankle   half elbow
massage me with your camphor tears
  salute the patina and concrete
of my rat tail wig
  face up   face down   piss
into the bite of our handshake

i am new york city
my skillet-head friend
  my fat-bellied comrade
citizens
  break wind with me

IN THE EVERYDAY ROUTINE

In the everyday routine
of a time clock
i punched in
only to be out
of my head
without
jumping the gun
by thinking

SATURDAYS

Why do people always choose saturdays
to wig out
I mean the ones who scream leave me alone
i hate your guts
why do they always choose 2:05 pm saturdays
to say get the hell outa here
I mean the ones kicking walls
slamming doors
crushing skulls
why do they always have to choose saturdays for
me to lift my window and yell
shut the fuck up

UNDER THE EDGE OF FEBRUARY

Under the edge of february
in hawk of a throat
hidden by ravines of sweet oil
by temples of switchblades
beautiful in its sound of fertility
beautiful in its turban of funeral crepe
beautiful in its camouflage of grief
in its solitude of bruises
in its arson of alert

Who will enter its beautiful calligraphy of blood

Its beautiful mask of fish net
mask of hubcaps mask of ice picks mask
of watermelon rinds mask of umbilical cords
changing into a mask of rubber bands
Who will enter this beautiful beautiful mask of
punctured bladders moving with a mask of chapsticks

Compound of Hearts   Compound of Hearts

Where is the lucky number for this shy love
this top-heavy beauty bathed with charcoal water
self-conscious against a mosaic of broken bottles
broken locks   broken pipes   broken
bloods of broken spirits broken through like
broken promises

Landlords   Junkies   Thieves
enthroning themselves in you
they burn up couches they burn down houses
and infuse themselves against memory
every thought
a pavement of old belts
every performance

a ceremonial pickup
how many more orphans   how many neglected shrines
how many stolen feet   stolen gums
stolen watchbands of death
in you how many times

Harlem

hidden by ravines of sweet oil
by temples of switchblades
beautiful in your sound of fertility
beautiful in your turban of funeral crepe
beautiful in your camouflage of grief
in your solitude of bruises
in your arson of alert
beautiful

LYNCH FRAGMENT 2

Autumn in New York 72

I am bleed mouth nod
from an oath in sorrow

i command both rise and fall
through melancholy links
of refugee sweat

i succulent republic of swamp lips
push forward my head through
windshields of violence
to baptise in a typhoon of night sticks

Scream on me

I've gasolined my belly against suspects
and flown away tears across
the dry rust wings of a roach god

Attention all units

i call to the fumes
drawn back against steel
against invisible fuck of a cry
to remove its road block flesh of a flunky
and let that rotting become feast
on sapphire of my adobe fangs

i am zest from bad jaw quiver
of aftermath

Come Celebrate Me

ORCHARD STREET

Here is my card
here is my cup
i trust in god's trust
in me
    Thank you mam
it's only a smile
next to tape measures and short dogs
no passport
no visa
but where are we going anyhow
nowhere rag over my heart
    Nowhere

3 DAY NEW YORK BLUES

It's tuesday night
in ole possum face new york city   sweet daddy
    spit upon sadness
in this fist of three vines of two dark lips of
sunken blisters in my need more   need more
need more lovin sometimes baby please please please

And already it's wednesday mornin
in the deep end of my river
and like a woman
locked out doors in a storm
    i got those mean wet kill me kill me
    stroke me baby do me tonight blues

May i present thursday
in moonshine of my weepin willow
in the lonesome road of my groanin
moanin   sanctified   dignified   sweetsmellin
hoochicoo

Comes Friday
and this life beggin request
dead and gone
in noon time of my frisky whiskey money bag
cuttin mood

Juice up new york   Juice up

  Cause i got a fine warm satisfyin
screamin deep sea divin good feelin papa
hoppin   skippin   jumpin   flyin
back home to me

TO A FRIEND

Don't speak to me about
the mutilation of things through
ectoplasms of unmarked armpits
   tear slime of suffering

Why in the bar of ravishing symbols
under balconies of flowered eyes
purple colored sac factory of bruises why
this inauguration of tender ruby lips against
pine smelling rags of river flames
   not yet calm in delicate yawning lobes
of fecunded sound
   a few steps into bronze
the good luck cry of death
   current among chemicals

Why under the inspiration of tragedy
gram for gram
between notches of totem flesh and crumbs
obscene to bank tellers
should i drool beneath the corduroy mind of sabotage
like a substitute piece of plaster

Don't speak to me about these mutilated things
no longer fever of my fever of
my mouth of laughing nails
climaxed in the voice of a worm
postured against storm

APPEARANCES

You can beat down
the crabs on your hairs
if you want to
but it's the matters
in your eyes
that make you
uncordial

A NEW COLOGNE

You cover the kisses
of sailors and soldiers
with fumes from stashed dollars

the exploding scent of white shoulders
on tweed tongue of your rubber cup

you radiate in a mist of ambush
the jungle torn eyes
and desert boot flowers of shalimar

You are pellet deluxe of ricochet
the atomizing dew of youth blood
cream sachet of tabu acids
oriental sunlight

You are the new cologne
the fire itself
smell the stains on those panties
the long lasting sensual soap on those bodies

Intoxicating   Flaming   Provoking

A flare-up of a fragrance
you are called
Napalm
beauty house for fresh enemas

AND ANOTHER LOOK AT YOU

And another look at you anticipation
strung out and silent
your eyes between bent legs
covered by the show of hands
fabulous on the outside of gangosa

What do i care
face of metal buttons
nose of chain
roasted dreams
you annoy me with your plastic hair
and cotton scalp
hugged up with fear
and the flesh of fears world
fatigued by dentyne

Ask me why i take your complaint
on chin of my dilapidated ass of
prowling fish markets without revenge

Ask me why my convulsions
why my infatuations
why my dialect
why my warts without vaccine
what do i care if you ask me
why my navel is copper with hatred

AMERICA 1973

There is No wounded knee in america
only wounded arches and wounded ankles
in platform shoes

THESE ARE THE TIMES

These are the times of sterility
of hormone shots and lobotomies
of dehydrated funk and stagnated
celebrities
these are the times of solitary confinement

IT GOES DEEP

It goes deep
this pantomime tonguing
of the soul
not as a comeback
but as a tribute to resistance
against master priest
of our mother's ambushed flesh
life into
headrags of our love
reorganized

PHRASEOLOGY

I say things to myself
in a bitch of a syllable
an off tone wisp remarkable
in weight and size
completely savage to the passing of silence
through mass combinations of moisture
uncaked in pockets of endless phraseology
moving toward sacred razors
like air like untangled bush
over a piece of dead scar
instant in another smashed ear lobe
shivering between word echoes of
word shadows
jugular veins of popular contradictions
well dressed and groomed in the mirror of language
transparent and useless against
the impulsive foam
of a spastic

LAW AND ORDER

We know the official puke
of official appointees
the stiff shirts of desperation
the knotted ties of failure
the baggy pants of arrogance
the smelly socks of panic
the ordinary shoes of law and order
with their toes of pyorrhea
inflaming the consciousness
of an unpaid bill

WHEN I THINK

When i think of death
waiting in the hands
of some mercenary
the cultural look
of imperialism upon the plains

listen when i think
in the forceps of these thoughts
singing as if they were only
pearl handle pistols dipped in ink
or chlorine tears
on my feathered pelvis exhaling
once upon the mugging of my knock-kneed lips

When i think in allendes in african mine workers
in atticas in nerudas in septembers
suddenly upon this page of crosseyed symbols

Listen when i think of the suffering
in these thoughts
disappearing as if it were only a rusty nail
dipped in copper
or iodine blood
on my fish-meal flesh striking
once upon the kidnap of my gold shaped heart

When i think in the brass and textile
purina of these thoughts
death waiting in the hands of some colono
the shitty look of coup upon the plains

Listen when i think in the nitrate
of these thoughts
no getting around it
my wine glass is empty

CALL THE NIGHT

Listen to arks of filed down teeth
clapping   snappin
beneath masks of calabash eyes
screamin

Call the night   Call the night

And in this retreat
thrilled by my own poking chops
against sliding necks of wiping sounds
i strolled on discharging mud paths
through the delta of my mind

Call the night   Call the night

And in mouth of my protective cult
between blades and tail feathers
in the back yard of my yam

I weep with music
crack with thunder
and dance with the shadow of my leg

Call the night   Call the night

Hear this cherry-throated
guitar god-son of poverty
passing lonesome leaves of pain roots
between the blues and me

Call the night   Call the night

I said love me in stretched out ruins of my belly
and let me feel my flesh come true
cause i got a very special need

to have a real experience with you
next train please

Call the night   Call the night
next train please

Call the night   Call the night

BACK HOME IN BENIN CITY

Here in my lateness
in nerves of my sweetness
churning in the fact
of my flooded sadness
hour to hour
i am arriving at the fork of my blues
standing on ramps of torn mouths
sometimes confused
sometimes free
the heat of my soul at the entrance
of my mistreated heart
bound and gagged between torsos of studded knives
and lizard tails
stroking sperm compositions
in ear shots of oily red altars
the smell of iron bells
afternoon street of dying dogs
sacred shells and dodo leaves
the air fonky and soft
the music up and low down
the homeland poised between lungs
tense in the memory of fever
hot in the chest of a returnee

ORISHA

Across the flesh and feeling of soledad
tornados of blackness
patoised in its beauty
in its luminous fuchsia lagos nights
ruby darkness

criss-crossing in front of the music
in front of my pigeon toed solitude
another bush of praise
another battle ground for accents
insurrecting against brainwash and breakdowns
white bucks and famished lyrics
spellbound and peglegged
on cartridges of gunpowder teeth
Windpipes of burgundy lands
burning veins of respect forward into the blues
into pulsating ear of my cobra skin heart
immense in its infancy of these few words
Orisha   Orisha   Satchmo   Orisha

LIBATIONS

I witnessed
   the lynchings of Jonathan of George
and heard bulldozers coming
   for our ghetto tears

and i said to myself then:

   without libations and flames and sacrifice
without understanding and dreams
   emotion and protest
without struggle
   there will be no childhood to grow among
the corn and cassava
   watered by brown blood
shelling between zones

IFE NIGHT

Big beautiful bronze man
your love is as close
as the life-death shrill
from old folks in paradise
young as beginning rains in Guinea-Bissau
and strong like a million quivering
frog-throats wailing through
the night wells of Ife

How deep this time of us
dancing beneath Mozambique
against moon confessing flames
bouncing baby heart-beat
ocean tears of mud
to a strange snake of a new mask
arking the brain neck
of our song

We Remember Our Brother

AMÍLCAR CABRAL

Murdered January 20, 1973
by portugese agents

WARRIOR HEART

You Left Us A Courageous Life

A Beautiful Memory

A Liberated Territory

Our struggle continues in your guiding spirit

he armed struggle for the complete freedom of

our people

Rest in peace our brother
until we meet again

Long Live The Liberation Movements

Long Live Our Warrior Hearts

SONG FOR KWAME

You appeared in every feast
every crime
every spell
every chopped tongue of a tribe moaning
to themselves growing dim
    you appeared when laughter became crust
and crust became scrotum
rolling inward from constipation
    from fibroids of a festival without
    dried bats and posing martyrs
You appeared
    on the muted front of pigmented lungs like
puberty bones heated between
war cries and cold ash
    a praise song to puny legs
    to flab filled sorrow becoming
    violent within beandrop of a moment
barefoot and magic
above money changers and thunderbolts
emerging from death rattles
    from flames of raked cheeks into
beaded skulls of oil   blood   time
    the revealer
    the transformer
    the invader
sucking through grave yard pots of human heads
into kente cloths of our communal tears
    oh shy one
    spirit one
    one alone one
whose odor anoints bladders
salts brains
smelts together bodies
into one protruding navel
You have fallen

You are gone
and like grain inside rivermouths
of our nostrils we grow you
in the poolroom thoughts of our blackskins like
a ceremony of secret alleys
    beneath lips of cork
    ears of omen
    eyes of coin
scarification of sacred rouges
muscatels of rocking sadnesses
    you are growing under the gin-head-mask
    of beer breaths like a love shout from
    the black-belt of broken nipples
    dominating madness
you have fallen
you are gone
you are ancestral placenta
reassembled on the fifth day
of the flatted fifth scream
spreading like fire
    through isolated profiles of sanctified
    invalids
through ruffled gums of broken hearts
recording blackness in morning airs of endurance
    a urine test of lamentations
    into python skin moons sacs crying
    at the entrance of fish-like tombs
spirits frames of fire into
legends of hard luck wine
    carried in worms
entwined in stars
    visible between shedding skins
adorned with bricks
    closer to scorpion lips
of smelly guns
    fire
that knows the origin of cooked names
of rented rooms and velvet caskets
    flaming through night holes of wolftickets

through day ladies in ragged drawers through
    sentimental crocodile men
fire
    from the royal quarters of mercy
into the foul scent of being colonized too long
    fire
the blood of vision
the vision of Nkrumah
    the fallen
    the gone
    the grain grown bullets
    inside rivermouths of our
    nostrils shooting
You have fallen
You are gone
you are grain grown bullets
inside rivermouths of our
nostrils shooting

BRICKS

New York
I'm embellished
by your face of plaster
your scaffolds of greetings
shriveling in me
like corkscrews
the nasal of your voice
arriving in my hips an epidemic
your asphalt arms
embracing me in their
reputation
I kiss your bricks

FEATHERS

Excite my breasts
and patrol my vagrant heart
bloodshot tongue of veins
today
stands
the wet kiss liver of passion
against charcoal gums
of my soul's teeth
Oh the fatness of love
(compared to tumors fly away my friends)
these scabs have taken eyes
and navels have taken off shades
to look experience in its nose
bartender of bars
a drink to the length of that
dog called loneliness
the sparrow mouth ruby
dry feathers on my lover's step

STANTON STREET

Friends
terror entered me
in white gloves
leaving ant ridden memories
of strange latrines
on cane of a half skull

I was in symbol
of yesterday's shaven head
all things flashing ebony
when refrain
this half skull sucked up
secreting crows
of loose men
three fat ones
held over in bribes
of red ivory

And crossed by revenge
of my high butt
i could not see into
half skulls water boy
sweet heart of broken cups
standing outside naked
rusted
painful
unclean

INDELIBLE

Listen i have   a complaint to make
my lips are covered
with thumb prints
insomnia sips me
the volume of isolation
is up to my thyroid
and i won't disappear
can you help me

AND ALWAYS

And always having to speak
in spaces
when i'd rather cut up your clothes
and throw shoes at your head
is too much for now
so fix me a drink
my hands are in need of something
something to wipe with my mouth
one on the other
when we reach march
april may june

NATIONAL SECURITY

If you take these capes
of wet sheets and broken glass
these tom hearts of meshscreens
these decorated skins of 2nd degree burns
and toilet tissue armbands
If you take these football helmets
towels and broom handle headdresses
these bullhorn mouths of mace
these spinning bullets full of navels and hostages
If you take these ornamental gifts
to the governor of shellshock
you will be rewarded
with the momentous eyes
of society's autopsy
attica

CONSULTATION

I have lived in circles of solitude
in support of my involved laughter
emerging from words
from an atmosphere of folded hands
and the half lip stroke of burnt respect
becoming noble while pounding an old love bone
in withered consultation
and without warning
i wiggle through dead hairs of dead gods
no change in volume
i too can be pain in the face of your body
speak to me about this confinement
this deep revelation
between pauses
and the earth fonk of discharge
pearl tongue submissions of enslaved tears
manhood   womanhood   childhood
the zig zag message from my teeth
heard by my lips
bold against painted spirits
of hunchback fear
    (as if i couldn't fly away from this road show
    of passing syringes)
No
it is the convulsion of limbs lying
in pose of a person
empty of all confidence
that will make the ritual invasion of death
spread like grease
through scalps of decorative hairdos

SO LONG

My man loved me so much
he wanted to kill me
cause he loved me so good
he wanted to die
cause he loved me without sorrow
so sad without tears
he loved me to kill to die to cry
so much he wanted to scream
cause i loved him too much i
drank his tears
loved him too much
i ate his strength
loved him too much i stole his joy
i loved him to drink to eat to steal
cause we loved so much
so good to love to love
so long to love
so long

LEXINGTON/96 STREET STOP

New York
he was caught in a penitentiary of tears
  passionate to no one
he drank red soda pop
and became parolee to paranoid desperation

Tonight my wife died he said
and i'm about to waste this air this
sound this policeman with his
fucking face of stink breath harassments

Caught in a penitentiary of tears
  passionate to no one
his heart became a massive grave of electricity
from which no trains run
his eyes a spray gun of graffiti exiled between sockets
he's in the maximum security of himself
unknown janitor from angola where
his head lay planted in coffee fields
as his body stands constricted with sweat
seeping inward to fertilize suppression
hold back the liberation of himself
turned earth he says
look at this mother fuckin cop
with his no lip grinning invitation
to a duel

i am savage of subways yes
filled with old funk and
saltpeter tears yes
my bowels salute you in your justice
in your technical sadness of paper i.d.'s
man my wife died tonight
in a hospital not 30 minutes ago

and you stand here on this platform
in your mustache madness
handing me a ticket for drinking red pop?

MAKING IT

I know they want me to make it
to enter eye droppers and invade pills
    turn around or get shot
I know they wanna vaccinate me with
the fear of myself
so i'll pull down my face and nod
I know they want me to make it
    but i'm not in a hurry

I REMEMBER

I remember through remains
of my lip hanging cigarette
three days before your ass was dog tagged
and corsage of my acrylic tears
said to my good looking flesh of green tattoos
throw back your coat
and your face got hard as rock candy
and tight like alum pussy
as my pointed toe pointed heel high top silvers
pushed back their buckles
and my champale and bubble gum sweat flew
to the surface of my rhinestone crabs
and my belly cincher bra pincher
popped up their dukes
and my voice more precise than the wind said
come on motha fucka
kiss me

BLEECKER STREET

i got a dog
i got a cat
i got a rat
i got cockroaches
and guess what
i have more trouble
out of you
than i have
out of them

ORANGE CHIFFON

If orange chiffon sadness
flowed from my chin of three bumps
and sat in the armpit of a worn-out douche bag
looking back at the system
opening like unfamiliar smells of dead cimarrons
in my two hands of empty tribal reserves
the cap and blanket of my thirst
   would i hold back
my jelly-bean shrine of menstrual blood
to wipe skag from curve
of a lone pubic hair
and sink into anesthesia of my launch pad
   would i push back the desert
and begin my shake dance with a flask
of empty buzzard grunts
if orange chiffon sadness
flowed from my uka of purple hearts
and my shadow half the size of two dates
broke

HERALD SQUARE

Tell us about that shaking ensemble
of itching flesh
its inner thrill of warmth
its deep smell of instinct
the counter grunt of thunderbird radiation
between legs of strolling monsters
and the ruination of insult
fishing confessions from a coronation of crumbs
exalted through pigeon eyes

ASSETS

I got a sore throat
sore back
shit running everywhere
afterburner
a pink pad on
and none of it looks good on paper

BOWERY STREET

new york
won't you confess
your private affairs
inside booth ears
of a leather uterus
who cares about the bumps on your tongue
cup of spit listen
i was bending against the railing
when i saw
go down shadow of your thing
and thanks to corn meal
i tell you this
not in falsetto
not in swine posture
but in my devotion to snot
we resemble

HOMICIDE 1973

He died from
a bullet wound
in the back
fired by a plainclothes
policeman
in Queens New York
don't forget 10 year old
Clifford Glover

DO YOU THINK

Do you think this is a sad day
 a sad night
full of tequila full of el dorado
 full of banana solitudes

And my chorizo face a holiday for knives
 and my arching lips a savannah for cuchifritos
and my spit curls a symbol for you
 to overcharge overbill oversell me
these saints these candles
 these dented cars loud pipes
no insurance and no place to park
 because my last name is Cortez

 Do you think this is a sad night
  a sad day

And on this elevator
 between my rubber shoes
in the crème de menthe of my youth
 the silver tooth of my age
the gullah speech of my one trembling tit
full of tequila full of el dorado
 full of banana solitudes you tell me
i use more lights more gas
 more telephones more sequins more feathers
more iridescent head-stones
 you think i accept this pentecostal church
in exchange for the lands you stole

And because my name is Cortez
 do you think this is a revision
of flesh studded with rivets
 my wardrobe clean

the pick in my hair
    the pomegranate in my hand
14th street   delancey street   103rd street
    reservation where i lay my skull
the barrio of need
    the police state in ashes
drums full of tequila   full of el dorado
    full of banana solitudes say:
Do you really think time speaks english
    in the men's room

MEN'S SETTLEMENT HOUSE

Today on this day of old boots
filled with sores
full of eyes
coral like beads on my arms
like used razors in alcohol
and tampax in a cross
on the face of a young blood

I sit with a paper cup of slogans
in dog mange smell
of my cough syrup look

We don't have a damn thing
so maybe you could spare a quarter
for a sandwich
or a drink of wine or something
no

Swell up?   grease up
who gives a fuck 85¢ worth

And if I stretch my lips forward
to whisper through your grass covered ears
made of clay to be broken
can i borrow a cigarette

Face of perfect locks listen
it's too much flesh in this bombshelter
for you to like my occupation
so sleep it off

This sidewalk is without drink
this lobby is without food
this voucher hauling ass to reach me with

a fetish of hasbeen   has never been
and ain't gon' never be is also without hope

So swell up   grease up
who gives a fuck 85¢ worth
even if you have a cigarette

AND FROM YOUR MOUTH

And from your mouth
the dental records of life
will be fished up from
the hudson river
or a penny arcade
or maybe
a greyhound bus station
or some other place taking responsibility
for your kind of heat and flesh
and submission and fumigation
of such a wish

IT'S NOTHING

It's nothing
this tragedy in our arms
we can invent new bones
new fleshes
new flowers against madness
another red dress
another apple jack
another mug from
the neck bend of our conflict
yes
we can tolerate a still heart
against our ears and
relax with the crusted
confessions of a blood cake
it's nothing

TAPPING

for Baby Laurence, L.D. Jackson
and other tap dancers

When i pat this floor
   with my tap

when i slide on air
   and fill this horn intimate with
the rhythm of my two drums

   when i cross   kick
scissor   locomotive

   take four for nothing
four we're gone

when the solidarity of my yoruba turns
join these vibrato feet
   in a Johnny Hodges lick
a chorus of insistent Charlie Parker riffs

   when i stretch out for a chromatic split
together with my double X
   converging in a quartet of circles

when i dance my spine in a slouch
   slur my lyrics with a heel slide
arch these insteps in free time

   when i drop my knees
when i fold my hands
   when i decorate this atmosphere
with a Lester Young leap and
   enclose my hip-like snake repetitions
in a chanting proverb
   of the freeze

I'm gonna spotlite my boogie
    in a Coltrane yelp

echo my push in a Coleman Hawkins whine

i'm gonna frog my hunch in a Duke Ellington strut

quarter stroke my rattle
    like an Albert Ayler cry

i'm gonna accent my march in a Satchmo pitch

    triple my grind in a Robert Johnson blues

i'm gonna steal no steps

    i'm gonna pay my dues

i'm gonna 1   2   3

    and let the people in the apple
go   hmmmp   hmmmmp   hmmmmmp

MOUTH ON PAPER

(1977)

FOR THE POETS[1]

Christopher Okigbo & Henry Dumas

I need kai kai ah
a glass of akpeteshie ah
from torn arm of Bessie Smith ah

I need the smell of Nsukka ah
the body sweat of a durbar ah
five tap dancers ah
and those fleshy blues kingdoms from deep south ah
to belly-roll forward praise
for Christopher Okigbo ah

I need a canefield of superstitious women a
fumes and feathers from port of Lobito a
skull of a white mercenary a
ashes from a Texas lynching a
the midnight snakes of Damballah a
liquid from the eyeballs of a leopard a
sweet oil from the ears of an elder a
to make a delta praise for the poets a

On this day approaching me like a mystic
number oh
in this time slot on death row oh
in this flesh picking Sahelian zone oh
in this dynamite dust and dragon blood and liver cut oh

I need cockroaches ah
congo square ah
a can of skokian ah
from flaming mouth of a howling wolf ah
the smell of Harlem ah
spirits from the birthplace of Basuto ah

---

* This poem was titled "Kai Kai (For the Poets)" when used in *Poetic Magnetic* and the album *Maintain Control.*

mysteries from an Arkansas pyramid   ah
shark's teeth   ah
buffalo   ah
guerrillas in the rainy season   ah
to boogie forward ju ju praise for Henry Dumas   ah

In this day of one hundred surging zanzi bars   oh?
in this day of bongo clubs moon cafes and paradise lounges   oh
in this day's pounded torso of burgundy mush   oh
in this steel cube   in this domino   in this dry period   oh

I need tongues like coiling pythons   ah
spearheads gushing from gulf of Guinea   ah
the broken ankles of apartheid ah
to light up this red velvet jungle   ah
i need pink spots from the lips of trumpet players   ah
the abdominal scars of seven head hunters   ah
a gunslit for electric watermelon seeds   ah
to flash a delta praise for the poets   ah

Because they'll try and shoot us
like they shot Henry Dumas   huh
because we massacre each other
and Christopher Okigbo is dead   uh-huh
because i can't make the best of it   uh-hun
because i'm not a bystander   uh-hun
because mugging is not my profession   uh-unh

I need one more piss-ass night to make a hurricane   a
i need one more good funky blood pact
to shake forward a delta praise for the poets   a

On this day of living dead Dumas
on this day of living dead Okigbo

I need kai kay   ah   i need durbars   ah
i need canefields   ah   i need feathers ah
i need cockroaches   ah i need eyeballs   ah
I need buffalo   ah

i need spirits   ah   i need hurricanes ah
I need   ah
to make a delta praise for the poets   ah
  ah ah ah ah ah
i need spirits   ah   i need ankles   ah   i need hurricanes   ah
i need gas pipes   ah   i need blood pacts   ah   i need   ah
to make a delta praise for the poets   ah

BROODING

They're brooding in Rosedale
with pipe-bombs in their mouths

Brooding in Boston
with darts   between their teeth

Brooding in Connecticut
with curses on their tongues

Brooding with the smell of rat's piss in their hearts
brooding with the breath of red whiskey in their spit
brooding into madness into death into sheets   drying up
    while brooding brooding brooding brooding brooding

These bloodthirsty people

They're brooding in North Dakota with grenades in their hands
brooding in the Carolinas with torches in their ears
brooding in Alabama with water hoses still under their hoods
brooding in Louisville with gasoline in their beer cans

brooding in New York City with long nails shooting from their hockey sticks
brooding in Puerto Rico with sterilization on their minds
brooding in South Africa with cactus missiles perched on their thighs
just brooding brooding brooding brooding brooding

They're brooding with purple veins of the bible shooting from their noses
brooding with brass knuckles on their toes
brooding with badges under their chins
brooding with bricks in their baby carriages
brooding with prayers in their belts
just brooding brooding brooding brooding brooding

They're brooding with stiff upper lips for brooding
they're brooding with rules for brooding

they're brooding with heli-cannons for brooding
they're brooding with hate in their eyes for brooding
they're brooding with withered wreaths on their heads for brooding
they're burning books while brooding
burning buses while brooding
throwing stones while brooding

These bloodthirsty people

They're brooding beyond the deadline
for brooding brooding brooding brooding brooding

GIVE ME THE RED ON THE BLACK OF THE BULLET

for Claude Reece Jr.

Bring back the life
of Claude Reece Jr.

I want the bullet from his head
to make a Benin bronze
to make an explosion of thunder
to make a cyclone

I want the 14 years of Claude Reece Jr.
shot on the 15th day of september
shot in the back of his head
shot by a police officer in Brooklyn
shot for being black

Give me the black on the red of the bullet
i want to make a tornado
to make an earthquake
to make a fleet of stilts
for the blackness of Claude Reece Jr.
the blackness called dangerous weapon
called resisting an arrest
called nigger threat

I want the life of the blackness of Claude Reece Jr.
i want the bullet from his head
to make a protective staff for startled children
to make hooks and studs
for warrior masks

Give me the bullet with the odor
and the smoke and the skin and
the hair of Claude Reece Jr.
i want to make power
to make power for
the blackness of Claude Reece Jr.

the blackness called pent-up frustration
called unidentified negro
called nigger revolutionary

I want the life of the blackness of Claude Reece Jr.
i want the bullet from his head
to make a protective staff for startled children
to make a Benin bronze
to make an explosion of thunder
to make a cyclone
i want the bullet to bring back the blood
of Claude Reece Jr.
i want to make justice

I want to make justice for
the blackness of Claude Reece Jr.
bring back the bullet with the blood of the blackness
of Claude Reece Jr.
i want to make justice
i want to make justice for the blackness of Claude Reece Jr.

MERCENARIES & MINSTRELS

A mercenary like Rolf Steiner
will split open your head with a bottle of I.W. Harper
in a liquor store in boston
he will shoot through every cell in your body
and blow you up for kicks on pay day
he'll cut off your legs
fire-up your thighs
and twist your balls
into an american eagle and swastika emblem
for this bi-centennial

So don't tell me to be cooperative
and let the SS colonel knock me off
don't tell me that this plantation is changing
and so i should be cool and let the paratroopers fuck me
don't tell me that i'm just a plain ordinary citizen
because the mercenaries of the world don't give a shit

They have teeth like firing squads
naked women like red devils with rancid breaths
thoughts like infested rivers of dismembered bodies
jokes like invasions into angola
faces like ten german shepherd dog tongues
look Steiner is washing his mouth with the blood
of five more africans
his combat boots go berserk up ass holes
there's no controlling this bereted pimp
when the smell of dark flesh enters his brain
he goes crazy
gasoline spurts from his navel
rockets launch from his eyelids
he's a butcher a killer
with a sweet tooth especially for niggers
so don't tell me
to get down on my knees

and roll around singing mammy like ben vereen
because Steiner oils his lips
with fear sweat from armpits
he belches bullets and smokes toe nails
his torso is lit with neon machine guns
he's an expilot in love with war
he's a mercenary who cares only about killing
he's an addict addicted to twisting balls into
an american eagle and swastika emblem for this bicentennial
so don't tell me to suck on a flagpole   coming
through the sockets of a death skull and be cool

DRYING SPIT BLUES

Tonight the whooping moan of invading blues
    with its clef of troubled hearts
with its double stomp burn of woman flesh
    spitting with the whirlwind of spitting cobras
spitting with the meaning of Anna Nzinga
    flashflooding blues
of great blues migrations
    the great blues of howling sudan
great blues in a conflict of nubian throbs
    among the faces chiseled from memphis
among the cataracts spitting from ethiopia
    the great blues of drying spit
with its escalator of razors
    forefinger of pistol whips
quadrangle of knuckle bones
    basin of fish hooks
equator salt
    the whooping taste of invading blues
of broken whistles
    radiated fox holes
a grenade of camel hair
    calypso of neckscars
old blues
    intravenous blues
blues with a procession of blows
    the blows in mouth of the goatheads of death
a commemoration to famine
    right up to our chests
afterskulls of invading blues
    of bombed out groans
150 rockets between screams
    meat hooks smelling into smells of needle-tracked ribs
dead crows   fried feathers   spoiled calamares
    and eyes of sculpted slugs

and silver ants on lower lids painted charcoal
and long teeth in amber jels
    and tongue flaming tongue of sweetheart rings
of ruby snakes with veins of iridescent smoke studs
    a squadron of lips made of cockle-burrs
    a salty dirge of sapless pinchers
a mirage of pulsing green roosters
secret dogs
polychrome spirits
    head-quart of bullface throat slitters
right up to our chins
    sparkling without lizard juice
mutilations without mucous
    a concave of widowfish entering flies
a circle of jackals cocked on the moon
    a cylinder sun without holes
and once again warships rush to other ports
and once again relief is too late
and once again a shriveling solution
    the code name for buzzards
wrist-bones on altar of another jaw
    illuminations
right up to our nostrils
in howling sudan
    in nubian throbs
in faces chiseled from memphis
    the shrinking shrines of whooping flesh
of invading skeletons
    of spreading saharas
of drying spit
    tonight's Blues

SO MANY FEATHERS

You danced a magnetic dance
in your rhinestones and satin banana G-strings
it was you who cut the river
with your pink diamond tongue
did the limbo on your back
straight from the history of southern flames
onto the stage where your body
covered in metallic flint
under black and green feathers strutted
with wings of a vulture paradise on your head
strutted among the birds
until you became terror woman of all feathers
of such terrible beauty
of such fire
such flames
all feathers Josephine
This Josephine
exploding red marble eyes in new york
this Josephine
breaking color bars in miami
this Josephine
mother of orphans
legion of honor
rosette of resistance
this Josephine before
splitting the solidarity of her beautiful feathers

Feather-woman of terror
such feathers so beautiful
Josephine
with your frosted mouth half-open
why split your flamingos
with the death white boers in durban south africa
Woman with magnificent face of Ife mask
why all the teeth for the death white boers in durban south africa

Josephine you had every eyelid in the forest
every feather flying
why give your beaded snake-hips
to the death white boers in durban
Josephine didn't you know about the torture chambers
made of black flesh and feathers
made by the death white boers in durban
Josephine terror-woman of terrible beauty of such feathers
I want to understand why dance
the dance of the honorary white
for the supporters of apartheid in south africa

After all Josephine
I saw you in your turquoise headdress
with royal blue sequins pasted on your lips
your fantastic legs studded with emeralds
as you kicked   as you bumped   as you leaped in the air
then froze
your body breaking lightning in fish net
and Josephine   Josphine
what a night in harlem
what electricity
such trembling
such goose pimples
so many feathers
Josephine
dancer of the magnetic dancers
of the orange flint pelvis of the ruby navel
of the purple throat
of the feet pointing both ways
of feathers now gone
Josephine   Josephine
I remember you rosette of resistance
southern flames
Josephine of the birdheads, ostrich plumes
bananas and sparkling G-strings
Josephine of the double-jointed knees
double-jointed shoulders   double-jointed thighs
double-jointed breasts   double-jointed fingers

double-jointed toes double-jointed eyeballs
double-jointed hips doubling
into a double squat like a double star into a giant double snake
with the double heartbeats of a young girl
doubling into womanhood
and grinding into an emulsified double spirit
Josephine terror-woman of feathers i remember
Josephine of such conflicts i remember
Josephine of such floating i remember
Josephine of such heights i remember
Josephine of so many contradictions
of so many transformations i remember
Josephine
of such beauty
Josephine of such fire
Josephine of such sheen
Josephine of such
feathers i remember
Josephine Josephine

IN THE LINE OF DUTY

In the line of duty
i had to recite into the right eye of a midget
i had to recite into the left ear of a dog
and there they were
a pair of recital boots
made of leather whips
squeaking and echoing
into armpits of my nervous wreck
at noontime on the job in the line of duty
i recited my emotions
into their lunches
i recited empty spaces between the spaces of their bites
and there they were
a pair of eggs
made of old gasses
blowing rhythms
into thighpits of my eating sweat
at noontime on the job in the line of duty
i shoved my battle scars into their belches
i wiped my X on their blah blahs
and quilted images between their bow wows & tee hees
and there they were
a midget made of hiccups
a dog made of sirens
backfiring into my stomach
at noontime   on the job   in the line of duty

OGUN'S FRIEND

Metal Workshop

I saw your eyes like bumps of flint
i saw your shoes like high-top boulders
i saw your hands like faces of fire
i saw your fingers like axes of Shango
i saw your body like a rocker of steel

Yo
i heard a hum down there
i heard a rumble down there
i heard a ghost down there
i heard a thunderbolt expel down there
i heard a anvil in the night go hummmmmmmm
down there

Hey whose metals are shouting so loud
they must be the tapper that Ogun knows

whose are those beads so hot and black
they must be brass for Ogun to fill

who's that worker with corrugated gums
it must be the worker that Ogun chose

who's that one with feet like flames
it must be the welder that's Ogun's friend

Yo
i smell a chicken in here
i smell some charcoal in here
i smell a goat in here
i smell some wax in here
i smell a dog in here
i smell some clay and some oil and some blood in here

Hey i see your chains like links of teeth
crowbars
i see your coils like female pouches
barbed wire
i see your grills like braided snakes
fish-net
i see your ladder like a totem of pliers
crocodiles
i see your pipes like razors on tusks
wine bottles
i see your scissors and your keys on the table in there
uh-huhn

Yo
you got pant legs made into hats
you got diamond plates made into walls
you got straightening combs made into steps
you got hammer-heads made into skulls
you got flat-rings made into ears

Pant legs diamond plates
straightening combs hammer-heads
flat-rings
yo

I feel your flux
i feel your sander
i feel your drill bit
i feel your grinder
i feel your drill press
i feel your hack saw
i feel your brick ax

Yo
i saw your windows like sheets of steel
i heard a gong down there
i saw some navels like bushes of wire
i heard a bird down there

Hey
you got lizard tongues made into tongs
i feel your bald spot
you got snakeskins   covered in bronze
i feel your chin marks

lizard tongues   bald spots
snakeskins   chin marks
yo

i smell some fish in here
i see a rail down there
i smell some toes in here
i see a horn down there
i smell some funk in here
i see a knife down there
i smell some ratheads in here
i see a person down there

Whose that one so brown and fine
Ogun's friend
who's that one in green on green
Ogun's friend
who's that one who eats so fast
Ogun's friend
who's that one with toothpaste lips
Ogun's friend
who's that one who spits on tools
Ogun's friend
Yo Ogun's friend

I KEEP THE TREMOR

Exhibition of Early American Art

I keep the tremor in my nose
when doors open to metal fragments
and red from the penis
enters lace
that combines mud-asphalt
with a swallowing of fire-flies
and they want me to shut off the odor
relax, spread, pull the tremor from nose
  an old silver saxophone crushed like foil
against wrinkled lids
metallic lids of starvation
blinking to my mouth
through plastic goblets
through glory glory hallelujah
through bye bye blackbird
through the pain in my ass
sitting between antique scarves
of a bicentennial
fingers in nose
and nothing on the tip

GRINDING VIBRATO

Blues Lady
with the beaded face
painted lips
and hair smeared
in the oil of texas

You were looking good and sounding beautiful
until the horseman wanted your thunder
until the boa constrictor wanted your body
until syringes upright hyenas
barbwired your meat to their teeth
pushing behind your ears
inside your mouth
between your vagina
scabs the size of quarters
scabs the size of pennies
the size of the shape of you
all pigeon holes and spider legs colonized woman
funky piece of blood flint
with blue graffitied arms
a throat of dead bees
and swollen fingers that dig into a swamp of broken purrtongue

Spotted stripped blues woman
who was looking good and sounding beautiful
with those nasal love songs
those strident battle-cry songs
that copper maroon rattle resonator
shaking from your feet to your eyes
the sound of water drum songs
grinding vibrato songs to work by to make love by
to remember you by
Blues song lady who was looking good and sounding beautiful
until you gave away your thunder
until you gave up your spirit

until you barbwired your meat to teeth
and became the odor of hyenas
uprooted woman with the embalmed face
pall bearer lips
and hair matted in the mud of texas
how many ounces of revolution do you need
to fill the holes in your body
or
is it too late to get back your lightning
is it too late to reconstruct your song blues song sister tell me
is it too late for the mother tongue in your womanself to insurrect

I'M NOT SAYING

I'm not saying that i'm bitter
so why tell me about telling
someone else about it
let's not lose our tempers
or our statistics over whose smell
became pungent before the others
let's not loose each other over
these choice of words
devoted to someone else
after all my life is not dependent
on your gestures
and your gestures are not dependent
on my smoke
so why blink

ALBERTA   ALBERTA

Mother of Martin Luther King

A helmet of dilated orbs
   dilated orbs   dilated orbs
a cylinder of sawed-off teeth
   sawed-off teeth
a torpedo of bulldogs   bulldogs   bulldogs
   target   target
into Alberta   Alberta ?

Alberta
   horizonal darkness
shaking three times in the head
   three times in the head   three times in the head

Alberta
   a deep holler compounded
with goober oil   with roses
   with blood   with warriors
rising beneath the surface of her body

Alberta
   slow spiritual
below the flame
   Alberta
M.A.K.   Blues
   into Baule woman of mud   Alberta
woman with holes of electric currents Alberta
   fertility woman
ringing three times in the earth
   three times in the earth   three times in the earth
Alberta
   spirit with waist beads of ebony clay
Alberta
   with brass face bells
Alberta
   womb of red and purple masks

Alberta
 in a secret society of tears Alberta
tears that are tidal waves
 tidal waves in the name of Harriet Tubman
in the name of Yaa Asante Waa
 in the name of Betty & Coretta & Myrlie & Pauline

Alberta
 flat-mouth machete Alberta
Alberta with luminous ears like steel doors
 breaking along the lines of the goggles
over the eyes of Marcus Chenault Alberta
 breaking in front of the compulsion on the trigger
of the finger of Marcus Chenault
breaking the worms on the brain in a trance
of the possessed victim Chenault
 Chenault of the enormous skull
Chenault of the puffy cheeks
student Chenault
 hoodlum Chenault
Marcus Chenault assassinator of mothers
between the gun and thirty minutes of life
left in Alberta King

Alberta Alberta
 soloist with eyes pointing down

Alberta Alberta
 dancer in a choir of shrieks

Alberta Alberta
 flesh embedded with broaches Alberta

Alberta Alberta
 great tattooed beauty called Mama King

Alberta Alberta
serene intense Alberta
Alberta indelible Alberta

Alberta encircling
  the tribe of sons
who kill for the sake of a purse
killing for the sake of a purse
who kill for the sake of rape
  killing for the sake of rape
who kill for the sake of killing themselves
  in one pair of goggles
  one pair of pants
  one gagging tongue
  three lobes of colonization and condolences
to the family of King
to the family of Chenault
to the family of the deacon and the wounded
in ebenezer church with Alberta

Alberta
  with the high pitched voice of an organ
Alberta precious love Alberta
  Alberta
in sculpted hairdos
Alberta in amber nose rings   Alberta
  striking three times in the tongue
Alberta   Alberta   Alberta
  horizonal darkness   darkness
compounded with goober oil   goober oil   with roses   roses
with blood   blood   with ashes   ashes   and charcoal   charcoal
and Harriet   Harriet   and Yaa   Yaa   and Betty   Betty   and
Coretta   Coretta   and Myrilie   Myrilie   and Pauline   Pauline
and Albert   Alberta   Alberta   Alberta

DRUMS EVERYWHERE DRUMS

Drums everywhere drums
drums that remain
to booster thighs in its radar
in its thump of a bass without
being beggar
sunlight   midnight having to be barfly
having to be bullfrog
having to be drums
                                        drums
burnt drums to clear the skin among dreams
flint of antibiotic dawns
potash and cinnamon   sperms rising
with an algebra of swamp drums
no longer pyrex teeth
topaz excrement
angular nightmares
no longer ax-shaped lips
pierced corten buttocks
at the bottom of fermented mud drums

Drums flowing with a mask of zircon tornados
pickup band holding spirals of whiplash
in its bric-a-brac in its eyefold of mashed tendons
rimless springs
entrances funneled with catafalques of
embroidered signal drums

Drums made from rivers
made from a multiplication of dance steps
made from catfish heads in a tongue's embrace
made from a rosette of orange rosin cradle cap
with impulse spotted like seclusion and
revolution decorating its drum
with memory grease made from Nat Turner's body
drums preoccupied in cheeks of ancestors

twirling into footprints into snare drums into ceremonies
into shoe shine rags
the dust on those skins on those reeds
arranging armatures of black feeling
into street octaves of liberation drums of
membranes close to the sun's memoirs
and life duct of this brillo atmosphere
drums the size of flea bites drums that are fly heads
cork and plantain drums vase oil drums and
flannel flame wreaths of iridescent toenail drums
Everywhere drums

Drums
brushing whiskers of imagination
into ink ripples of compelling pompadours
drums grinding into steel
silver wires out of nostril bells
embalmed with images inoculating drums into feet spikes
of new canoes and new patterns
of new hurricanes
drumming with red palms of passion
drumming with massacred villages in Mozambique
drumming with uncombed look of a message
moving through heartbeats of six female drums
everywhere drums

Drums of acrobatic wombs
of bladders and trumpets engulfed
in a drum of opening elbows
the alto wind of sapling drums
fluorescent drums of benzine marshes
barracuda drums
in asphalt drums of nipple star drums of hunger drums
indexed between ovums
between floral ligaments
and the rhythm of rickets
drumming in a hollow of blues
baritone callus on rainbow covenant
of pickled heart drums

breast wheel of drums
fished up through pores of pimento
through ovations of bloated gills
babbling goiter drums holding
fissures of thumps in a coil of favelas
drums
the frequencies in position
drums
the sulphurated humidity of brooding rolls
broken pistons and cockpits of drums
remaining with pablum
with fluorine
with city whistles and forks entering drums
of borax and wild hairs
turbo-jetted throat drums
chrome-studded fangs of stomping stampedes
into tom-tom diaphragms
of black diamond pearl drums
everywhere drums
peninsula of my berserkness drum
axle of my hydraulic cough drum
diatonic drums
crazybone of my hyenaic laughter drum
thrill of a triad of electrode drums
everywhere drums

Drums in rufescent blades of Roxbury wind
tall cool fine drums
cry drums scream drums
dream interpretation of jungle spells and
tenement fire drums
searching through the buckeye drums
reaching for washboards of African blood drums
laughing drums emerging drums
precisions of blackness drums
drums whispering drums climbing
drums migrating into pedals and moods
of finger-popping tambourine drums
brick drums   crawfish drums

drums of new belches   drums with old mercurochrome
undulating armpit drums
cubano drums
sparrow leg strokes of tongue-tied drums
opal pool cues
ground nut pyramids
hey peewee from Panama drums
sanukadei   sanukadei
and my wide mouth paradiddles of adupe adupe drums

And these bragging drums of sparkling cans
and these home-brew tear-jerking drums
and this bong bong deep in the cowbell of Zimbabwe
and staccato beating drums
crossing the Limpopo
crossing death-drums foreskin drumming against drums
Fierce drums
growling drums
echo drums
over mojo whoop whooping drums
out of coo coo ka hooka drums
ear drums   khaki drums
drums made of dynamite
drums made from elephant yelps
Fulani drums   Fon drums   Ga drums
drums of new juniflips
drums of ancient mardi gras
Asantehene drums Senufo drums
and my indigo lip-smacking conga drums
tightening
drum rhythms
into mush-mouth rhythms child-birth rhythms
Ibo god house rhythms
melancholy bellies crossed in a knife of rhythms of rhythms of rhythms
from baba's calabashes of rattling rhythm drums of
drums to drums of brass cymbals of drums
dazzling with hummingbirds
with guava skins   with cowrie shells

with jellyfish   with kola nuts
with cobalt and uranium and
Mandingos on the road to kokomo drums
everywhere drums
spit drums from Oduduwa drums
everywhere drums
domo domo domo domo domo domo drums
Oduwa drums   everywhere drums   everywhere drums
Ekuse

ROSE SOLITUDE

for Duke Ellington

I am essence of Rose Solitude
my cheeks are laced with cognac
my hips sealed with five satin nails
i carry dreams and romance of new fools and old flames
between the musk of fat
and the side pocket of my mink tongue

Listen to champagne bubble from this solo

Essence of Rose Solitude
veteran from texas   tiger from chicago   that's me
i cover the shrine of Duke
who like Satchmo   like Nat (King) Cole
will never die because love they say
never dies

I tell you from stair steps of these navy-blue nights
these metallic snakes
these flashing fish skins
and the melodious cry of Shango
surrounded by sorrow
by purple velvet tears
by cockhounds limping from crosses
from turtle-skinned shoes
from diamond-shaped skulls and canes
made from dead gazelles
wearing a face of wilting potato plants
of grey and black scissors
of BB shots and fifty red boils
yes the whole world loved him

I tell you from suspenders of two-timing dog odors
from inca-frosted lips
nonchalant legs
i tell you from howling chant of sister Erzulie

and the exaggerated hearts of a hundred pretty women
they loved him
this world sliding from a single flower
into a caravan of heads made into ten thousand flowers

Ask me
Essence of Rose Solitude
chickadee from arkansas that's me
i sleep on cotton bones
cotton tails
and mellow myself in empty ballrooms
i'm no fly by night
look at my resume
i walk through the eyes of staring lizards
i throw my neck back to floorshow on bumping goatskins
in front of my stage fright
i cover the hands of Duke who like Satchmo
like Nat (King) Cole will never die
because love they say
never dies

NIGHTTRAINS

When i blow open green bottles
straight across hump of a frozen tongue

when i shove brown glass
through skull of a possum
and pass from my ears a baptism of red piss

when i cry from my butt like a jackal
and throw limbs of a dying mule into the river

when i split venom from the head
burn codeine into a cosmetic paste
and grieve into a wax of dried bulls

when my mystical bunions jam eyes
into searching spit of a starving wolf
into cosmic lips like monkey genitals

And i receive my pickled turned skeleton of rusty chains
in the bodega
i receive a symbolic heart made of five middle fingers
in the bodega
i receive a teeth parade of yellow roses to leave the bodega
and cross the rio grande
onto the flatbed bones of a musty nighttrain

I say
to see me loosen jaws like a snake
to see me exhausted after a few strikes
to see me pay dirt to the ice hog
in my masai-pachuca-doo
squatting on a pillow of old zoot suits
squatting among the names and breeds
breaking down cheeks dotted

on this night train
and i say i dream of the 1943 riots
I say i dream in a hailstorm of riots
And i say riots dream into a mass of skins stooping
on flatbed bones of a funky nighttrain

And when i siphon sweat for fuel
from this patron saint of chronic diarrhea

When i turn this rubber face into a spotted puma
and take on the forceful winds of the prune pickers

When my laughter dominates the last seat
And i burn labor contracts into brown port caca

Then i approach in mother of pearl and human blood
in father of smoking and coughing throats
in my jelly of coyote strings
who is to say what when i approach

I mean somewhere along the road in this cold cold chicken shit
somewhere along the road in this wasted body
somewhere along the road eat stocks, bonds feathers
somewhere along the road confiscate borders from wild dogs
somewhere along the road shove them into the imperial valley
somewhere along the road cry hard
and let this night train sink its
rundown rectum of electric chairs into heaven
and say fuck it

I see a way through the maroon glass of this milky way
I say i see a way through for the cradle of hulls
sticking through these indigo ankles
I see a way through
for these torn shoes stinking like dead cats
I see a way through for these blood-streaked legs
I say i see a way through
for these pus-riddled holes in their suction-cup lips
and when i pass through toothless combs coming from armpits

of the bodega
when i pass through bats on corkscrews coming
from the bodega
when i push my mortified flesh from this bodega
and walk with the mildew of an old zoot suit
walk tall in my mud-packed-masai-pachuca-doo
walk among the survivors from the musty nighttrains
fuck it
I say dreams are like riots
i say we dream in a hailstorm of riots
and i say riots dream into a mass of skins
coming from flatbed bones of the funky funky nighttrains

COMMITMENT

for Paul Robeson

You stand out in your passport
a committee of one
and I like that
a committee of one who
covered a lot of territory
the territory of dedication
a dedication to the freedom of your people
I knew you in that way
as an example
the example of a prominent artist
complete with talent and revolutionary gestures
and I like that
making connections
being progressive
the story of struggle instead of the story of success
I knew you in that way
in the way of the spirituals I loved
even though you didn't sing in the style of my choice
but what does style have to do with commitment
after all contributions go beyond songs
and I like that
the fact that you interpreted
the symbol that your photograph had become
a powerful force significant to masses of people
I understood you in that way
as a person complete with confidence and political intent
never holding back
never selling out
the story of dignity instead of the story of fame
I knew you in those ways and I like that

IN THE MORNING

Disguised in my mouth as a swampland
nailed to my teeth like a rising sun
you come out in the middle of fish-scales
you bleed into gourds wrapped with red ants
you syncopate the air with lungs like screams from yazoo
like X-rated tongues
and nickel-plated fingers of a raw ghost man
you touch brown nipples into knives
and somewhere stripped like a whirlwind
stripped for the shrine room
you sing to me through the side face of a black rooster

In the morning   in the morning   in the morning
all over my door like a rooster
In the morning   in the morning   in the morning

And studded in my kidneys like perforated hiccups
inflamed in my ribs like three hoops of thunder through a screw
a star-bent-bolt of quivering colons
you breathe into veiled rays and scented ice holes
you fire the space like a flair of embalmed pigeons
and palpitate with the worms and venom and wailing flanks
and somewhere inside this fever
inside my patinaed pubic and camouflaged slit
stooped forward on fangs
in rear of your face
you shake to me in the full crown of a black rooster

In the morning   in the morning   in the morning

Masquerading in my horn like a river
eclipsed to these infantries of dentures of diving spears
you enter broken mirrors through fragmented pipe spit
you pull into a shadow ring of magic jelly
you wear the sacrificial blood of nightfall

you lift the ceiling with my tropical slush dance
you slide and tremble with the reputation of an earthquake
and when i kick through walls
to shine like silver
when i shine like brass through crust in a compound
when i shine   shine   shine
you wail to me in the drum call of a black rooster

In the morning   in the morning   in the morning
gonna kill me a rooster
in the morning
early in the morning
way down in the morning
before the sun passes by
in the morning   in the morning   in the morning

In the morning
when the deep sea goes through a dog's bite
and you spit on the tip of your long knife
In the morning   in the morning
when peroxide falls on a bed of broken glass
and the sun rises like a polyester ball of menses
in the morning
gonna firedance in the petro
in the morning
turn loose the blues in the funky jungle
in the morning
I said when you see the morning coming like
a two-headed twister
let it blow let it blow
in the morning in the morning
all swollen up like an ocean in the morning
early in the morning
before the cream dries in the bushes
in the morning
when you hear the rooster cry
cry rooster cry
in the morning   in the morning

I said
disguised in my mouth as a swampland
nailed to my teeth like a rising sun
you come out in the middle of fish-scales
you bleed into gourds wrapped with red ants
you syncopate the air with lungs like screams from yazoo
like X-rated tongues
and nickel-plated fingers of a raw ghost man
you touch brown nipples into knives
and somewhere stripped like a whirlwind
stripped for the shrine room
you sing to me through the side face of a black rooster

In the morning   in the morning   in the morning

MADNESS WITHOUT HEAD

They say it swoops down at midnight
in a throat to throat search

They say it swaggers forward softens up the system
and installs gratitude behind the eyes of a dreamer

They say it hides in the entertainment section
of an electric cage
and enters through a voice of apologetic tremors
and gyrating lips

They say it's a form of madness
the kind of madness disguising its mouth as a wagon wheel
a madness carving its tonsil into a machine gun
the madness painting itself black
and filling the balcony with darkness
the madness singing its heart out to the balcony through
the wagon wheel in machine gun moans
and when the moans become flames and the darkness dies
then this madness closes its mouth
pulls back its heart
takes off the wagon wheel and puts on another pair
of lips and a rose
and then madness presses its lips to the rose and
starts a light show
and then madness fills the auditorium with lightness
and then madness becomes a soul lightener singing
through the lips of the rose in the light
of america the beautiful
and then madness pretending to need love
is infiltrated with applause
and then madness infiltrated with applause
and believing its own publicity
walks the waters in a fashion show to New Zealand

and then madness escalated with dreams
becomes too big for its lips
and then madness losing its lips becomes a security risk
and then madness sinking into grief without lips
becomes too little for its wigs
and then madness without wagon wheel   without applause
without dreams   without lips   all alone now
sticks its head in the oven
and then madness losing its head becomes
madness without head
a madness that can't eat itself up
a madness that'll run in circles forever

the madness that swoops down a midnight
in a throat to throat search

They say it swaggers forward   softens up the system
and installs gratitude behind the eyes of a dreamer
they say it interrogates the soul
and waits in the shade during the heat of initiation
they say it hides
in the entertainment section of the electric cage
and enters through a voice of apologetic tremors
and gyrating lips

they say it's a form of impersonation
the kind of impersonation they call madness
the madness known as forever madness

CAROLINA KINGSTON

We know you by your dance Carolina Kingston
with your carved legs
and guitar face
and feet like two warpaths
arriving from angola
in night-flesh of a new migrant
Carolina Kingston
fetish neck priest woman
imbangala woman who do battle the white man's god
yea   plenty macking motherhood
packed in your grief house   yea
Carolina Kingston advancing through ports
through fields   through mills   through railroads
into eighty million arms like radar
and protrusions the size of oceans
like faucets of blood
no blood without faucets
no faucets without the tap of Carolina Kingston
zambesi mouth woman
with your raw slit moan
and loud breath mooch
and smell of talcum powder skin
against skin of your turpentine worker
you Carolina Kingston
surviving in mountains
in forest   on riverfronts   and the mohawk valley
and the commanche bar
and the splash down from egyptian coffins
into johnnie walker red
with your dip   with your strut
with your two names and beginning of the guitar faces
advancing the savannah through your mojo bones
black fringed snaggle tooth sudan queen laughing
in the blue gardenia cafe   yea
plenty eyesockets carved from your ice house yeah

Carolina Kingston
We know you by your deep scars
by your mellow whooping heart beats crying in their big lips
we know you by the perfume hairs pressed in this book
you have teeth in the arena of good luck
your pelvis is a drum now
yeah plenty hot flashes left in your ju ju house
and tomorrow be the one you give it to
no complaints   no regrets
too many sisters gone mad already
what you say Carolina Kingston
with your elegant frog voice
and feet like two iron pins
advancing through waters in a regatta of conqueror roots
fierce-mouth woman who do battle the white man's patterns
You Carolina Kingston
with your spotted hands
and purple ebony solitaire eyes
how can we amplify your entrance
peace in the canyon
queen of the trembling women in pompadours
angel in a girdle of steel strings
whisper to us sister Carolina Kingston
the drummers are waiting by the roadside
come forward
with your peach brandy spit
in rosebush smell of your banjo bones
come forward
and let the repetitious light from your infra-red tongue shine
through your blue monday face of splintered guitars
release your belly of balafons through the fingers of Olodumare
you are Carolina Kingston from desert to grassland to rainforest
to night-flesh from angola dancing on fish-heads   yeah?

FLAME

And it's familiar
this fact of flame
of indulging images
the salty dust devil winds
spitting into silver helmets
through shit splattered wings
the beginnings and endings
in which i salute the sun
because i know it has to come today
because a dream is like a nail
because this room peels back the hole in my cup
and so i tell you whoever you are
plastic pen, paper, dictionary
i tell you
the policemen sing
the sanitation men whistle
the distended body of military parades
fly flags in wounds of dead words
and the sad look of tribal warfare
points every second between sockets
into the same flame of the zero hour
and i know it has to come from me

CHOCOLATE
CHOK-OH-LAH-TAY

Hey Chocolate
they say in your high-blooded fingers
full of fetish dolls
hurricanes run

And on those fuchsia-dotted lips
where sad African ballads drink
solitude intensifies

And with your teeth down deep in these overtones
you form a snake each night that spits

And I hear a spell shaking
Vera Cruz almost bending
flying crying aye aye aye

aye Chocolate
they say in your mouthpiece
full of baby talk and conga beats
superstitious flames cut through sentimental
rainbows full of love affairs intruding
and formless realities sloping
weaving overlapping half-moaning
you blow your axe aye aye aye

Chocolate
they say through your open horn full of dancers
laughter comes
and in your purple velvet mute
you keep a walk so fine
a rhumba so strong
your yuka in root
a green smell   a low pitch
a shrilling vibrating cry
stridulating through the swamps through the city

through the time effects
you keep the mambos inflamed
you keep the sambas in tune
you keep a tango in slides aye aye ayee Chocolate

They say
into your breath full of wa-wahs women scream
and with your knees dipping deep into these spirits
you carve your shout
and I hear the signals barking
blood vessels almost breaking libating on the sands of Havana
crossing fast blades falling hot brass melting
tongue forks tuning holding spreading leaping
squawking rhythms rising modulating salsas striking
aye ya ya ya ya ya yo Chocolate
lyrical Chocolate Choc-o-late Chocolate
I like the way you play your horn
through the bell through the navel through the impulses who
through the sweat through the veins through the felt-covered boom
you keep the tangos in oil
you keep meringues in chrome
you keep a cha-cha implunged aye aye aye aye Chocolate

They say in your cheeks full of staccato
a witch doctor lives
and between your orange-striped gums
where circles rotate
secret ancestors knock

And I hear you grinding spinning
parading through the crowd like a hawk flaming
smoking
you blow your axe aye aye aye
aye   Chocolate I like the way you blow your horn man

YOU KNOW

for the people who speak the you know language

You know
   I sure would like to write a blues
you know
   a nice long blues
you know
   a good feeling piece to my writing hand
you know
   my hand that can bring two pieces of life
   together in your ear
you know
   one drop of blues   turning a paper clip
   into three wings and a bone into a revolt
you know
   a blues passing up the stereotype symbols
you know
   go into the dark meat of a crocodile
   and pinpoint the process
you know
   into a solo a hundred times
   like the first line of Aretha Franklin
you know
   like Big Mama Thornton
you know
   i sure would like to write a blues
you know
   if i could write me a blues
you know
   a blues that you could all feel at the same time
   on the same level like a Joe Louis punch
you know
   a punch that could break a computer
   into an event like Guinea Bissau
you know
   if i could write me a blues

you know
    a nice long blues
you know
    an up to the minute blues
you know
    a smack dab in the middle of depression blues
you know
    a blues without incidental music
you know
    without spending time being incidental
you know
    if i could write a blues
you know
    a blues without the popular use of the word love
you know
    without running love love love in the ground
you know
    a serious blues
you know
    a significant blues
you know
    an unsubmissive blues
you know
    a just because we exist blues
you know
    a blues
you know
    a terrible blues about the terrible terrible need
    i have to write the blues
you know
    if i could write a nice long blues
you know
    a nice long blues
you know
    it sure would feel good to my writing hand
you know
    you know
you know

FOR THE BRAVE YOUNG STUDENTS IN SOWETO

Soweto
when i hear your name
I think about you
like the fifth ward in Houston Texas
one roof of crushed oil drums on the other
two black hunters in buckets of blood
walking into the fire of Sharpeville
into the sweat and stink of gold mines
into your children's eyes suffering from malnutrition
while pellets of uranium are loaded onto boats
headed for France for Israel for Japan
away from the river so full of skulls
and Robben Island so swollen with warriors
and the townships that used to overflow
with such apathy and dreams
and i think about the old Mau Mau
grieving in beer halls
and the corrupt black leaders
singing into police whistles
and i think about the assembly line of dead "Hottentots"
and the jugular veins of Allende
and once again how the coffin is divided into dry ink
how the factory moves like a white cane
like a volley of bullets in the head of Lumumba
and death is a death-life held together by shacks
by widows who cry with their nipples pulled out
by men who shake with electrodes on the tongue
and Soweto
when i hear your name and look at you on the reservation
a Xhosa
in the humid wrinkles of Shreveport Louisiana
walking down fannin street
into the bottom hole in the wall of endurance
i smell the odor of our lives together made of tar paper
the memories opening like stomachs in saw mills

the faces growing old in cigarette burns
and i think about the sacrifices made in Cape Town
the sisters being mauled by police dogs
while the minister of justice rides
the tall ship of torture
down the hudson river in New York
while vigilantes under Zulu masks
strike through the heartland like robots
in military boots with hatchets made of apartheid lips
and Soweto
when i look at this ugliness
and see once again how we're divided and
forced into fighting each other
over a funky job in the sewers of Johannesburg
divided into labor camps
fighting over damaged meat and stale bread in Harlem
divided into factions fighting to keep from fighting
the ferocious devils who are shooting
into the heads of our small children

When i look at this ugliness
and think about the Native Americans pushed
into the famine of tribal reserves
think about the concentration camps full of sad Palestinians
and the slave quarters still existing in Miami
the diamond factories still operating in Amsterdam in Belgium
the gold market still functioning on wall street
and the scar tissues around our necks
swelling with tumors of dead leaves
our bodies exploding like whiskey bottles
as the land shrinks into the bones of ancestor "Bushmen"
and i tell you Soweto
when i see you stand up in the middle of all this
stand up to the exotic white racists
in their armored churches
stand up to these landstealers, infant killers, rapists and rats
to see you stand among the pangas the stones
the war clubs the armadillos dying along this roadside
to see you stand with the ocean the desert

the birthright of red cliffs
to see you stand with your brave young warriors
courageous and strong hearted
looking so confident in battle marks coated
in grief and gunmetal tears
to see you stand up to this epidemic of expansion
and flame passbooks into ashes
fling stones into the mouths of computers
to see you stand on the national bank of america
like monumental sculpture made of stained bullets
to see you stand empty handed
your shoulders open to the world
each day young blood falling on the earth
to see you stand in the armed struggle
next to Mozambique, Angola, Namibia, Zimbabwe
Soweto i tell you Soweto
when i see you standing up like this
i think about all the forces in the world
confronted by the terrifying rhythms of young students
by their sacrifices
and the revelation that it won't be long now
before everything
in this world changes

JAYNE CORTEZ

FIRESPITTER

FIRESPITTER

(1982)

OPENING ACT

To be the opening act
and absorb all slobber
all praises
all stares
all insults in a rhythm tube of
fallopian teeth

To be the opening act
and not forget the odor of cockroaches
in a diamond miner's eyeball
flame of a dead flint
listen to this suspect number one
because to be the opening act
and plant feet in asses of corrupt politicians
without a time clock without correct wages
without profits without bitterness
without a breeding place for pain
is a bitch
so pass the word around

To be the opening act
and know when to duck when to salute
when to cover up
when to fight
when to scream when to dive into your solitude
and detoxify whistles in your kidneys
salt dry curses in your eardrums
and then laugh into the drunken gallbladders of the night
you have to be rich in blood vessels to
bury that act in someone's mouth at 3 o'clock every morning
so don't fuck with me
I want to be the opening act between this planet and the sun
in health   in sickness   in death
I said primp on your own time baby
because I'm walking the entire motion of space

in rawflesh of this opening act to end all acts
and I don't have to impose myself on anybody
so throw your wig into the ocean
I know I'm the opening act of acts here
because all of a sudden
someone blew smoke in my face and yelled booooo

FIRESPITTERS

Festac 77

Firespitters
spitting across the desert
into feverdust rituals on Badagry road
a sanctified road full of ghostwriters
gin drinkers
lips spreading like
stripes and medals from the chest of my father
knife swallowers
wine tappers
torches gleaming like
the gold tooth of my mother
Firespitters
spitting across syncopating roaches into
sunsets falling like orange tams
on the heads of sweating soldiers
tangerine spit balls
going down into sewers of dark stout
a loud baritone night entering us between
pine streaked thighs of big city funk
a festival of firespitters in a mucus of brass bands
Lagos
in your beautiful nasty self shake everything
we're here
moving through the red fog like a giant defense plant
we open our boot tops and bones like nightsticks throw
themselves into maneuvering shadows
we stand on the blunt wings of steel bees
a unit of bent fingers and torsos bending forward
like sharkknives
we have jet propellered tongues
ten fifths of lightning
battle stars   chlorophylled plungers   horizontal jaws
painted skins   swiveling pupils   gut blasting moans and
the supersonic sound of invisible orchestras
sweet spirits of Nupe
listen to the Firespitters

a caravan of
Firespitters
spitting into the river of asbestos
into the trade wind of coral snakes
into marrows of guinea fowl
into a meridian of rice
one hundred and ninety spits in
a village libating like Niagara Falls
we drink this three thousand and seventy five proof down-pour
spitting through chains of acrobatic fingers in green caps
going up into the chalk eyed smell of wintertime
a slurring soprano dawn entering us
on outskirts of big city dumps
Lagos
dark puree of flesh in a mask of spinning mirrors
shake everything in your beautiful nasty self
we're here

DETAILS OF RITUALS IN FESTAC VILLAGE 77

In the exaggerated thump of a passenger's heart
the confrontation
between foot soldiers and stone carriers
in afternoon smell of everybody's funk
the confrontation
between bus driver and boy scouts
on petrol line in a dust eater's mouth
the confrontation
between horn blowers and gun bearers
in wide angle lens of a photographer's mood
the confrontation
between lip—force and fast flash
in meal time rush of cafeteria push
the confrontation
between metal trays and human elbows
on clear tongue of a long verb
the confrontation
between hip pinching and face slapping
in metallic sweat of electrical storms
the confrontation
between sockets without fans and
fans without sockets
in heated evenings of flickering bulbs
the confrontation
between flinch once and blink twice
in midnight moon of breaking pipes
the confrontation
between flood tide and ebb tide
in morning scent of a bursar's breath
the confrontation
between dollar and naira
in compounded flesh of everyday life
the confrontation between this official
that official and these identification cards

in the taxi cab man's quote of outrageous fees
the confrontation
between boom boom   blip blip   bam bam   dash dash

INTO THIS TIME

for Charles Mingus

Into this time
of steel feathers blowing from hearts
into this turquoise flame time in the mouth
into this sonic boom time in the conch
into this musty stone-fly time sinking into
the melancholy buttocks of dawn
sinking into lacerated whelps
into gun holsters
into breast bones
into a manganese field of uranium nozzles
into a nuclear tube full of drunk rodents
into the massive vein of one interval
into one moment's hair plucked down into
the timeless droning fixed into
long pauses
fixed into a lash of ninety-eight minutes screeching into
the internal heat of an ice ball melting time into
a configuration of commas on strike
into a workforce armed with a calendar of green wings
into a collection of nerves
into magnetic mucus
into tongueless shrines
into water pus of a silver volcano
into the black granite face of Morelos
into the pigeon-toed dance of Mingus
into a refuge of air bubbles
into a cylinder of snake whistles
into clusters of slow spiders
into spade fish skulls
into rosin-coated shadows of women wrapped in live iguanas
into coins into crosses into St. Martin de Porres
into the pain of this place changing pitches beneath
fingers swelling into
night shouts
into day trembles

into month of precious bloods flowing into
this fiesta of sadness year
into this city of eternal spring
into this solo
on the road of young bulls
on the street of lost children
on the avenue of dead warriors
on the frisky horse tail fuzz zooming
into ears of every madman
stomping into every new composition
everyday of the blues
penetrating into this time

This time of loose strings in low tones
pulling boulders of Olmec heads into the sun
into tight wires uncoiling from body of a stripteaser on the table
into half-tones wailing between snap and click
of two castanets smoking into
scales jumping from tips of sacrificial flints
into frogs yodeling across grieving cults
yodeling up into word-stuffed smell of flamingo stew
into wind-packed fuel of howling dog throats slit into
this January flare of aluminum dust falling into
laminated stomach of a bass violin rubbed into red ashes
rubbed into the time sequence of
this time of salmonella leaking from eyeballs of a pope
into this lavender vomit time in the chest into
this time plumage of dried bats in the brain into
this wallowing time weed of invisible wakes on cassettes into
this off-beat time syncopation in a leopard skin suit
into this radiated protrusion of time in the desert into
this frozen-cheek time of dead infants in the cellar
into this time flying with the rotten bottoms of used tuxedos
into this purple   brown   grey   gold minus zero time trilling into
a limestone-crusted Yucatan belching
into fifty-six medallions shaking
into armadillo drums thumping
into tambourines of fetishes rattling
into an oil slick of poverty symbols flapping

into flat-footed shuffle of two birds advancing
into back spine of luminous impulses tumbling
into metronomes of colossal lips ticking
into a double zigzag of calluses splitting
into foam of electric snow flashing into this time
of steel feathers blowing from hearts
into this turquoise flame time in the mouth into
this sonic boom time in the conch
into this musty stone-fly time sinking into
the melancholy buttocks of dawn

BIG FINE WOMAN FROM RULEVILLE

for Fannie Lou Hamer

How to weave your web of medicinal flesh into words
cut the sutures to your circumcised name
make your deformed leg into a symbol of resistance
Big fine woman from Ruleville
great time keeper
and dangerous worker
I use this hour
to eat from your spirit
dance from mouth to mouth with your holler
hold fingers together in remembrance of your sacrifices
And I have chosen to wear your riverstone eyes splashed
with Mississippi blood
and your sharecropper shoes braided with your powerful stomp
and now in your riot stick neck smeared in charcoal burns
and in your bones that exhausted
the god of whiteness in Sunflower County
I will push forward your precious gift of revolutionary courage
Thanks to the southern knife with terracotta teeth
magnificent ancestor
warrior friend
most beautiful sister
I kiss the mud of this moment

IF THE DRUM IS A WOMAN

why are you pounding your drum into an insane babble
why are you pistol-whipping your drum at dawn
why are you shooting through the head of your drum
and making a drum tragedy of drums
if the drum is a woman
don't abuse your drum   don't abuse your drum
                don't abuse your drum
I know the night is full of displaced persons
I see skins striped with flames
I know the ugly dispositions of underpaid clerks
they constantly menstruate through the eyes
I know bitterness embedded in flesh
the itching alone can drive you crazy
I know that this is America
and chickens are coming home to roost
on the MX missile
But if the drum is a woman
why are you choking your drum
why are you raping your drum
why are you saying disrespectful things
to your mother drum   your sister drum
your wife drum and your infant daughter drum
If the drum is a woman
then understand your drum
your drum is not docile
your drum is not invisible
your drum is not inferior to you
your drum is a woman
so don't reject your drum
don't try to dominate your drum
don't become weak and cold and desert your drum
don't be forced into the position
as an oppressor of drums
and make a drum tragedy of drums

if the drum is a woman
don't abuse your drum   don't abuse your drum
                    don't abuse your drum

ONCE UPON A ROAD

It was fun
traveling through the heart of this country
just what I needed
enough gasoline
to speed along the highway
in the winter morning
so crisp and white and dirty and cold
my poetry trying to escape the chill
but anyway
it was fun purging the heart of this country
wow
what a beer mug against
mug of a drunk lumberjack on
his way to South Africa
what electricity in mouth of a disco band so full
of the frenzy of nothing
what a great feeling to
look over shoulders of a liberty statue
look up into the oxidized head of
a country so pure in dumbbells
ding dong
what a crowd of Mr. and Mrs. Blank faces going off to war
such a promotion of fear
such fleshless featherless balls
you make me laugh right in the middle of
this fucking poem
and that's not a device to get your attention
once upon a road
there was a country in the heart of
the Crow the Sioux and the Kickapoo

HAVE A GOOD DAY

Smell the stinking cargo of hunger
sent from textile mills and petroleum companies
sent to us with a fingernail of water
half a fleck of dry chili shadow
and have a good day

Hear the outpouring of eyes
coming from rubber plantations
and iron companies
coming to us with a delegation of spit balls
two poppies made of tomato skins
and have a good day

See the cult of cocoa stealers
the obscene men running goldmines
and lime factories
descending on us with a platter of syphilis
one dose of radioactive fallout
and have a good day

Feel the penetration of brutality
sent from school systems and copper refineries
sent to us with a handout of fresh hickies
a snapshot of broken thumb prints
and have a good day
have a good day
Oh yeah
Take all your personal belongings with you
and have a good day

SOLO FINGER SOLO

When evening goes down into its jelly jelly jelly
into drain pipe cuts and stitches and vaccinations
protruding from arms

And spirit of the five by five man pushes
his sweet potatoes in the air
feather daddy leaps into a falcon of tropical bird squats
rubber legs swing into off-beat onijos onijos
then into your solo finger solo
the blues chantress jumps up and
repeats her nasal volcanic chant calling

Count Basie   Count Basie   Count Basie

And Count Basie
you burn through this timbale of goose flesh rhythms
a drop of iodine on your starfish lips
the intonation of your kiss of melodica trilling
into a labyrinth of one o'clock jumps
into corpuscle flashes of the blues torpedo
the erupting volcano of the blues shouters chanting your name

Count Basie   Count Basie   take em to Chicago Count Basie

And Count Basie
you punctuate this strong bourbon mist of gamma globulin breath
a mixture of chords like serpentariums coiling
from the deep everglades of your body
and when the luscious screams of three headed root doctors split
Kansas City reeds in unison with this triple tapping
double stopping   slow grinding   loosey butt night swinging
with the blues chantress
erupting volcano of the blues torpedoes chanting your name

Count Basie
you reach through the bottom of the music
way down beneath cross rhythm vamps
below air stream of the lowest octave
into depths of a sacred drum
and Count Basie   Count Basie   Count Basie
how powerful and dignified and exquisite and direct and sharp
your solo finger solo is

COBRA CLUB

To dance the razor-drill dance in the cobra club
suck off the rain-crows holler
pull into a fantail paper-lip-smacking-reefer straight out
at midnight

for you on double elbows in a butane truck

I have the crazy bones laughing in alligator stomps
I have the railroad tracks you call my thighs
flat-talking like sepia trumpets
I hold the scorpion and tequila in my mouth
we embrace the paranoid sea
the tip of a stinging kilimanjaro licked

Let it dry like fly specks between cyclones
in this lobe burnt pepper day
in the dizzy spells falling head
in belly bush navels with sesame crabs

There will be other chicken wings at the window
other leaves turning back into mosquito drums
other legends in dark stockings rolled down
you will tangle in the long rope solitude menses
of solitary funguses
you will eat buckshots off the evening
and wear them like flea bites in new cities
we will blow through this gravel pit shadow of poverty together
like a rada of black rum flowing with the depths
of this cobra club funk
An alkalized cadenza of stale metallic tongues pushed back

THE RED PEPPER POET

for Léon Damas

If you see a cycle of heavy breezes
blowing backward
into massive loops of heat
crossing two oceans after sunset
if you see an avalanche of clouds
pushing forward into jet streams with syncopated thunder
before sunrise
if you see a long stroke of black lightning
flashing in the sky
like a fast flying train
on its way to Savannah at noontime
if you see a medley of slow moving currents
spinning into a hum of furious tornados
at midnight
Tell everybody
The Red Pepper Poet
moving like the eye of a hurricane is going home

Listen to the mud flow into its deep zydeco
the high speed drills in their tapping shoes
storm   flesh   flame
ethiopian ash rings
in this luminous hour of potassium bones
with wings like a magma of hot tears
flooding into mouth of the cayenne river

Listen to the shrill evening falsettos
and the filing down of teeth
hatchet dancers carving up shadows
knife men entering with lips of purple plated chrome
scar tissues opening their pigments
into the 21st century
Boom
Shoot off the guns for this elder

put your hair into the earth
and fill the night with fire ants

Go ahead
and show your respect for this freedom fighter
this great warrior
dangerous orphan
ibeji among ibeji
the Red Pepper Poet with the bull-roarer tongue
Go ahead
shoulder to shoulder
exile to exile
Dance for the Red Pepper Poet who fought so well
so long   so many places   so many times in
this world of so much suffering
Boni   Boni   Boni   Boni

Won't you dance for this mean banjo player
this dignified volcano
with his hat pushed to one side and his eyebrow up
Won't you dance for the Red Pepper Poet
with the bull-roarer tongue
Go ahead   move into the flow of the deep zydecos
into the shrill evening falsettos and the grinding down of teeth
Go ahead and decorate this ground with tobacco leaves
with sea shells   with broken bottles
with tiger balm cans   with books   with wooden daggers
with dollheads   with cornshuck
and a tall glass of scotch and soda
Go ahead and let the old-time rhythms roll
for this great pain-carrier poet
who carried his pain into the forest
like earth carries the amazon river
carried his pain
like a sizzling fever carries a hidden jungle
like the sea carries fish glue
and we carry the intensity of these
fragile vaporous magnetic words of revolt between

anthills of ice-covered poverty
and fire coals burning next to iron spikes
on this day mixed in plantago weed
the smell of snake root
rain feathers
rusty nails in solitude of
a smoking typhoon drilling backward
in backwater lashes of hurricane sweat
triple time on stilts across a mardi gras mass
in angles   in circles   in green paste   in purple agua
Zoom

It's the agility of these popping veins
the strong knuckles of endurance
the expanding neck of unpublished flights
that we push together the amber oils up
split into drops one shake
dissect the meaning of the strategy of Damas
arriving on the concourse
the odor of rum and manioc in his hair
Strike up style spellbinder
You had it
and everybody loved the thickness of your accent
the ritual look of fierce crocodiles crossed in your eyes
the secret memories and sacred visions knotted in your smile
the indestructible timing of your spirit
and your natural slashing attitude
Red Pepper Poet with the bull-roarer tongue
Throw off the flames
flame thrower with your dark flesh barrel house band come
and blow into our ears now blow

If you hear a solo wind
in sandpaper socks
sanding sounds of superheated stone songs
against sulfurous falling cells on
dry crust dogs
at the pulse of the hawk's scream
at the moment

when fifty drums hemorrhage
in the middle of the rhythms
when the hurricane turns
at the yoke of the curve
among dead spiders
at the end of the choice
when everything drops into your mask
in that position beyond all grief
at that second
this very instant
Won't you dance for the Red Pepper Poet
with the bull-roarer tongue
Go ahead
push your chair forward
and dance for the great warrior poet
who fought so well   so long   so many places
so many times in this world of so much suffering
Boni   Boni   Boni   Boni   Boni

They want the oil
But they don't want the people
They want the oil
But they don't want the people
They want the oil
But they don't want the people
They want the oil
But they don't want the people
They want the oil
But they don't want the people
They want the oil
But they don't want the people
They want the oil
But they don't want the people
They want the oil
But they don't want the people
They want the oil
But they don't want the people
They want the oil
But they don't want the people
They want the oil
But they don't want the people
They want the oil
But they don't want the people
They want the oil
But they don't want the people
They want the oil
But they don't want the people
They want the oil
But they don't want the people
They want the oil
But they don't want the people
They want the oil
But they don't want the people
They want the oil

But they don't want the people
They want the oil
But they don't want the people
They want the oil
But they don't want the people

IT CAME

It came through the frizzled feathers of sparkling hens
through blood red blood of asphalt earth
through navels infested with intestinal worms
through skulls infused with electric shock
It came
through the vibrating hum of empty stomachs
through raw buttocks slashed against rubber hoses
through a trench of wounded infants near Cassinga
through the last breath of the dead among dead bodies in Chimoio
It came
through boiling beer on scalded feet
through corn meal and maggots
through outbreaks of malaria and typhoid
through bombsplinters and blinding lights
through the quivering convulsive and hemorrhaging heads of
two hundred thousand refugees in transit
It came
through the splash of plastic gloves on the shallow water
through chests and legs and mutilated fingers floating in the water
through eyepits of parasitical flies raging in the water
through chemicals illuminating in the water of the river
It came
through shattered bones of protesting students
through nasal spines in cockroach shit
through tropical babies in polluted milk
through the english knot of a hangman's rope
through testicles shaking into mouth of a supreme court of
supreme coldness
It came
through the smell of blue stones and used rifles
through the naked root of new trees and missiles
through a soldier's uniform
through a farmer's implement
through a white starched waiter's shirt
through a miner's helmet

through a woman's skirt
through Bindura and Pungue
and a curfew of darkness
the bazooka of victory came
Oh   Zimbabwe it came

FOR A GYPSY CAB MAN

And you say you love the South Bronx
and you say you love Brooklyn
and you love Harlem
Well we love you
Mr. Gypsy Cab Man
Loose lips fast talk sudden stops potholes

And you say you came from Africa
and you've been here working evenings
going to school days
for ten hard years
Now with a wife
two children
and three degrees under the belt
you say it's time
to pack up and go home
Mr. Gypsy Cab Man

Loose lips fast talk sudden stops potholes

We want to wish you
all the happiness in the world
Best wishes for a safe journey
Congratulations
and thanks again
for your long struggle and cooperation
for your system of communications
and your solidarity
to the South Bronx
to Brooklyn
to Harlem
to us Mr. Gypsy Cab Man

Loose lips fast talk sudden stops potholes

Thank you for your praise songs to the road
for your tweezer of luck
locking doors
for your laughter   your anger
your loud wail
of political thoughts

And thanks for turning your automobile
into an ambulance
into a fire engine of red stallions
into a combat car of constant motion
and endless horn signals

Mr. Gypsy Cab Man
friend and collector of green cards
thanks

Loose lips   fast talk   sudden stops   potholes

And you say
in spite of the hassles and the hazards
you say you'll miss the South Bronx
you say you'll miss Brooklyn
and you'll definitely miss
these Harlem people
Well
we sure will miss
riding through the streets with you
Mr. Gypsy Cab Man

Loose lips   fast talk   sudden stops   potholes

RAPE

What was Inez supposed to do for
the man who declared war on her body
the man who carved a combat zone between her breasts
Was she supposed to lick crabs from his hairy ass
kiss every pimple on his butt
blow hot breath on his big toe
draw back the corners of her vagina and
hee haw like a California burro

This being wartime for Inez
she stood facing the knife
the insults and
her own smell drying on the penis of
the man who raped her

She stood with a rifle in her hand
doing what a defense department will do in times of war
And when the man started grunting and panting and wobbling
forward like
a giant hog
She pumped lead into his three hundred pounds of shaking flesh
Sent it flying to the Virgin of Guadelupe
then celebrated day of the dead rapist punk
and just what the fuck else was she supposed to do?

And what was Joanne supposed to do for
the man who declared war on her life
Was she supposed to tongue his encrusted toilet-stool lips
suck the numbers off of his tin badge
choke on his clap trap balls
squeeze on his nub of rotten maggots and
sing god bless America thank you for fucking my life away

This being wartime for Joanne
she did what a defense department will do in times of war

and when the piss-drinking   shit-sniffing guard said
I'm gonna make you wish you were dead black bitch come here
Joanne came down with an ice pick in
the swat freak motherfucker's chest
yes in the fat neck of that racist policeman
Joanne did the dance of the ice picks
and once again
from coast to coast
house to house
we celebrated day of the dead rapist punk
and just what the fuck else were we supposed to do

BLOOD SUCKERS

In Miami
the blood suckers came sucking in full speed
twisting and sucking into
a urethra of decapitated shrimp heads
tongue slashing and sucking into
a matrix of turtle shells
rising up and sucking through
a perforated sac of southern crosses
drawing blood and resucking
the dried mutilated scalps of a Seminole nation
moaning and groaning and sucking on mucus from
nipples of tropical storm troopers
grunting and chewing and pissing on
the artificial hides
of stuffed alligators
Corrupted suckers dropping down and sucking
all the way through Brownsville to Coconut Grove
Blood Suckers
sucking on the joints of steel horses and trembling
sucking gopher meat from
the plastic womb of St. Mary on
the dixie highway and hallucinating
sucking on the moon over Miami
muck fire in the everglades sucked
Florida folks sunbathing on the swanee river sucked
telephoto lens sucked
deposits of uranium sucked
veins of manganese sucked
dry lizards jelly sucked
chrome nickel mercury sucked
tax payers money sucked
A sucking extravaganza
in the brown coral coop of peruvian breasts
in the spanish moss wings of moorish armpits

tobacco ensemble fantasia
Blood Suckers
sucking slow motions sucks on the ends of
throbbing hoodoo spikes
sucking on the cracked heels of ancient bolito winners
sucking through the rotten banana farts of
a jesuit priest
sucking through the contracting pupils of vicious watch dogs
then fabricating sucks with
the Dupont suckers at the test site
Blood Suckers
sucking on high powered rifle butts and splattered glass
sucking on a column of smoking mickey mouse dolls
sucking on a sea sick refugee in the gulf stream
sucking on the panama canal treaty
sucking on sixty bars of gold
sucking on a thousand tons of rubble and disfigurations
sucking at the Mr. Universe pageant
sucking with the firestone tire company executive suckers
sucking with a security force of forced suckers
sucking with a conglomerate of born again christian suckers
sucking with the general dynamic suckers of blood suckers
Blood Suckers
sucking and sweating and hooting and balling themselves
into knots on the red tide slime of Miami beach
A casino full of suckers turning tricks of justice and
vomiting into a palmetto of fluoridated snake ash
Addicted suckers
fucking and pecking and choking themselves to death in
the weasel stink of little Pretoria
Blood Suckers
sucking with an asshole full of radioactive rust and
exploding way down in the dumps of Love Canal
expanding themselves and vigorously sucking on
a medley of birth defects
stealing land and sucking into
a grand jury of broken cow teeth
yelping and belching and collapsing in

the dark blue quick sand
of Liberty City
screaming and squabbling and wallowing and
suck suck suck suck suck sucking
all the way down in buzzard shit

I SEE CHANO POZO

A very fine conga of sweat
a very fine stomp of the right foot
a very fine platform of sticks
a very fine tube of frictional groans
a very fine can of belligerent growls
a very fine hoop of cubano yells
very fine   very fine

Is there anyone finer today   olé   okay
Lucumi   Abakwa   Lucumi   Abakwá
Oye
I see Chano Pozo
Chano Pozo from Havana Cuba
                                        You're the one
You're the one who made Atamo into
a tattooed motivator of revolutionary spirits

You're the one who made Mpebi into
an activated slasher of lies

You're the one who made Donno into
an armpit of flammable explosives

You're the one who made Obonu into
a circle of signifying snakes

You're the one who made Atumpan's head strike against
the head of a bird   everynight   everyday
in your crisscrossing chant
in your cross river mouth
                                        You're the one
Oye   I say
Chano
what made you roar like a big brazos flood
what made you yodle like a migrating frog

what made you shake like atomic heat
what made you jell into a ritual pose
Chano   Chano   Chano
what made your technology of thumps so new so mean
I say
is there anyone finer than Chano Pozo
                                        from Havana Cuba
Oye
I'm in the presence of ancestor
                                        Chano Pozo
Chano connector of two worlds
You go and celebrate again with
                                the compañeros in Santiago
                                    and tell us about it
You go to the spirit house of Antonio Maceo
                                and tell us about it
You go to Angola
                                and tell us about it
You go to Calabar
                                and tell us about it
You go see the slave castles
you go see the massacres
you go see the afflictions
you go see the battlefields
you go see the warriors
you go as a healer
you go conjurate
you go mediate
you go to the cemetery of drums
                            return and tell us about it
Lucumi   Abakwa   Lucumi   Abakwá   Olé   okay
Is there anyone finer than Chano Pozo
Oye   I say
did you hear
Mpintintoa smoking in the palm of his hands
did you hear
Ilya Ilu booming through the cup of his clap
did you hear
Ntenga sanding on the rim of his rasp

did you hear
Siky Akkua stuttering like a goat sucking hawk
did you hear
Bata crying in a nago tongue
did you hear
Fontomfrom speaking through the skull of a dog
did you hear it   did you hear it   did you hear it

A very fine tree stump of drones
a very fine shuffle of shrines
a very fine turn of the head
a very fine tissue of skin
a very fine smack of the lips
a very fine pulse
a very fine encuentro
very fine   very fine
Is there anyone finer than
                    Chano Pozo from Havana Cuba
Oye   I say
I see Chano Pozo

THERE IT IS

My friend
they don't care
if you're an individualist
a leftist a rightist
a shithead or a snake
They will try to exploit you
absorb you confine you
disconnect you isolate you
or kill you

And you will disappear into your own rage
into your own insanity
into your own poverty
into a word a phrase a slogan a cartoon
and then ashes

The ruling class will tell you that
there is no ruling class
as they organize their liberal supporters into
white supremist lynch mobs
organize their children into
ku klux klan gangs
organize their police into
killer cops
organize their propaganda into
a device to ossify us with angel dust
preoccupy us with western symbols in
african hair styles
inoculate us with hate
institutionalize us with ignorance
hypnotize us with a monotonous sound designed
to make us evade reality and stomp our lives away
And we are programmed to self-destruct
to fragment
to get buried under covert intelligence operations of

unintelligent committees impulsed toward death
And there it is

The enemies polishing their penises between
oil wells at the pentagon
the bulldozers leaping into demolition dances
the old folks dying of starvation
the informers wearing out shoes looking for crumbs
the life blood of the earth almost dead in
the greedy mouth of imperialism
And my friend
they don't care
if you're an individualist
a leftist   a rightist
a shithead or a snake

They will spray you with
a virus of legionnaires' disease
fill your nostrils with
the swine flu of their arrogance
stuff your body into a tampon of
toxic shock syndrome
try to pump all the resources of the world
into their own veins
and fly off into the wild blue yonder to
pollute another planet

And if we don't fight
if we don't resist
if we don't organize and unify and
get the power to control our own lives
Then we will wear
the exaggerated look of captivity
the stylized look of submission
the bizarre look of suicide
the dehumanized look of fear
and the decomposed look of repression
forever and ever and ever
And there it is

NO SIMPLE EXPLANATIONS

to the memory of Larry Neal

There are no simple explanations
not for the excesses
not for the accumulations
not for the lips of magnetic lava
not for the liver of explosive slits
not for the heart
          ready to shoot off like a volcano
There are no simple explanations

The altar will not fit another skull
and there are no more volunteers
no mixture of eyelashes and drops of blood
                              in the circle
no alliances drinking together
                    in a night of dead events
no bullet proof faces in the air
no mask of erosion fermenting in slobber
no fetish trunk of sacrifices in disguise

Only the space of exasperation left by the advance
only juice from heat of its possession
the injunction of shadows
collectivity of ants
tongue of deified soot
flesh of incarcerated bones
but no simple explanations

Not for madness
reproducing itself through the uterus in the throat
not for sharks
having feeding frenzies in the middle of foreheads
not for
sentimental pass words of vomit splattering pages
No simple explanations

Let the index finger
take responsibility
for its smell
let the chickens protrude from drums
let the lagoon the boat the ancestors
enter pores of a poet of pretty smiles

This piece is passing up the motif of sorrow
let it pass
let the words split and erupt and dry
into snake pulsations
Spit three times
into ruby dust of your own snot
and paste it
on callous of your self-conscious itch

I say lung fire of mouth-piece tremble
still warm and metal stone
conjuration and syntax
inverted stump under solitary root
of erratic falcons
weed of pain of rupture of panic
let it go down
like body and soul
in the horn of Coleman Hawkins
Sink into the insurrection of red shanks
into the high pitch voltage of mosquito hums
into liquified ankh of egyptian flames
sparrow house bubble of quiver
let your divination fall
like body and soul
in the horn of Coleman Hawkins

Ritual fart
and navel of rebellious stink
urination and energetic repulsion
poetic orgasm and guttural belch of erotic storm
let your dynamism grunt

I say
make it shake forward like shimmering tumors of okra stew
shake forward on a speckled canvas of menstrual bandages
shake into sucking tubes of midnight flies
into the sub-dominant tilt of flinching eyeballs
into the intrinsic elasticity of violent impulses
Conform to evolution of your own syllables
to revolution of your own stanzas
because
suddenly it will be too soon
suddenly it will be too late
suddenly it will be too sudden
and there'll be no tuning forks left
in palm of a poet on a cold morning
no deposits of fat left
on neck of a blues at the crossroads
no spell of inspiration waiting
at foot of a cocaine pyramid
no ju ju leaves hidden
in the center of the whirlwind

Only abusive forces in absolute opposition to revolts
only burial grounds of radioactive mud
only bellies of unfinished poems
and time dismantling itself between invisible sticks
but no simple explanations

Not for the flesh of incarcerated bones
not for the tongue of deified soot
not for the womb of hoodoo hollerin' bebop ghosts

No simple explanations

FESTIVAL FUSIONS 81

My festival is a parading pant leg of vomit
my festival is a permanent archive of scar tissues
my festival is a configuration of
hieroglyphic toenails on stilts
and this is the clay sun of Arawak teeth
this is the foam ash of Congolese soap
this is the pyramid sky of negritude lips
this is the awesome jungle of charcoal feathers
this is the smoking torpedo of steel drums
and those are the bloated vulvas of ceremonial paste
those are the pancreases of inflamed hawks
those are the avalanches of leaking saxophones
and this is
the invisible coyote howling
                    in my mouth of canker sores

this is
the invincible tornado blowing
                    through my flesh of protruding ants
this is my festival in its ritual bone of violence
in its torso of condensed passion
in its constellation of compressed sadness
in its cohesion of suffering
in its duration of endurance
in its frenzied mask of pure terror
stand back
This festival is
          scratching like a frizzled chicken in a cockfight
this festival is
          fermenting like pulque in a skin bag
this festival is
          twitching like the tongue of a hungry jaguar
this festival is
          stinking like heat from a stink war

this festival is
humming like a swarm of amplified bumble bees
this festival is
trembling on the tip of the burn of
butt popping boils
My festival of sucked out breasts
my festival of epileptic fingers
my festival in its sacred accumulation of slashes
my festival in its tee shirt of ashes
my festival turning into a forest of urinating shadows
my festival breaking through a combustion of
incoherent gusanos
my festival consolidating its weight into
the scrap iron metabolism of lightning
look out
This naked festival body is chalked up and ready
this naked festival body is codified in black metallic soot
this naked festival body is splattered in sex juice
this naked festival body is a secret nest of hoodoo lye
this naked festival body is embedded with scorpion dust
And these are the fruit flies in the puke
these are the tonal attitudes in revolt
and what an infestation of
stalled trucks in the horseblood
what a suicide pack of distorted expectations in
the valley of shark pus
what a shrine of matted hair styles swinging on
the bandstand
what a flock of police badges flying
such a spark of boldness
such a jump up of ligaments
such magnetic gyrations
such potent coagulations
what a dialogue what a laxative
what a powerful fission falling on
heads of the cockpowers of spectacular fuckups

MILWAUKEE

I will not shovel 24 inches of snow
from this Milwaukee
even if
chairman of the local F.B.I.
is black
so throw all the unions out
I don't need the angry fart of a corpse
to get my head bad
not me
I know why testicles crack in
the jingle bells of a silent night

BLACK FEATHERED MULES

Responsibility will mount you in red satin sheets
you will fall into empty silos along the highway
and in the putrid smell of your own tongue
you will not be a worker a fighter or an ant
so stand up in your black feathered mules
and confront it
tonight
the helicopters are patrolling the neighborhood
spirits are sipping alcohol from your liver
radiation is leaking into your mouth
and blood is caked on head of a dead fly in your nose
so stand up in your black feathered mules and
don't say another fucking word

COAGULATIONS:

NEW AND SELECTED POEMS

(1984)

STOCKPILING

stockpiling of frozen trees
in the deep freeze of the earth
stockpiling of dead animals
in the exhaust pipes of supersonic rockets
stockpiling of desiccated plants
on the death root of an abscessed tooth
stockpiling of defoliants
in the pine forest of the skull
stockpiling of aerosols
in the pink smoke of a human corpse
stockpiling
of agent orange agent blue agent white acids
burning like the hot hoof of a race horse on
the tongue
stockpiling
Look at it
through the antibodies in the body
through the multiple vaccines belching in the
veins
through the cross-infection of viruses
stockpiled
in the mouth
through the benzine vapors shooting
into the muscles of the
stars
through the gaseous bowels of military
fantasies
through the white radiation of delirious
dreams
Look
this stockpile marries that stockpile
to mix and release a double stockpile of
fissions
exploding
into the shadows of disappearing space

Global incapacitations
Zero
        and boom
This is the nuclear bleach of reality
the inflated thigh of edema
the filthy dampness in the scientific pants
                                        of a peace prize
the final stockpile of flesh dancing in
the terrible whooping cough of the wind
And even if you think you have a shelter
that can survive this stockpiling
                                        of communal graves
                                        tell me

Where are you going
with the sucked liver of mustard flint
the split breath of hydrogen fumes
the navel pit of invisible clams
the biological lung of human fleas
the carcinogenic bladder of sponges
lips made of keloid scars
memory in the numb section of the chromosomes
            Just where do you think you're going
                                        with that stockpile of
                                        contaminated stink

Listen
When I think of the tactical missiles plunging
        into the rancid goiters of the sun
The artillery shells of wiretapping snakes hissing and
                                                vomiting
        into the depths of a colorless sky
The accumulation of fried phosphoric pus graffitied
        on the fragile fierceness of the moon
The pestering warheads of death-wings stockpiling
                                            feathers upon feathers
                                            in the brain
And the mass media's larvae of lies stockpiled
                                            in the plasma of the ears

And the stockpiling of foreign sap in the fluxes
of the blood
And the stockpiling of shattered spines
in chromium suits
under
polyurethane
sheets
I look at this stockpiling
at this rotting vegetation
and I make myself understand the target
That's why I say I'm into life
preservation of life now
revolutionary change now
before the choking
before the panic
before the penetration
of apathy
rises up
and spits fire
into the toxic tears
of this stockpile

THEY CAME AGAIN IN 1970 IN 1980

You didn't send for them
but in the name of god and progress
they came again
Missionaries and scientists arriving
with television sets and microwave ovens
Military advisors landing
with a party of born-again puritans
Bible societies blowing in
with a battery of translators
Bankers coming with loans
with indian-head nickels
Bulldozers entering the undergrowth
from two points in the river
Death exchanging drinks
at the first whiff of petroleum
And in the name of god & progress &
stuffed pockets
after so much torture
& so many invasions in the blood
your veins are
air strips for
multinational corporations
Your native sweat is
aviation fuel for
drilling rigs
Your compound is like
a French Devil's Island
And when the eagle flies through
the Amazon rain forest on friday
everything falls into
the pulp of the ferment of your lips
to kiss the landscape goodbye

ACCEPTANCE SPEECH

And now to overcome what ?
The secretary's face
The publisher's glasses
Two intellectuals winking to
          each other across the table
A vibration of tv voices
Spectators covered with ball point pens
Pigeons waiting for Amtrak trains
Impulses sent to slash the belly
          carve out the navel
          tear down the day
          plunge into the midnight dump of dead
                                        chickens
                                        to overcome what?
Frivolous gestures of a woman so unnaturally bloated
i'm exhausted
Dying laugh of a man so rotten in the eyes
i hide on the first bus leaving
Stammering dirge of a child so active with fear
i tremble without trembling
exist without existing
overcome without overthrowing
and for that
i'm supposed to thank the producer for
                                  making it possible
Thank some god for making it happen
Thank my sore butt for thanking you in
the combat tooth of every missing word doing
          time on this rag of discharge reflecting
                                   back into repression
                    back into sexual crust of
                                     dazzling pigs
to say thanks for filth of rocket sweat in the vulva
Thanks for nostril feathers of metallic boogers in
blood

Thanks for rectum of imperialist flames in shit
Thanks for glow of agent orange pus in orbit
Thanks for the shivering hole of pink foam on fire
Thanks no thanks
          and don't touch it
                              ass in front of pain
                                        don't
                                        touch it.

COMPLICITY

Who likes to glitter
Who likes to smell blood
Who likes to be real imperialistic
real corrupt
Trade all the gold for a mercedes-benz
Trade all the oil for a peugeot
Trade all the uranium for a rolls royce
Trade all the peanuts for a villa above the Riviera
Trade all the cocoa for a ski lodge in Grenoble
Trade all the traditional art for a case of champagne
Trade all the cobalt for a swiss bank account
Who will buy the outmoded mold
Who will buy the outdated rust
Who will make a billion dollar deal
to store radioactive waste
Who likes to glitter
Who likes to smell blood
Who likes to be real imperialistic
real corrupt

PLAIN TRUTH

They say
jab the pencils
in your tongue
Smash windows
Scream
Holler
Tear up the room
Knock down the books
Hold your mouth open with
a stick
Roll over in a rage
Push your private pain
into a collective sadness &
explode
They want you
to hate yourself
in the fly
of their masturbating teeth
Electrocute yourself
in dryness
of their syntax
Suck
their national standard
of
dead metrical feet
and free-base into
refugee camp
of a make-believe
think-tank
They say
walk with
depressive effects
of
a
toxic
cloud
in
your
skull

Keep that
vaginal
aerosol spray
hissing in
the pussy
Store that
contaminated
fetus
of dioxin in
the womb
line those lungs
with the snowflakes
of asbestos
and nuke up to see
the glory
of the coming
of the lord
They want you
to be product
consumer
and public authority
all together in one package
without choice
without change
without a human transforming action
Just enter
emulate & exit
Just puke in
pay off
punk out
and
as soon as you receive
the triple internal illumination
of yourself
as a lunatic
just know
it's a direct hit
in
the
head

IN A STREAM OF INK

Written for the print portfolio produced by
the Bob Blackburn Print-Making Workshop

So many elbows on the bandstand
        so many ideologies grafted together
So many memories coexisting
        so many extensions breaking off
So many scuffles redefined
        so many secretions interlacing
So many whistles hidden in the flesh
        so many exaggerated organs on the horizon
So many tongue tampering strategies on the
        toothbrush
        so many questions bleeding between dentures
So many uncontrollable punches on the circuit
        so many edges
So many fringes
        so many zones
So many flashpoints plunging
        into the rhythm of the moment
                of so much diversity
that even the finest cloth ever stuffed
into the last tremor of a corpse
can become the rarest vein in the eyeball of
compression
and robot mucus on the sex pulse of nostalgia
can turn into a nuclear warhead of hot semen
and steel dust on the ass of a common pimp
can become a presidential pompadour of acid rain
and the strongest teeth in the grin of humiliation
can become the toothless gums of a fuchsia volcano

Because anything and everything is possible
in this collection of umbilical sweat
bursting forth like a mound of a thousand palm leaves
waving into the space of the night of assaulted bones
Shapes accumulating like ancestors

in the purple velveteen shadow of leather lungs
A ceremony of rakes and rollers crosshatching
into a gel of artificial light
          Clusters
                    Patterns
                              Infiltrations

The weight of five overlapping facial configurations
split and glued onto a spleen of lingering odors
Textures   Contours   Colors   Juxtapositions
Half lip   half eye   half day   half tones baptising
in the turquoise darkness of a train serenade and
in the center of another slab of epidemic wax
a release   a transfer   an accusation
a corrosion of marks
head units and gyrating limbs parading
in a stream of black ink
       Elevations
                    Stilts
A promenading surface of erotic strokes
Rebellions carried on the felt tip of an evening sunset
Images
climbing in and out of sensations
in and out of distortions
in and out of the static of chartreuse lightning
With flint and graphite and soot and the knife
       grinders grinding into a paint of pink champagne
With smoke and stone and grease and the magnification
       of multiple grooves pressed on a generation of profiles
With bleach and dye and hemp and the metallic inflammation
       in eyeslit of a sub-zero bump
With volume and theme and
       the spinning suction cup of Yucatan flames
With flag and map and
       dialogical coagulations on mute of a frozen plate
With lines
         contracting   expanding   going deeper
                    into the damp sound of the paper

curving crossing shifting slicing
into the quiver of a human impulse
coiling zig-zagging swirling
into the bite of the process
pushing piercing swinging from inner
limitations into outer limits of space
eliminations
in a stream of ink

And it's a collographic jungle of cuts
A photographic blister of red dots
Deformed *cabezas* that are secret wells
Mouth murals of flashing metals
A codex of hidden structures
A refuge for absurd feelings
Gouges
Terrains
Bodies in relief
Bodies absorbed in copper
Bodies subdivided into bodies
Attitudes
Definitions
Dreams
stretching through a labyrinth of shades
Everything intensifying in this
charcoal sandstorming desert
The buzz in the ear
The blow torch blow of barracuda breath
Barbwire posing on a mask of zinc windows
Apprehensions Footprints Invasions
The stench of withdrawal and regeneration
A convulsion of currents A conduit of
confabulations
Exhaust pipe of lavender flowers
Impressions
from coins from keys from anthills
from fifty-five polluted singing winds in a
stream of
so many calculations

So many conjunctions
so many uninhibited gestures
So many toxic runoffs
so many self-inflicted etchings
So many reef devastations
so many identification stones smoking
So many tilted forms feathered
so many insertions inserted
So many conceptions communicated
so many enclosures
So many events
so many blunted instruments scraping
into the rhythm of the moment
of so much diversity
in a stream of ink

WHEN I LOOK AT WILFREDO LAM'S PAINTINGS

They have breasts shaped
like papayas like grapefruits like
spades & shovels & picks & mangos

They erupt
and swirl into baby tornados
They mutate and chalk into
burnt out bulbs of
decorated pus in paint

They merge and melt into other forms
Swallow themselves and gush forward

They connect their sockets
to spermatic strings
of dried centipedes
moving in half steps toward
center of the darkness of the dot
to become ancestral shadows
saturated between Damballah's tattooed toes
and Oya's fishhook fingers
between Ogun's rust colored neck
and Oshun's wine coated tongue
between Shango's red leaves matted to
tiny pyramid teeth of a barking sorcerer
and Yemaya's silver-rimmed eyelids expanding
and contracting into a cyclonic breeze of
double-headed bats

They burn up the brushes
with raffia swishing and shooting from
buttocks of vibrating nostrils
with knee-caps swelling on stilts of
bowlegged nails
with grinning horses galloping from

navels of frying fat
with purple stems of cane protruding from
green lips of machetes
with zigzagging flamingos fluctuating on
the roof tops of Matanzas

They billow and overlap in broaches of
charcoal spittle
They cross and dissolve into
a fleet of orange blotted organs
They have their bull horns
their yellow snake arrows
their triangular forest skulls
their blood vessels sprouting from daggers
their upsidedown faces in pelvises rotating
and perforating in spider specked sex of the gouache

I AND I

for Michael Smith

We had a nice time together
traveling laughing eating drinking
reading our poetry
in jam sessions
carving up rhythms
carving up syllables
carving up time
I and I
Now they say
you be dead in your dreads Michael
Stoned to death
by some treacherous Black brothers
in your own country
of Jamaica
And hey
You were worried about the White Man
about not receiving berries from
grave of a Russian writer
about the theft of black talk
in mouth of a punk rocker
about the customs officer
who tried to block your re-entry
into Paris
Yeah man
It must've been
a mean verbal extension
of the dozens
that you laid
on those reactionary elite politicians
to cause such a tremor of hate
to flare off
and become fanatical in them
and in their followers
who had already suffered
from a loss of consciousness

a loss of purpose
a loss of self
And I can just see you
tearing the night up
with the intensity of your stare-down
tearing it up
with your blistering cadre
of rebellious rhymes
And it is what it is
from this word to that word
from that event to this event
from here to there to where
men with occupations emphasizing the
precisions of
death
rather than the precisions in life come
out through the bacteria of walls
not to hear the sound of your reggae sound
not to see you smile your natural smile
not to understand the concept of your conceptual
ways of dealing
but to familiarize themselves with the functions
of shutting off voices shutting out faces
shutting out names
And it is what it is
in front of that kind of energy of confusion
that mysticism of madness
that homicidal hipness which
you yourself alone tried to penetrate as
the build up between dominance and resistance
threw down
at full cry
And the cross-road-smells collided and flashed back
to the day you demanded to be treated like a human being
back to the day you entered the ritual compound to be
an African saluting Africa
back to the day you declared yourself a poet with
a message from the people enslaved in poverty
back to the day you called for justice

That was the day you became a threat to
the lifestyle of the bourgeois class of beggars
                                        in Babylon

That was when they decided
you were an insane dangerous infant   opposed
to their neo-colonial out-house mentality
That was when they vowed to
blow away the Stagolee in your mental fire
To put paraquat in your holy weed
to turn the erotic vitality of stone
into signifying stones
into tribal stones
into a stigma of stones
against your complexion of Blackness
against your language of revolt
against your spiritual defiance
against the slash of your limping
                              leg of steel
And it was a rain of boulders shooting
in and out of your skull
                          like bombs
A burst of red lava in the air
A greenish bolt of lighting
          in the center of the unity of space
Your baby teeth going back into the earth
back into the hearts of the poets
who break open their lines to
sing your wolfing wolof words
straight through the pathological
invasions of the hour
straight through the emergency wards
of agitated officials
straight through the bull's-eye of the cyclone

SOLOMON MAHLANGU FREEDOM FIGHTER FROM MAMELODI

They tried to force Solomon Mahlangu
to swallow their shitball ideology of apartheid
Tried to make him a burning carrier
of their bantustan madness
Tried to contaminate him
with their infectious passbook plague
They wanted him to be
a castrated lopsided afrikaans speaking scavenger
a drunk wornout mimicking collector of fascist
culture
a sticky unborn unconceived spot on the reservation
But he went outside of their wants
outside of their needs
and built up a defense system
against the secretion of insanity and fear
Vaccinated himself
against the inflamed mucus
of Pessimistic White Inept
Reactionary Arrogantitus Syndrome (PWIRAS)
Became immune
to the compounds used to separate people
Sprinkled his body
with the blood of other revolutionary warriors
And by the time his fist flew up
and his heart shot forward
like ten king cobras
in the pre-dawn spit of April
he had already
gone beyond the realities of life

PUSH BACK THE CATASTROPHES

I don't want a drought to feed on itself
through the tattooed holes in my belly
I don't want a spectacular desert of
charred stems & rabbit hairs
in my throat of accumulated matter
I don't want to burn and cut through the forest
like a greedy mercenary drilling into
the sugar cane of the bones

Push back the advancing sands
the polluted sewage
the dust demons   the dying timber
the upper atmosphere of nitrogen
push back the catastrophes

Enough of the missiles
the submarines
the aircraft carriers
the biological weapons
No more sickness   sadness   poverty
exploitation   destabilization
illiteracy and bombing
Let's move toward peace
toward equality and justice
that's what I want

To breathe clean air
to drink pure water to plant new crops
to soak up the rain to wash off the stink
to hold this body and soul together in peace
that's it
Push back the catastrophes

EVERYTHING IS WONDERFUL

Under the urination of astronauts
and the ejaculation of polluted sparrows
and the evacuation of acid brain matter
everything is wonderful
except for the invasion and occupation
of Grenada and Panama
except for the avalanche of blood coagulating
in El Salvador
except for the brutal apartheid system
raging in South Africa
except for the threat of intervention
in Nicaragua
except for the war of repression
in the Sudan
except for Pinochet killing again in Chile
except for the famine in Ethiopia
except for that
and the torrential rainfall
of cluster bombs falling in Beirut
everything is everything
wonderful and wonderful

EXPENDITURES
ECONOMIC LOVE SONG 1

MILITARY SPENDING HUGE PROFITS &
DEATH

MILITARY SPENDING HUGE PROFITS &
DESTRUCTION

MILITARY SPENDING HUGE PROFITS &
DEATH

MILITARY SPENDING HUGE PROFITS &
DESTRUCTION

MILITARY SPENDING HUGE PROFITS &
DEATH

MILITARY SPENDING HUGE PROFITS &
DESTRUCTION

MILITARY SPENDING HUGE PROFITS &
DEATH

MILITARY SPENDING HUGE PROFITS &
DESTRUCTION

MILITARY SPENDING HUGE PROFITS &
DEATH

MILITARY SPENDING HUGE PROFITS &
DESTRUCTION

MILITARY SPENDING HUGE PROFITS &
DEATH

MILITARY SPENDING HUGE PROFITS &
DESTRUCTION

MILITARY SPENDING HUGE PROFITS & DEATH

MILITARY SPENDING HUGE PROFITS & DESTRUCTION

MILITARY SPENDING HUGE PROFITS & DEATH

MILITARY SPENDING HUGE PROFITS & DESTRUCTION

MILITARY SPENDING HUGE PROFITS & DEATH

MILITARY SPENDING HUGE PROFITS & DESTRUCTION

MILITARY SPENDING HUGE PROFITS & DEATH

TELL ME

Tell me that the plutonium sludge
in your corroded torso is all a dream

Tell me that your penis bone is not erupting
with the stench of dead ants
that your navel is not the dump site
                                        of contaminated pus
that the spillage from your hard ass
is not a fallout of radioactive waste
Tell me it's a lie
Tell me it's a joke

Tell me that you don't have to fuck yourself on
the reactor core of an intense meltdown
                                        to show your importance
Tell me that you have no desire
to be the first one to fuck
                    into the fission of a fusion
                                        of a fucking holocaust

Tell me i'm hallucinating
Tell me i'm fantasizing
Tell me i'm delirious
Tell me you know peace is better than war
that total decolonization is better than war
that the elimination of hunger is better than war
that the moon merging into the shadow of the earth
                                                    is better than war
That night moving into day
and day moving back into night is better than war
That the sound of the human voice in its calmness
in its shrillness
in its monumental invention of pitches
                                                    is better than war
that the arrival of rain

the smell of something familiar
the blood circulating in your legs
the visitation of the sun
the conjunction of rivers
the vexation of your special nerve and
hope rising from the soul of your nose
                    is better than war

Tell me that the tonnage of nuclear sweat
in your prostate gland is all a mistake
tell me that your vagina
      will not be
            a bursting silo of blue flames
that your chest
      will not be
            an infested swamp of vomiting mosquitos
Tell me it's a mirage
Tell me it's absurd
Tell me you really have no intention of being
a homeless   nameless   sexless piece of shit
                    somewhere over the rainbow

Tell me that you have no need to get high
                off the fumes of a neutron bomb
Tell me that you're not going to peel off your skin
and be a psychedelic corpse in the holy water of
                        patriotic slobber
Tell me it's ridiculous
Tell me it's ludicrous

But don't tell me that you think you're immune
      because there is no immunity
No immunity to the hydrogen dust
   moving like a cloud
         of a hundred trillion infuriated rhinos
No immunity to the fireball smoker
                        of abdominal organs
No immunity to the fetishes wrapped
                        in uranium crates

No immunity to the downwind flames
of invisible radiation
No immunity
and you know it
i know it
the computer knows it
everybody knows it

So tell me that you're going to pull away
from the corrupt gluttonous controllers of profit
Tear open the condescending attitudes
full of green ashes
Separate yourself from the solitude of stagnation
Don't tell me that you want to sink into the stink
of exotic weapons
Don't tell me that you want to quiver into the heat
of missile repulsion
Don't tell me that you want to disappear
into the pessimistic past
of your own self-interest

Tell me i'm dreaming
Tell me i'm hallucinating
Tell me i'm fantasizing
Tell me it's unthinkable
Tell me it's unrealistic
Tell me it's all in my imagination
Tell me you never heard of such a thing
Tell me it's a misunderstanding
Tell me it's not a human need
Tell me it's a crock of shit
Tell me it's propaganda
Tell me you really intend to go forward
Tell me
Tell me
Tell me

POETIC MAGNETIC:

POEMS FROM *EVERYWHERE DRUMS*

& *MAINTAIN CONTROL*

(1991)

POETRY MUSIC TECHNOLOGY

In a recording session or musical setting many important things just happen. Even though I have a certain amount of material prepared, the real structure is created while working. In performance I usually read from a manuscript, recite lines from memory and spontaneously compose on the spot. By using music and technology I'm trying to extend the poet's role, which means, the poet in this situation becomes the band, the pen, paper, books, research, instruments, words and all the possibilities of the technology. The poet is in control. One of the highest compliments given in the arts is when an artistic work is said to be not only excellent but also has beautiful poetic qualities. This compliment usually suggests that the work is more sensitive, has more insight and is at a higher level of expression. I am trying to move this combination of poetry, music and technology to a higher poetic level. It's the poetic use of music, the poetic use of technology, the poetic orchestration of it all.

In 1964 I started reading my poetry with music. I have worked with musicians in Africa, Cuba, Brazil, England, France, Italy, Canada and throughout the United States of America. In 1980 I formed a band and named it The Firespitters. *Poetic Magnetic* contains poems from the last two recordings: *Everywhere Drums* and *Maintain Control.*

The Firespitter Band: Denardo Coleman, Al MacDowell, Charles Moffett, Jr., Bern Nix and guest.

JAZZ FAN LOOKS BACK

I crisscrossed with Monk
Wailed with Bud
Counted every star with Stitt
Sang "Don't Blame Me" with Sarah
Wore a flower like Billie
Screamed in the range of Dinah
& scatted "How High the Moon" with Ella Fitzgerald
as she blew roof off the Shrine Auditorium
                    Jazz at the Philharmonic

I cut my hair into a permanent tam
Made my feet rebellious metronomes
Embedded record needles in paint on paper
Talked bopology talk
Laughed in high-pitched saxophone phrases
Became keeper of every Bird riff
every Lester lick
as Hawk melodicized my ear of infatuated tongues
& Blakey drummed militant messages in
soul of my applauding teeth
& Ray hit bass notes to the last love seat in my bones
I moved in triple time with Max
Grooved high with Diz
Perdidoed with Pettiford
Flew home with Hamp
Shuffled in Dexter's Deck
Squatty-rooed with Peterson
Dreamed a "52nd Street Theme" with Fats
& scatted "Lady Be Good" with Ella Fitzgerald
as she blew roof off the Shrine Auditorium
                    Jazz at the Philharmonic

ADUPE

(ah doo pway)

1981 and
I did not find Nicolás Guillén
but I found Cuba
the Cuba in Nicolás Guillén
but I found Cuba
the Cuba in Nicolás Guillén's poetry
poetry dedicated to his two selves
his two sides
poetry in half notes
in eighth notes
in 6/8 time
poetry moving backward & forward like war dances
poetry doing the Rara in an African vocabulary
& I said
adupe   to Nicolás Guillén
Nicolás Banjo Guitar Mbira Guillén
improvising like the great instrument he is
in Yoruba
in Spanish
in Son
not exotic but Zydeco
not Miami but Havana
not tweet tweet but Mau Mau
adupe to the man from Camagüey

This morning
I went into the Paris of his poetry
& came out with poets clinking glasses to
nouveau beaujolais at Roquets
I pushed into favela of his poetry and
emerged with carnival costumes for
one hundred year celebration of the abolition of slavery
I looked through his blunt poetry and
saw exiles smiling like rusty bulldozers and acting
like disjointed chiefs of staff

like broken stags roaming in
everglades of khaki teeth & clandestine scrotum
I walked through seance house of his poetry and came upon
a fiesta sizzling in the bubble chamber of Aztec clouds
I dived into political content of his poetry and
discovered mysterious caves with odors of rotting imperialist dust
I looked at shell lined pelvis of his poetry and saw
infra-green heat of human capacity snaking down through
underground galaxy
of atomic clocks
I moved into stamina of his poetry and returned
with boxing gloves smelling like Santería shrines
I ran along the Malecón of his poetry and found
a poverty imbued with the power to drive straight through
a northern frente frio
I stood in stadium of his staccato yelping poetry and heard
messages coded and covered with drum heads from Oyo
and I said adupe Nicolás Guillén
adupe
for the cavalcade of leaves & moaning doves &
regalia of punching bags
adupe
for the musky cyclones in bolero jackets &
smoke filled consultation of yagruma trees
adupe
for the call & response of collaborating oceans &
the rooster juice splashed on feet steeped
in rumba motivations
adupe
for the great poem confrontations of Nicolás Guillén
adupe

Determination belongs to Guillén
Revolutionary thought belongs to Guillén
Solidarity belongs to Guillén
Gulla Efik Ewe Fula Fulani Twi belongs to Guillén
Mende Mandingo Mossi Umbundu Suk belongs to Guillén
Bomba la conga bomba belongs to Guillén
Negrismo Socialismo belongs to Guillén

Completeness of life in poetry belongs to Guillén
Nicolás Banjo Guitar Mbira Guillén
digging up roots and making his mark making his mark
breaking those chains and making his mark making his mark
mixing up rhythms and making his mark making his mark
talking to his people and making his mark making his mark
working with his work and making his mark making his mark
Nicolás Banjo Guitar Mbira Guillén
Nicolás Banjo Guitar Mbira Guillén

MAYBE

LIBERTY
JUSTICE
EQUALITY
MAYBE
IN
THE
21st
CENTURY
MAYBE
ON
ANOTHER
PLANET
MAYBE
IN
OUTER
SPACE
MAYBE
MAYBE
MAYBE
NO
EQUALITY
NO
JUSTICE
NO
LIBERTY
WHAT
KIND
OF
DEMOCRACY
IS
THIS

WHAT'S HAPPENING

What's happening
You'll know what's happening
when you see Pedro the poet
selling condoms and poetry books
and hear the man of god
choking on his sexual contradictions
you'll know what's happening
when you see computers going to sleep on
shoulders of their secretaries and
hear workers dismantling governments
in Europe
in South Africa
you'll know what's happening

What's happening
An intellectual is marching around like
a great humanitarian but won't pay his
child support that's what's happening
And on the lower eastside of New York City
a Doris Day look alike is imitating the voice of
Louis Satchmo Armstrong while
the minister of unnecessary information
gets his hair curled
That's what's happening
The musicians are making facial expressions acting
like they're really playing something complex
                        and are not
That's what's happening
& me? Me?
I have already dropped a half inch of
slobber on a certain line
I have already placed parachutes on
two mountains of paper
OK. It's only one word in three hours
but look at you

look at you
Your job is to be a singing raisin
He's a dancing cornflake
You're a smiling commode
She's a walking roll of toilet tissue
He falls on the beach like
a sack of empty bullet shells
She's forced to sit like a ground based
missile interceptor in the tourist area while
commander in chief invades Panama and
shoots Panamanians democratically to
enforce human rights and burn up another flag
That's what's happening
And there are other drug dealers butting
heads in the dark
other equal opportunity killers on
the horizon
other fraudulent financiers manipulating money
and doing the hand jive
other corrupt hotel chain owners with
nice clothes and dirty drawers
That's what's happening
Meanwhile
the meter "maids" are still giving parking tickets
and the gospel singers are still taking cliches
and beating them to death
and the xmas tree crews are out discovering the
deepest hole of their consciousness in the donut shop
and little ladies in long coats are walking in
competition with big ladies in tight pants
and here we are between the emergency exit of
a closing bank
and the ambulance entrance of an aging nuclear reactor
waiting for the economic recovery of our dreams
and that's what's happening
that's what happening

MAKE IFA

Make Ifa make Ifa make Ifa Ifa Ifa

In sanctified chalk
of my silver painted soot
In crisscrossing whelps
of my black belching smoke
In brass masking bones
of my bass droning moans
In hub cap bellow
of my hammer tap blow
In steel stance screech
of my zumbified flames
In electrified mouth
of my citified fumes
In bellified groan
of my countrified pound
In compulsivefied conga
of my soca moko-jumbie
MAKE IFA MAKE IFA MAKE IFA IFA IFA
In eye popping punta
of my heat sucking sap
In cyclonic slobber
of my consultation pan
In snap jam combustion
of my banjonistic thumb
In sparkola flare
of my hoodooistic scream
In punched out ijuba
of my fire catching groove
In fungified funk
of my sambafied shakes
In amplified dents
of my petrified honks
In ping-ponging bomba
of my scarified gongs
MAKE IFA MAKE IFA MAKE IFA IFA IFA

EVERYBODY WANTS TO BE SOMEBODY

Everybody wants to be somebody
in the mouth of someone
someday   someway
in the USA
in the USA
Everybody wants to be somebody
on a magazine cover
Everybody wants to be somebody
on television
Everybody wants to be somebody
in the mouth of someone
someday   someway
in the USA
in the USA
but nobody wants to struggle
to be somebody
Nobody wants to suffer
to be somebody
Everybody wants to be somebody
if somebody is someone
but nobody wants to be no one
if no one is nobody
in the USA
in the USA
everybody wants to be famous
famous
but nobody needs it
Everybody wants it
& everybody should be recognized as something
Everybody has the right to be something
but nobody wants to just be something
Everybody want to be something famous
but nobody needs it
Everybody wants it
Nobody needs it
Nobody needs it

NELSON MANDELA IS COMING 2

Mandela is coming
Mandela is coming

As a result of mass demonstrations
as a result of strikes boycotts and sanctions
as a result of organizing in exile
as a result of international support
as a result of grass root revolts
as a result of armed struggle
as a result of progressive democratic thinking
as a result of revolutionary commitment
as a result of the sacrificial blood

Mandela is coming   Apartheid is going
Mandela is coming   Apartheid is going
Mandela is coming   Apartheid is going

They told Nelson Mandela not to open his mouth
about freedom
They told him he'd better capitulate to oppression
But Mandela refuses to be brutalized into submission
Mandela did not let himself be beaten down by insults

Mandela made the sacrifice
and the sacrifice made Mandela
Mandela makes progress for the movement
and the movement makes progress with Mandela

Mandela is coming   Apartheid is going
Mandela is coming   Apartheid is going
Mandela is coming   Apartheid is going

Mandela knows law
Mandela is a lawyer
Mandela knows tradition

Mandela is a traditional chief
Mandela knows how to organize
Mandela is organizer for the ANC

Mandela is coming   Apartheid is going
Mandela is coming   Apartheid is going
Mandela is coming   Apartheid is going

& as a result of mass demonstrations
as a result of strikes, boycotts and sanctions
as a result of organizing in exile
as a result of international support
as a result of grass root revolts
as a result of armed struggle
as a result of progressive, democratic thinking
as a result of revolutionary commitment
as a result of the sacrificial blood
South Africa will be free   Africa will be free

Mandela is coming   Apartheid is going   Mandela is coming   Apartheid is going
Mandela is coming   Apartheid is going   Mandela is coming   Apartheid is going
Apartheid is going   Apartheid is going   Apartheid is going   Apartheid is going

MAINTAIN CONTROL

Where are you going   Where have you been
Where are you going   Where have you been

When you rush to the job
& time clock the card
then step up production
to pay for corruption
but have no deductions
to pay for your pension
pay for your pay cut
pay for your strike fund
to Maintain Control   Maintain Control   Maintain Control

Where are you going   Where have you been
Where are you going   Where have you been

When you throw down your coat
& kick off your shoes
& drink down your booze
& turn on the beat
& strike up a groove
to wear out your feet
& wear out the drummer
trying to wonder
what is that number to   Maintain Control
Maintain Control   Maintain Control

Where are you going   Where have you been
Where are you going   Where have you been

When you eat up the eats
& drink up the drinks
& smoke up the smokes
& crack up the crack
& blot out your visions

& blot out your values
but find no solution
to your pollution
to Maintain Control   Maintain Control   Maintain Control

Where are you going   Where have you been
Where are you going   Where have you been

When you numb down your brain
& dilate your eyes
& coke up your nose
& asbesto your sniff
& procaine your lips
& jolt up your heart
to stagnate your life
        & push out your violence
use up your body
        & push out your violence
count up your gadgets
        & push out your violence
lock up your face
        & push out your violence
litter up the planet
        & push out your violence
push out your violence   push out your violence

To Maintain Control?   Maintain Control?   Maintain Control?

Where are you going   Where have you been
Where are you going   Where have you been

& what have you done
& who made you do it
& what did you see
& who made you see it
& what do you need
to pull up your courage
& what do you need

& how will you get it
to maintain control
of who's in control
to maintain control
of what's in control
to maintain control
Maintain Control   Maintain Control   Maintain Control

BRIEFING 1986

Many mysterious people hide out
in the remote white areas
of South Africa
Some speak the Afrikaans language of Apartheid
Others speak the English language of Capitalism
Most are very reactive very repressive
Very racist and very very violent

They whip out their tongues like
pre-historic reptiles
slashing & thrashing Black youths to pieces
They wade through funeral crowds
tearing off heads and
chewing through armpits of Black mourners
They load their victims up with
tear gas and rubber bullets
and sit on borders
scooping out marrow and
eating dead Namibian corpse
They are the biggest bone collectors in the world
And they spare no expense to
Keep their one-way flow of
white propaganda flowing through
mouths of international entertainers

And because they create fetishes out of
gold mines
Black gold miners
migrant mining compounds and
widow reserves
they have been most successful at
avoiding European condemnation &
in widening their trails of corruption through
resolutions & calls for economic sanctions
and in keeping their brains stuck in

the inaccessible swamps of white afrikaner nationalism
and in making the perpetuation of supremacy a way of life
and in convincing the Western Block to support them for
their strategic location

And no
it's not unusual for them to
display photographs of
Africans killing Africans
of Black soldiers stealing from refugee camps
of Black armies keeping the military institution of
colonialism alive
because their rumps are filled with negatives of
fake Black liberation groups
They are the producers of war zones and squatter camps
They arm & pay Jonas Savimbi to disrupt Angola
They organize & pay Portuguese speaking black & white
mercenaries to destabilize Southern Africa
They use people like Gatsha Buthelezi
and the Inkatha Zulu delegation
to provoke riots & deradicalize Black townships
They design & sell new & old forms of tribalism
Their mixture of European tribal life-styles
rely on a policy of Black tribal separation

And because they're cold-blooded killers
with notorious reputations for
breaking up families
and for murdering men like Steve Biko
jailing leaders like Nelson Mandela
hanging poets like Benjamin Moloise
banishing and brutalizing women who
reject their ideology of apartheid
and calling it their holy duty
they think
they can preserve
their wild broderbantustan butts
and bulldozer lips forever
They think

they can be
the great civilizing messiahs of genocide
quoting scriptures and praying
in the ashes of Black African children
praying for a baptismal feast of
more special privileges
praying that countries such as Mozambique
won't be able to sever labor links of dependency
Praying that wars bacterial contamination
drought and nuclear threats
will keep all of Africa fragmented
Praying that they can go on praying and
refining their techniques of lying and praying
and capitalizing on whatever they can capitalize
and prey upon
in hopes of retaining power
in hopes of securing their survival
in hopes that all their hopes won't fall
under the blue funk of smoking stones in
a hopeless state of terror
in hopes that a holding reform pattern of hope
will hold them together in a Republic of Hope
but only we know what's happening
on the hopeful side
And since they're not progressively hip enough
to understand revolutionary expectations

And are not religiously righteous enough
to read hieroglyphic graffiti
and since they would rather steal land
suck on precious metals and
live off the high wages of cheap labor
instead of accepting one person one vote
then let's hope
they'll be technologically sophisticated enough
to sail through the air on corrugated rooftops
Let's hope they'll be intellectually educated enough
to flee on the Bantu express
Let's hope they'll be economically solvent enough

to shimmer in the dust storm of their plunging
defense budget
Let's hope they'll be independently boerish enough
to confront the extinction of their savagery
and physically fit enough to swallow
the bloody stools of their beloved system of apartheid
Let's hope for that dark day of liberation
for that gloomy day of unification
for that black day of transformation
for that drunk day of modernization
for that bleak day of peace and happiness and
all the beautifulness in the universe

DEADLY RADIATION BLUES

I've seen rubble left by earthquakes
seen erupting volcanos & devastating avalanches too
I've seen typhoons rising from oceans
seen tornados ripping hurricanes howling
and forest fires out of control
Now a nuclear reactor is exploding
and i've got those Chernobyl Three Mile Island Blues

I've seen flash floods & landslides
seen streets turned into red rivers roaring
I've seen thunderbolts & cyclones
and seen blizzards & sandstorms blasting & blowing
Now a nuclear reactor is exploding
and i've got those Chernobyl Three Mile Island Blues

I've seen reservoirs dry up
and knew that moisture in the soil could cease to exist
I've seen objects destroyed by lightning
seen humans stripped of flesh   trees stripped of leaves
bones stripped of bones in a drought
Now the rain showers are coming with radiation
and i've got the Chernobyl Three Mile Island Blues

I've seen photos of Nagasaki & Hiroshima
I've heard cries swirling from a chemical plant in Bhopal India
I've seen radioactive dust in Nevada & Utah
Heard screams echoing in from the Ural mountains too
Now a nuclear reactor is exploding
and i've got those Chernobyl Three Mile Island Blues

I've thrown away milk & lettuce
washed my hair my hands & my shoes
but the winds keep shifting & drifting
and i've got those Chernobyl Three Mile Island Blues

Reactors breed plutonium
blood cells pay their dues
radiation keeps leaking & seeping
and i've got the Chernobyl Three Mile Island Blues

Nuclear power plants can't be dismantled
no way to dispose of the waste
we've got to shut down those reactors
or have the Chernobyl Three Mile Island Blues

Deadly radiation levels high
deadly radiation flying in the sky
deadly radiation swarming with debris
deadly radiation dropping in the sea
deadly radiation forming other clouds
deadly radiation steaming in the bowels
deadly radiation falling through and through
and i've got the Chernobyl Three Mile Island Deadly Radiation Blues

COMMITMENT 2

Paul Robeson stood out in his passport
a committee of one
a committee of one who covered
    a lot of territory
the territory of dedication
a dedication to the freedom of his people
I knew him in that way
as a prominent artist
complete with talent with democratic ideas
    and revolutionary gestures
Never never holding back
Never never backing down
Never never selling out
    Projecting the story of dignity and love
    instead of the story of greed and corruption

And I want to be warm like him
funloving like him creative like him
unselfish like him
with his kind of awareness
his kind of generosity his
kind of critical understanding
kind of strength kind of vision kind of energy
kind of power kind of spirit kind of courage
kind of sensitivity yes
    Never never never holding back
    never never never backing down
    never never never selling out
Always projecting the story of dignity & love
instead of the story of greed and corruption

I knew him in that way
in the way of the spirituals I love
even though he didn't sing in the style
        of my choice

But what does style have to do with commitment
After all contributions go beyond songs
          & I liked his baritone bass speaking and
          booming out in artistic brilliance
A protest against hatred and fascism
A protest against racism and oppression
A protest against terror and fear
His song was an intense song of ancestral memories
His song was a song of faith and resistance
His song was a song of hope and creativity
Always making connections
Always being progressive
Always trying to live the life of struggle & determination
instead of the life of glitter and degradation
and I like that
the fact he could interpret the symbol
that his photograph had become
A powerful force significant to masses of people
I understood him in that way
as a person complete with confidence
               and political intent
Never holding back
never backing down
never selling out

Projecting the story of dignity and love instead of
the story of fame and corruption
I knew him in those ways
               and I like that
              Never never holding back
              never never backing down
              never never selling out

FRAGMENTS

Sculpture and Drawings
From the "Lynch Fragment" Series

By Melvin Edwards
With the Poetry of
Jayne Cortez

FRAGMENTS:

SCULPTURE AND DRAWINGS FROM
THE "LYNCH FRAGMENT" SERIES BY MELVIN EDWARDS
WITH POETRY OF JAYNE CORTEZ

(1994)

ALSO

also the ironess of iron
the metaphorical behavior of tools
horseshoehammerheadaxes
plus the language of pumps & vises
& the high carbon ghost from Tijuca

WE ARE

We are two bones
in the same clamp
two cults hanging from
the same tree

MY FACE

my face mask made of window screening
my barbwire hair glowing with coconut oil
I have the charred surfaces
wounded tree trunks
& spit riding on the cheekbones of
a new locomotive
jack up the jack base
& wait for me in the swamp
I am flying back with the teeth of fifty bloodhounds

UNSEXED

Unsexed by
the infra-red light of
red hot crowbars
Unsexed
in the direct sunlight
of butcher knives
Unsexed on the roof of
a christian church
Unsexed
on passenger bridge number 6
Unsexed
in railroad station number 2
unsexed in tunnel number 5
Unsexed
& then lynched
on the balcony of the courthouse of justice

CLARIFICATION/1984

No denture cleanser
can remove stubborn stains of greed
from plaque filled plates
of a self appointed god
no bullet proof vest
can hide repulsive flesh
of a violent fascist heart
no presidential cooking recipe
can eliminate problems of starvation & poverty
no missile making program
can kill unemployment
no first lady
kissing shaven head of a black santa claus
can erase memories of slavery and lynchings
no propaganda machine of lies
can bring back forty thousand people
murdered in El Salvador
and no school of prayer
can pray away lead embedded bones
of families buried in ditches in Guatemala
and no extra thick disposable diaper
can absorb the stench of bloody krugerrands
in pants of the corporate bankers of war
and no bathroom tissue with lotion
can sweeten smell of the oppressive class of mercenaries
economically in control of capitol hill
& no super computer is super enough
to hold all the distortions coming from mouth
of the great communicator of disinformation
destabilization & deficits
and no invasionary unit of body snatchers
secretly moving from the shores of Grenada
to the shores of Tripoli to the shores
of Nicaragua to the shores of Southern Africa

and back to tamper in shores of our private thoughts
can take away the human impulse
to resist against exploitation & extermination
and in the double digit inflation
of your constipation
you know it

I WAKE UP EARLY

I wake up early in the morning
sit and think about
divination trays
cow bells
oil drums
the sky all rusty with gongs
I jump up as
day snaps back through
maze of ashy Nubian thighs
poems entering my head
from left side of midnight
I put them on paper
touch down
in lower register of the turmoil
let one shape
tell the whole story
like a Thelonious Monk plunk
the motion
clear
distinct
rooted in what it is
what it was the
instant I hit it
the moment everything said click
unpredictable
imagination sticking out its tongue
unrepeatable
sound boards posing like
the sun that changes
into a bird standing
on crocodile teeth
transmissions
acquisitions
use it

go beyond it
just write and let it happen
        hangnail in afterbirth
        saltfish motif on steel

KISSES

You fall on your knees
to kiss the ground
stolen from Indians
kiss the ground
where violent lynch mobs stand
where corrupt politicians catch planes
                                        to Swiss banks
but what does the ground
have to do with your kisses
          Were you born
          to just shoot up
          shoot down
          kiss the ground
          & call that a victory

A KISS

A kiss is not a kiss
if it means
death of your spit
donated to
a golden era
of classic cliches
fuck that old white magic
in its cigarette butt
& you know what I'm talking about
do not try to paste a dollar
on my clitoris
in the long term parking lot

I AM

I AM
THE BLOOD SPLATTERED LAMP
WITH THE REBELLIOUS SLEDGE HAMMER LIPS
HELLO SWEETHEART

MARIE SMITH

In remembrance of your knife
plunging into the body
of a rapist killer overseer
who you had to fight off
in the slave quarters
saturday night
girl
I celebrate your boldness

COMPARATIVE LITERATURE

Which god is in charge today
which deity is being called upon now
which one is constipated
which one is subversive
& into which coup d'état mouth will we bleed
& why are all the elements
                    singing in french like local heroes
why are all the subjects
                    laughing in english like woodpeckers
& did the signifying monkey really give aids
to the colonial administrator
                    Let's compare lacerations
I'm dancing with an anthropologist
smiling at a sociologist and
presenting my violent impulses to curator
                    at the museum of natural science
& what chemicals are they cooking up
what kind of viruses are they throwing around
what imported species are they tampering with
                    Let's put our masturbations on the airport table
                    Let's open our luggage in the claim check area
Did the signifying monkey really give aids
to the colonial administrator?

RUM

Tonight rum
carries the sanctions
the sourness
the sweet tooth of united extractions
rum carries the cyclone
the flood the armed struggle of
united sugar workers
rum at the throat entrance
and in the exit wound
rum labels tattooed on thighs
rum bottles holding up houses
rum in scars in bones at borders
converted from molasses into
gold dust, ivory, cassava, corn & rum
tobacco, salt, spices, slaves & rum
rum the circulator, rum the ventilator
rum the navigator
eggs, blood, fowl, ginger root & rum
rum for the trees for the ghosts for
the shrineroom rum
rum for the panyard for the transition zone rum
rum for the people
Caliban for literature
rum for reality
rum for the ruins
rum darkness rum lightness
rum over rum in rum with rum
rum

WHAT IS THERE

What is there to discover
from this steel face snake of a lover
internationally speaking for
pelvic examinations
very high up
in the oxygen cap
of metallic transfusions
instrumentally yours
source of fire
& muscle of introspective scissors

CULTURAL OPERATIONS 1992

The fishmongers are trying to sell fish
Ironmongers trying to sell iron
Poets are having beautiful springtime daughters
A sculptor is walking around astonished that he's 55
A painter overdoses on fumes from a pizza parlor
Eight year old boys are on stage
holding their crotches and rapping about
"i'm making love to my baby"
while armed Renamo bandits
who murder playmates
rape little girls
turn kids into killers
and force families to cook and eat remains
of dead relatives
are calling themselves
heroic freedom fighters
& the white South African government wants
to give up the word Apartheid
without giving up the gold,
the army & the real estate
& the new judge is showing his hairy teeth
to the Supreme Court
as the European Economic Community gang up to
keep racism in its body of segregated cash machines
and it's operation same old bullshit
operation same old right-wing multinational
think-tank manipulation of history,
geography and information
operation out-of-shape generals
still talking war & licking
plates in the cafeteria
operation desert dumbness
operation army for hire
operation pop star

still looking like
a walking flop house
operation thieves
still giving music awards
and patting each other on the back
for stealing and imitating their asses off
operation what does it matter
as long as the mob gets theirs
& the queen gets hers
& the X slaves continue to pay tribute
& the colonies continue to pay rent
& the International Monetary Fund &
World Bank stay intact
& there are no mass unruly defaultations
& no reorganizational plans of advancement on
front burner of an urban rebellion
& as long as we act as silly and mediocre
and corrupt and greedy and repressed
as we're programmed to act
and don't explode
& globalize that explosion into
a redistribution of all there is to redistribute
then everything remains what it is
& children you'd better hold onto your balls
because it's operation deforestation
operation deprivation   operation privatization
operation falsification   operation contamination
operation marginalization   operation militarization
operation polarization   operation subordination
operation toxification   operation destabilization
operation termination operation

DAY CUP

Day disappearing in the cup of
a homeless pair of dentures

Day riding on wounded cup of
the man who walks with
empty wine bottles tied to his
                                        sickle cell anemia

Day blowing its nose against burnt cup of
the woman infested with fireflies

A metal cup hanging from navel of
a man dodging immigrations
A rusted cup
sprouting from shoes of
a woman following her feet

Day breaking through the snoring cup
& the cup eating out of the head of sleepy day
are no surprise guests to the machete

STATES OF MOTION

Sun Ra left the planet in a pyramid made of metal keys
Willie Mae Thornton sailed away in an extra large
moisture-proof harmonica
Pauline Johnson flew off in a brass trimmed telephone
Thelonious Monk withdrew in a space ship shaped like a piano
Art Blakey departed in a great wood & stainless steel bass drum
Esther Philips bowed out in a nasal sounding chrome microphone
Charles Tyler, George Adams & Clifford Jordan reached another realm
in receptacles constructed like tenor saxophones
Okot p'Bitek shoved off in an attache case full of songs, books & whiskey
Léon Damas hit the road in a big black banjo
Audre Lorde departed wrapped in her book jackets
Dizzy Gillespie zoomed off in a sweet chariot shaped like a trumpet
Miles Davis left in a magnificent copper mute
Marietta Damas vacated the terrain in a beautiful house filled with
folkloric & electronic gadgets
Romare Bearden crossed over the rainbow in a blimp made of
his collages & etchings
Norman Lewis pushed away from the shore in a vault shaped like a bicycle
Ed Blackwell marched off concealed in an assortment of cymbals
Tchicaya U Tam'si floated away in a big heart shaped tuba
Vivian Browne departed draped in her painted forest canvases
Larry Neal went to the bush enclosed in two bookcases of poetry &
Bebop tapes
Kimako Baraka evacuated in a stone temple marked with Egyptian
hieroglyphics
Wilfred Cartey got away from the hurricane in an ocean liner made of
rum bottles
Johnny Makatini took off in a black, green & yellow rocket
Kathy Collins departed in a container made of unedited film clips
John Carter left in a fabulous silver clarinet
Evan Walker split in a boat that was shaped like a bird
Dumile Feni hurried to South Africa in one of his muscle bound
wooden sculptures

Peter Tosh reached the intersection in a bus filled with herbs &
political newspapers
Bob Marley retreated in a booming amplifier draped in
African flags tied with dreadlocks
Ana Mendieta made her exit as a bronze silueta
Michael Smith left for the forest in one huge audio cassette case
Elena & Jawa Apronti traveled from Accra in compartments made of
ceremonial umbrellas
Bill Majors rode off into the sunset in a highly polished brass
mercedes benz
Coco Anderson went to the festival in a fixture shaped like
a yam wrapped with eight patch-work quilts
Franco Manqwana rolled off in a king-size purple guitar
Nicolás Guillén went to the rendezvous in a grand rumba cow-bell
Tamu Bess traveled home in a queen-size computer plastered with eyeglasses
Flora Nwapa crossed the horizon concealed in pages of her new novel
Sarah Vaughan ascended in a misty glass recording booth
Gilberto de La Nuez disappeared into one of his paintings in Havana

CHEERFUL & OPTIMISTIC

even though I have this radioactive cloud
above my head
I'm cheerful & optimistic
even though my reproductive rights are threatened
I'm cheerful & optimistic
even though I have toxic sludge on my Xmas shoes
I'm cheerful & optimistic
even though my confirmation dress is in such a mess
in this acid rain
I'm cheerful & optimistic
even though I eat purple dioxin king crab legs
from Exxon Alaska
I'm cheerful & optimistic
even though the self-appointed saints of our time:
Saint Jonas of Savimbi, Saint Joseph-Michel François of Haiti
& Saint Gotcha of Buthelezi are sprinkling us
with their filthy holy water of human destruction
I'm cheerful & optimistic
even though I'm having polluted fish for dinner tonight
I'm cheerful & optimistic
I'm cheerful & optimistic like my computer
so cheerful so optimistic so cheerful so optimistic

SOMEWHERE IN ADVANCE OF NOWHERE

(1996)

ABOUT FLYIN' HOME

What would you say to yourself
if you had to lay on your back
hold up the horn
& play 99 courses of
a tune called Flyin' Home
exactly as you recorded it
55 years ago
& what would you think
if you woke up in the afternoon
& your head was still spinning with
voices shouting
Flyin' Home blow Flyin' Home
& what would you do
if someone whispered in your ear
hug me kiss me anything
but please don't play Flyin' Home
& what if a customer said:
tonight I'm having sex with
a person who has been up
in a flying saucer
so please funk me down good with Flyin' Home
& what would you think
if someone started singing
Yankee Doodle Dandy
in the middle of your solo on Flyin' Home
& what if you had to enter
all the contaminated areas in the world
just to perform your infectious version of
Flyin' Home
& what if you saw yourself
looking like a madman
with a smashed horn
walking backward on a subway platform
after 50 years of blowing Flyin' Home
& what would you think to yourself

if you had to play Flyin' Home
when you didn't have
a home to fly to
& what if Flyin' Home became
your boogie woogie social security check
your oldie but goodie way out of retirement
& was more valuable than you
I mean somewhere
in advance of nowhere
you are in here
after being out there
Flyin' Home

VISITA

1981
in Cuba
looking for
the great poet
Nicolás Guillén
in La Habana
in El Vedado
& on street corners
with 'Johnny Ordinary'
in bars with
'Johnny Nobody' &
between receptions & presentations
at Union of Artists & Writers
in office of Vice Minister of Culture
in the forest of ruffled tail feathers
at Tropicana night club
& in Santiago
Santiago de Cuba
where José Martí is buried like
                    a perfect poem
where spirit of Antonio Maceo sits like
                    a bronze sunrise
where beauty of Mariana Grajales who
saw her fifteen sons fall into
claws of fifteen buzzards
                    circulates
where blood of heroes illuminate in
deepness of Moncada Barracks
where old trova come leaping from new trova
& we are the trovas on the road to Bayamo
the road where I swear I hear
bass droning voice of Jesús Menendez
I swear I see those black facial gestures
meeting my facial gestures
in brightness of the cane field that

spins before me like a dream of
the sun dressed in fuchsia and
melting into folk lyrics of Camagüey
& merging with lime colored palm leaves
& blowing with tobacco smoke through
X cross section of
everything cross & criss-crossing like bulls
flywings   goats   dry grass   horses   gauchos
& this bus this guagua pulling
into city of huge clay pots
city of clear water
city of charcoal reddish mud
city of caramel sand
city with Indian name Camagüey
Camagüey city
birthplace of Nicolás Guillén
special like the clay pots
caramel like the sand &
in advance of walking on
        Trinidad cobblestones
& before passing Sani Spiritus
        Sierra del Escambray
then returning to
        La Habana
for homage
to Wilfredo Lam
it would be so nice
to meet Nicolás Guillén
here at the friendship house
or in a study circle
or with the Federation of Women
it would be so nice
to meet the poet who
gave us the Riddles
the Tropics
the Great Zoo
& Che Comandante
I would like to meet Nicolás Guillén

before leaving the
1952 turquoise Studebaker
the 1948 red painted Dynaflow Buick
the 1955 lemon yellow Chevy
& the steamrolling
diesel truck in the sky
honk   honk   honk
I would like to meet Nicolás Guillén while
I'm dazzling in the pure energy of Cuba
& getting the same serene feeling I get
after arriving in West Africa
no heavy load of racism on my shoulders
& while I feel happy
about nothing in particular
just happy
like a baby in the baby brigade
like children in child care centers
not fearful of knowing each other
just free & jaunty
you know jauntiness
not in the dumps of
constant depression
not hanging on edge
of an epidemic of stress
but cheerful & sunny
like sun bursting through pollution
on late stormy afternoons understand
not soft not hard core not threatened
but protected
& I would like to
meet Nicolás Guillén
in this mood
in this place
at this time

IN 1985 I MET NICOLÁS GUILLÉN

In 1985 I met Nicolás Guillén while
he sat with admirers in Havana
I met Nicolás Guillén
as he listened to
school children sing his poems
I met Nicolás Guillén
introduced by Nancy Morejón
to the delegation of
African American women writers
I met Nicolás Guillén
while he joked & flirted
& made poetry out of
simple human kinds of things
I met Nicolás Guillén
with his wit
with his smile
with his social criticism
& Spanish all fast
& dished up spicy

IN GILBERTO DE LA NUEZ'S STUDIO

I am full of Gilberto's paintings
full of his forests & figures of
emancipated African ancestors
full of his conga drums, dancing lines
& human songbirds singing in the plaza with
rumba bands playing 'Yolanda Yolanda'

It's a warm November morning in El Vedado
Gilberto has lost weight
his hands are shaking
he confesses his circulation is poor
and going to the doctor is complicated
due to lack of petrol and
shortages of medical supplies

I think goddam this stupid
U.S. blockade of Cuba because
Cuba wants to be Cuban

It's a warm November morning
I can hear Gilberto saying:
It's 1991 and I don't have
        enough electricity
I don't have enough food
I don't have enough of enough
but I'm still a revolutionary
in control of my own thoughts
I'm still a painter
in control of these brushes
and even though my health is bad
I still support the Cuban Revolution

WOMAN ON BURRO IN ASILAH

Your burro
is not
just some
happy-go-lucky model
in a fashion show
your burro is a mechanic
a gospel recording artist
with two tambourine ears
& a psychic who knows when you need
another pair of buttocks to exist in
another set of lips to whistle through
another group of fingers to shout between
your burro pounds the ground and sees
not only solitude is great
you sit on that burro
& in walks the environment
out step the confessions
& it's one fine laxative night
one more lovely field of lava
your burro pulling & plowing &
pushing forward like a space ship & grinning
& carrying you like a rainbow carries water
up the dirt path
down the paved road
around the planet
& back
to swallow the sunset
then start again
from exact spot
where I say to you
if my pen put in
same mileage a day
as your burro
without dropping dead from

exhaustion
I would show my appreciation
by celebrating
the next two centuries right now
& what a fucking wonderful event

DO NOT ALLOW

Do not allow flies to dominate your day
or let mosquitoes control your night
you are five slaps away from paradise
bring back the brown omelette
the green melon
& make that pony pull your wagon through
triangular sun sinking into
revolving earth
at the tone of trains whistling in from Tangier
at the sight of calamares frying between teeth
at the sound of your heart alive & thumping on
the water bottles of Asilah

ARIZONA 1985

Arizona
I have come
to sip
from your
coyote lips
I have come
to drink
from your
old Indian ears
and nothing else matters
because already
Afrikaner bosses
have shit on their shoes
in Pretoria
A gigantic female typhoon brews
in the Pacific
sparks are blowing
from fat face of Baby Doc in Haiti
& I am here
but I don't see
profile of Geronimo
carved in the mountain
I don't smell
black shake dancer's sweat
on this gravel
& where are those
spider women from Naco

Arizona
I had to fly
over smoking skies of Philadelphia
swim through stagnant waters of
breeding mosquitoes in New Jersey
walk through stinging sandstorms in Morocco

sit on the airplane
next to groups of
ku klux klanish speaking tourists
to get here
So I'm not in the mood
            to quiver and grow numb
                  with cockfighters
or get high &
sing along with
           mariachi bands
I'm not interested in
scribbling a few lines about
transnational solitude
        of your lavender pit
or concerned about penetrating
           your secret river of
           copper vomit and
    right-wing bird droppings

Arizona
re-introduce me
to the cliff dwellers
the water clan
the ghosts
in prehistoric caves
unfasten your cactus
your ore
your petrified forest
& give me
the Papago words of Papago
the Apache look of Apache
the Hopi view of Hopi
the Navaho dialogue with Navaho
Arizona
open up your silver slab of teeth

SHUT OFF THE SYSTEM

They're pulling
human pieces of flesh
from nervous rectum
of a Black Philly Flame of Hope
sue the city
the county
the state of bourgeois fear
don't give us
the classical story
of classical excuses
from
Mister Classical
drop-the-bomb-on-the-house-Goode
no good
cancel the classes
slash the certificates
seal up roof top to the planet

ANOTHER TROPICAL NIGHT

Another tropical night
in house of a poet of tropical nights

Draw back the sweat
the slurs the eyes
& tell me what I'm missing
me I won't touch it

Here in presence of everything smacking
I see the same mouth of spittle
on lisp of same old prayer
same gestures shoving cotton balls
up ass of same old muck
same nobody undulating with
the same old shadow of guts

And above moisture of hands
& tangle of tongues
no way out

Go ahead
ask me about the plastic flowers
break a melodrama in front of my face

Again song of violent clicks
in throat of poet of tropical nights &
are there nicknames for such inverted moments
such hyperactive jumping beans turning the other cheek

Be still sweet syllable shits
because tonight I'm going to swallow
earwax of every cult in this hole

WHAT DO YOU THINK

Centennial 86

What do you think
what are your thoughts

Should we halt this ceremony
in the chocolate green river
stop opportunity from
spinning its helicopter blades
shove bar-b-que ribs through
Ms. Liberty's nose
carry that platform off in
a blimp of orange leather lips
on this birthday celebration weekend of
bugles   warships   jerked beef
rubber diadems
& the feathery mouth of Lady Chipmunk

What do you think
what are your thoughts

Should we step into
iron shell of the statue
& salute the sculptor's vision
before another woman opens
her sandwich of vegetarian lizards
Should we sit
in front of orchestra B
& watch two presidents knock
tooth picks together in a hunger for dead trees
or return to our seats after
incense smoke blows from
combat boots of
sheet wearing vendors

What do you think

Should we fill the exaggerated bronze coiffure
with French wine
to keep grand colossal mademoiselle Liberty
drunk & waving bonjour
in the New York harbor forever

What are your thoughts
on this birthday celebration weekend
of brass bands hairy nostrils
& eagle face friendship grins

YOU HAVE

You have
so much oomph
so much gaucho itch
so much unchecked violence of
genitalia laugh
but do you have
a pass
to start
this affair
can you provide
urine samples
tattoo needles
one five minute high
a little inflammation on
the heart muscle
a little parental guidance
in the retina
a little salvation
for the secreta

POETRY

In fact
poetry
will not
strike
lightning
through
any
convoy of chickens

Today poems are like flags
flying on liquor store roof
poems are like baboons
waiting to be fed by tourists

& does it matter
how many metaphors
reach out to you
when the sun
goes down like
a stuffed bird in
tropical forest
of your solitude

In fact
poetry
will not
sing jazz
through
constricted mouth
of an anteater
no matter how many
symbols survive
to see the moon
dying in saw dust
of your toenail

SAMBA IS POWER

In Brazil
I sambaed on the road to João Pesoa
I sambaed on the beach of transparent crabs
I sambaed to sounds of iron bells
in State of Bahia
I sambaed while eating muqueca
while watching capoeira
while wearing Oxum belt made by
maker of ritual objects in Salvador
I sambaed through São Paulo airport
sambaed into dark-skin   light-skin   African
Indian   Portuguese situations of struggle
I sambaed into translations while drinking batidas
with writers at Eboni Bookstore
I sambaed while waiting for a short mustached
so-called mulatto who swore
he was a Yoruba Babalawo   I sambaed
I sambaed onto corner of handcuffed
Afro-Brazilian men
sambaed next to women who were
spinning pulsating & assaulting police cars
I sambaed into house of candomblé
into congress of Black culture
Into Perfil of African Literature
I sambaed
I sambaed next to the red buildings of Exu
I sambaed with Gege & Egbas
I sambaed into trance of Yemaya
I sambaed with Oko
I sambaed in front of the daughters of Santos
I sambaed against walls of political graffiti
I sambaed with Xango
I sambaed with Mae do Samba
My samba wrapped in Orixa ribbons

my samba mixed with human smells & feijoada
my samba infused with vatapá & caipirinhas
the uphill samba bursting out of my feet
the samba whistles hollering out of my navel
the samba fetishes buzzing high
in samba dome of my soul
as I sambaed & sambaed & sambaed & sambaed
I sambaed diagonally through Recife floods
sambaed upward through steel cages of Brasilia
sambaed away from alcohol fumes
in Copacabana
sambaed behind homeless children
with soccer ball eyes
sambaed past dealers dealing drugs
sambaed into costume room
in Comunidade Mangueira
sambaed in front of Protestant missionaries
who preached that samba is sin
but samba is life
samba is friction
samba is power
& I sambaed & sambaed & sambaed
sambaed into circles with Rei Momo
as he shook his heavy flesh in slow motion
sambaed next to young women quivering
their brown calves in quadruple time
my samba getting drunk off the high speed rhythms
my samba embedded with bass drums of cachca
my samba parading & scorching teeth of
the Rio de Janeiro sun
my samba absorbing the forest stench
of poet from Amazonas
my samba squatting down & wiggling up
as I sambaed the samba of my memory
the samba of my fantasy
the samba of my samba
because samba is life
samba is friction

samba is power
samba is everything
that's why I sambaed & sambaed & sambaed

THE MAN WITH ELEPHANTIASIS LEG IN RECIFE BRAZIL

This leg
oh yes
this leg he said
this leg is
a good-luck charm
a torpedo of fission
a hissing chain that
lays itself down to sleep across
entrances to city markets
oh yes
This leg is
a lipstick-wearing dancer in samba schools
a fat snake that zigzags and
sells poetry pamphlets to strangers before
stall keepers open teeth to yell 'guarana'
oh yes
This leg is more than
colonized chapel of parasites
more than any tree of
slashed flesh & calcified sap
This leg is not
just a man-made dam of
filarial worms & feathers erupting through
winter smells of leather
This leg is
the legendary limb that has
an ancient grandfather who
stands in a plaque
on wall of the British Museum
and a twin sister who
leans against buildings in Chicago
and one cousin who
sits in the shade next to
certain hotels in Egypt

oh yes
this leg
This leg is
a tropical garden
a gas pump
a mountain of sea-foaming blood that
sleeps after midnight
has no football in hell
no bicycle in heaven
but rises like
sweet sausage tongue of the sun
to spit out poems before
the rootmen scrape their barks to holler 'guarana'
oh yes
This leg
oh yes

NEW YORK'S BULLFIGHTER GUMS

New York's bullfighter gums
mashed up like red bananas
fiery sauce caked on
its rocket-shaped head
E train eyes rolling like
some big time frog from Uruguay
& I say
it's not impossible
to find deep fried romance
in this concrete ocean
of marinated snake juice
It's not impossible
to balance out life
in heated asphalt of
this suicidal lip track
let novocain & fortune cookies
have a recess in zero
because without naming
another name
without pointing
another finger
without blaming
this situation
on that contradiction
here's to friendship
dialogue   dreams
& the diplomatic pouch

THE SUMMIT

A meeting
between two men
two views
two arms devoted to racing
two old landfills dumped
in office of boozing eagles
in bureau of carousing penguins
vodka of my hiccuping pencil
scotch of my vomiting eraser
and everything depends
on this day's drunken storm of prayer
this day's ice-breaking calm
at the bottom of the summit
of polyester pants
tonight in cloudy eyes of irritated marines
tomorrow in dead spot of the index

THESE NEW YORK CITY PIGEONS

These New York City Pigeons
cooing in the air shaft
are responsible for me
stumping my toe
spraining my ankle
& getting sick on ammonia fumes

That pigeon roosting on the clothesline
stole my nightgown
Those pigeons on the street lamp
made me feel foolish
while riding in a black car
completely splattered
with their grey & white poo poo

These New York City pigeons
are not calm like pigeons of Oxala in Brazil
and do not croon like doves of Zimbabwe

New York City pigeons moan
strange   low   mournful   quivering cancer like moans
mixed with
hungry hyena barks
& gulping loss of the forest cries

New York City pigeons
are not relaxed like
pigeons sunning at
Marcel Duchamp swimming pool in San Francisco

New York City Pigeons are not happy like
pigeons standing on head of the woman
selling bananas on a street corner in Johannesburg

New York City pigeons
flap viral feather fungus dust from wings into faces

then sit on steps vocalizing & waiting
for the death of humankind
New York City pigeons
are not friendly like
pigeons eating flaky crescent-shaped rolls at
Hotel Du Piemont in Paris

New York City pigeons
are not content
like pigeons
posing for photos on arms
of men in plaza of Caracas

New York City pigeons
will lounge on ledges
& murmur profanity all day
will fight for fucking space in
the mating season
shit on air conditioners
& wipe their asses on windows
while big cockroaches
suck Sucrets in the dark

New York City pigeons
are not alert
like pigeons
sitting quietly on bicycles
in peace memorial park of Hiroshima

New York City pigeons
roll their pearly eyes
inflate their throats
& defecate on the shoulders of pedestrians

New York City pigeons
have no love for crumb-throwing pigeon lovers
& no year of the pigeon is celebrated
at least
not for these New York City pigeons

1988 NOW WHAT

So we get high
pick teeth
wiggle tongues
now what
I gave up
my blue cross
blue shield
certificate
of health
When
one
of
the most active
urine drinkers
in the west
became president
now what
dehorn a rhino
so somebody's dick
can get hard
Burn the planet up
in space
so somebody
can have
an orgasm
brilliant
great
toxic waste
now what
(my ass blew up last night
my breath stinks
& I'm here trying
to make the best of it)
now what

Are we
out of control
Is this extinction time
me
you
and
the elephant
now
what
what
now

SUPER POETS OF GUADALAJARA

Before you puff up
& become a flying peacock
surrounded by singing chickens
hear this
in Guadalajara
the super strong passionate
intensification poet is still
painter José Clemente Orozco
    The adult marimba players
    saying what they think marimbas
    should say
    if marimbas could talk
    behave like
    super humorous poets
Women holding audiences spell-bound
with their medicinal predictions while
pounding tortillas in Tonala Market
are called
super fascinating tone poets
    The men harmonically blending voices
    & splitting melancholy notes
    for video cameras every
    night in Mariachi Plaza
    are known as
    super sensitive poets with guts
Children who leave
tiny tin hearts on tourists' tables
transform themselves daily into
super professional beggar poets
    The politicians
    selling pieces of
    Mexico on
    the global market
    are not known as
    super poets
    but super greedy bandits

& it is not
poetry on the page that's hot
but poems written in stone by
super active avant garde poets.
Pancho Villa Vargos   Rosita Morales
Little Indio Nogalas & Mestiza Lopez
working at the cement factory and
having conversations with
Señora unfinished revolution

POET COVER YOUR FEET

It's raining excessively
on the Chelsea Hotel canopy
on hood of a sculptor's car
on sanitation trucks
on school bus windows
on fingers of a man picking his tooth
on coat of woman running with brown dog
on taxi cabs darting like yellow lizards to
avoid people waving in the rain
It's raining
& rocket launches are aborted in the rain
disgruntled employees go crazy in the rain
donut vendors fly up 7th Avenue in the rain
It's raining down on
black deep water umbrellas
on black & red Eshu umbrellas
on blood red Shango umbrellas
on honey gold Oshun umbrellas
on blue & white fertility umbrellas
on purple Ogun umbrellas
on melancholy green umbrellas
on the engineer of umbrellas it's raining
it's raining
at the drug & alcohol rehabilitation house
a brief afternoon downpour
splashes vomit on shoes of
one big shot censorship clerk
& a chilly hail pushes
untreated sewage into the sound
& It's raining
on midnight Island hoppers
on humorous strap hangers
on free love seats in the land fill
& rain has a wet ticket to paradise

rain has designer braces flashing
at the New York Secretary Show
rain is happy the rainbow has
a hole in its condom
rain is alive & storming with ecstasy
let's hear it for the rain

NEIGHBOR

Neighbor

everyday

you get up

coughing

harking

screaming at the dog

cursing yourself out

& for what

you are there

you see something coming

the event happens

and you can't go back to the beginning

THE DREAMS

I close my eyes
miss the right train
board the wrong bus
get lost   get drunk
rub down in cactus juice
dress up in wild turkey feathers
walk with vodun priest
into horrible charcoal mist
of a government assassination building

I clear my throat
scratch my belly
drop into dream of deflated whales
into sockets of inflamed cobras
my thigh a fly swatter of dead flies
my forehead a tuning pipe of unmelodious pinging
my uterus an enlarged ball of electric piranhas

I move
& the hole in the rug becomes
a transparent river of crocodiles
I stand on head of this hippo
to check out the tornado
of musical instruments
& with a dizzy sadness in my chest
I scream   I swallow   I moan
I hold smoke in my navel
spit ink into
my imaginary microphone fist
I whisper   I cough
I see my desk & papers gone
my passport torn & crushed
my tennis shoes frozen in ice
one half madwoman with baby says
she's Ogotemmeli

& boom
an abrupt change of pitch

A dark cave of talking rocks
an enormous bed of snoring camels
the house of wounded skunk
the old outspoken eagle squawks coming
from stomach of an unsatisfied bankteller on fire
& the midget says
imagination smiles
like a fat prostitute
& the waitress swears she has
the meaning of life & death
wrapped in four plastic baggies
I grin & drink white lightning
mixed with fried cabbage
bury myself like a frog
hear intoxicated ancestors talking backward
& there are yellow cows
with broken hooves dangling against the sky
men with alligator meat packed on their knees
women with dream policies between teeth
horses with ripped ligaments in pockets
& I sit & I watch &
I search my speech impediment
for discharging passengers
I invert the swelter in one nostril
I leap for air like dolphins
I turn loose ritual of turning loose
on sand bags
my flesh waiting
to be invaded
by cold blooded lizards
my fish stained napkin
ready for confiscation
my empty shoes
available for adoption
the ghost in my hair stinking

DEAR BANJO

Dear Banjo
I am staggering
like
unprofessional
exterminator
in fumes
blood shooting
toward me
in a flood of lights
cutting off
as I piss
& one pyramid splits

death shovels
walking from my vagina
xylophone keys puking
Beaujolais bottles exploding
turds overflowing
from toilet
of snake skin boots
my tongue
swallowing itself
in a bed of savage ants

DON'T ASK/1980

Don't ask me
who I'm speaking for
who I'm talking to
why I'm doing what I do in
the light of my existence

You rise you spit you brush you drink you
pee you shit you walk you run you work
you eat you belch you sleep you dream &
that's the way it is

In the morning
tap water taste fishy
coffee sits in its
decaffeinated cup
ca ca & incense
have a floating romance
& a stale wash cloth
will make you smell
doubly stale so
don't get kissed on the cheek
don't get licked on the neck

at 8 AM
the trains & buses are
packed with folks farting
their bread & butter farts
the gymnasium
is dominated
by the stench of
hot tennis shoes
& in one locker room
a few silly-talking
intellectual-looking
coke-drinking

cloth-dropping
paper-littering
spinach-pooting
smug arrogant women wait to
be waited on

& in another locker room
there are odors of
crotches & jock straps
bengay, tiger balm
& burning balls
sweat socks & sweat suits
of body-building
door-slamming
iron-pumping
phlegm-hawking men
all sour & steamy
& wrapped up together
in a swamp of
butt-popping towels
but don't let it
get you down
don't let it
psyche you up

Outside the ledges are
loaded with pigeons
clouds are seeded with
homeless people &
lyricism of the afternoon
is a sub-proletarian madman
squatting & vomiting
from his bowels
a brown liquid of death
in front of your house

& it's not happening because of you
those socks don't stink because of me
a bureaucrat is not a jerk because of us

I'm not this way because of them
you're not that way because of me
don't ask about influences

You rise you spit you brush you drink you
pee you shit you walk you run you work
you eat you belch you sleep you dream
& that's the way it is

ATMOSPHERIC BURN

for the Printmaking Workshop

A poem
of patriotic spitballs blowing
when the hour comes up
like flying saucer hairdo
        sparkling until
        five below zero
        then commercial break
the move
into menopause of warm snakes
a peck
into lightning zone of smashed bananas
        West of the big belch
        of unfinished identities
        & what did you expect
One sunrise
made of tomatoes & onions
Three poems
in porcupine skull under a wig in Harlem
Don't curse
it's cold in these red-stained ancestor trenches
Don't laugh
it's not so easy to reach
the upside-down tree rooted to
samba screeches of staggering shades
Don't shoot
arrest that dinosaur with the carbon monoxide breath
        Look
the circle frozen in its black jade asphalt
rolls through my collagraphic mouth
the blossoming knots stand like
UFO tracings
on my monoprinting teeth
the flag waves in
foreskin of my bullet train fingers
        then a dose of caffeine

an excess of poetic discharge
a flamestorm from
the next century of pimples
and once upon an atmospheric burn
the clock   the yawn   the commotion of paper voices

I HAVE BEEN SEARCHING

Rwanda Conflict

I have been searching
and searching and searching
since the day they said
you were tossed into a ditch by
a bulldozer
I have been searching all the ditches
trying to find you beneath
a million human bones
I have been searching between
twenty thousand bandaged skulls
I have been searching in a town of
fifty thousand jagged wounds
I have been searching in the ashes and
searching in the bloody footprints
and oh my friend
I have found nothing but
the song of dying
and the song of not knowing
the song of dying
and the song of not knowing

I have been searching and
searching and searching
since the day they said
they saw you standing there when
the assassins came in
they said you didn't have a chance to
hide
you didn't have time to run
they said they thought they saw
you standing there
and I have been searching
and searching and searching
and oh my friend
I have found nothing but

the sky all smoky with skin
the bulldozer of bones
the bloody footprints
and the factions within factions of factions of
factions of factions and
I have been searching but
I cannot find you anywhere
I have been searching and
searching and searching

TO CHRYSLER CIRRUS

Dear Chrysler Cirrus
Do not bother to schedule
a personal driving experience for me
in your luxury new coupe
I will not spread-eagle on your wheel
or let your corporation
fuck me in my ears
so you can hear the music better

I WONDER WHO

We have been calling across fields
& falsetto snapping & moaning
in deep Shona deep Edo deep Mandingo
before the erection
of artificial systems

& we have been building granaries
pounding grain
going from dry stream
to dry stream
since the beginning of
the illumination of stars

We have been pulling tons of wood
up the road
in the rain
in malaria land
for thousands of years

& we have been ploughing across deserts
linking events
& circulating information
since the division of night & day
day & night

Now I wonder
I wonder who will tell
all the Presidents Ministers & Chiefs
that can't decontaminate anything
to click their boots together & scram

I wonder who will make it happen

I wonder who will tell
all the missionaries to put

their satellite systems of surveillance
on their two religious feet
& split on back to where they came from

I wonder who will make it happen

I wonder who will tell
all the non-serious
scholars & expert invaders of indigenous cultures
to take their little bright ideas
shove them down their own throats &
cancel the habit of spreading shit

I wonder who will make it happen

I wonder who will tell
all the mercenary units
to take their
festive blood sausage farts
& the inexhaustible volume of human greed
that stinks of Jonas Savimbi's sweat
& blow out of Africa

I wonder who will make it happen

I wonder who will take
all the savage attachés & ton ton macoutes
& put them with
the industrial waste
that's buried in the tropics

I wonder who will make it happen

I wonder who will tell
all the undemocratic afrikaner trekkers
to have a good time
trekking on back to the Netherlands
& keep on trekking

I wonder who will make it happen

I wonder who will send
the bones of Cecil Rhodes
from Zimbabwe back to funk city in England
so the piranhas can have
a cannibalistic snack in front of
a topless princess on the Thames

I wonder why nobody ever did it

THE GUITARS I USED TO KNOW

Guitars
with excavated rhythms
with maps & bridges
& the sweetness of sugar from
Pernambuco
from Nacogdoches
from Itta Bena
from Chitungwiza
Guitars
with names like
Edolia Adelia
Freddie Mae Johnny Boy
Matakenya Machado
Zodwa & Letty Bea
Guitars
Guitars full of
inlaid shark fins
apocalyptic bloodstained fingerboards
intoxicated paradoxinated coils
indigenous fusionous realms
collisional digital switches
reverse reverb shrills on flatbed trucks
Guitars
The guitars trembling into
ultrasonic tempos into
insurrectional gestures into
scrunching wild-dog yowls
Yowling
with the mother-of-pearl habit
of living in isolation
with the plastic tradition
of being too sociable
with the inflammatory projections
hyperventilating into
trances stances romances guitars

The guitars I used to know
Guitars
arriving from Chicago
from Takoradi
from Casamance
from Texas
from Toledo
    & I can hear
    the guitars calling themselves Lightnin'
    I can hear the guitars calling themselves T-Bone
    I can hear the guitars calling themselves Minnie
    & I can hear the black lacquered guitars
    & the red guitars & the big brown rusty guitars
    & cadillac green guitars & majestic purple guitars
    & metallic blue   Guitars
acoustically dipping down whispering
"Don't make me wait too long now"   Guitars
electronically screaming
"I heard you beating your lover last night"   Guitars
zigzagging through the crowd & shouting
"I'm not losing my mind over you baby"   Guitars
marching around & yelling
"I'm gonna cut your power line"   Guitars
turning flips & whining
like ritual killers   Guitars
vamping on bandstands
& laughing like howler monkeys   Guitars
clearing paths
& humming like violins from Swaziland   Guitars
hollering half tone half step higher than
ordinary catastrophes   Guitars
circling with strings on teeth & crying ouch
Guitars
gigless   strapless
hanging upside down like
disembodied robots
between dilapidated flamenco boots
exhausted pubic bones
& torn alligator shoe tongues

Guitars
hanging upside down while
people imitate specialty of
the next machine   Guitars hanging
upside down before resurrecting & exploding
straight out into the air
of numb thumbs
of snap slaps
of steel squeals
of moan zones
of pecked necks
of drill trills
of joke smoke
of set frets
of ride slides
of squeeze freeze
of plunk funk
of ping ting
of ting ting ting ting
Guitars
I'm talking about
The guitars I used to know

WHAT CAN WE SING FOR YOU

What can we sing
for you
that you
have not already
sung
for yourself
in natural
supernatural setting
of world songs

we praise
your creativity
& say
someone
snatched your chance
someone
murdered your luck
& without a doubt
there is no
right moment
for a solo
that happens
because
it hears
itself
flying
before
taking
a smoke

THE ARRIVAL

Again
the arrival
the exit
memories dissolving
in frisky butt
of a wild goat
Traditions
rolling into
tight balls
of fried snot
A manuscript
of dead looks
dead struggles
dead erections
in dead holes
of waterless
deserts
advancing
into deserts
property
merging
with property
Stocks
climbing
straight up
on a tremor
of bones
come storm
come sun
come drought

I GOT THE BLUE-OOZE 93

I got the blue-ooze
I got the fishing in raw sewage blue-ooze
I got the toxic waste dump in my backyard blue-ooze
I got the contaminated drinking water blue-ooze
I got the man-made famine blue-ooze
I got the dead house dead earth blue-ooze
I got the blue-ooze
I got the living in a drain-pipe blue-ooze
I got the sleeping in a cardboard box
        waiting for democracy to hit blue-ooze
I got the 5 hundred year black hostage
        colonialism never never stops blue-ooze
I got the francophone   anglophone   alementiphone
        lusophone   telephone   blue-ooze
I got this terminology is not my terminology
        these low standards are not my standards
        this religion is not my religion and
        that justice has no justice for me blue-ooze
I got the blue-ooze
I got the gangbanging police brutality blue-ooze
I got the domestic abuse battered body blue-ooze
I got the ethnic conflict blue-ooze
I got the misinformation media penetration blue-ooze
I got the television collective life is no life to live
        and this world is really becoming
        a fucked up crowded place to be blue-ooze
  I got to find a way out this blue-ooze
  because the blue-ooze
  will make you sorry
  that you ever had
  the blue-oo-oo-ooze
  I got the blue-ooze
  I got the blue-oo-oo-ooze

WHATEVER FRIGHTENS

Whatever frightens
drunk crickets in dead reefer of your lungs
whatever fascinates alcoholic termites
on wooden tooth in your melancholy pimp mouth
whatever it is
the festival will start with
a twirling umbrella of rayon panties
a dark queendom of yawning vaginas
a urinating ear of hot asphalt words
that you can eat
in spanish fly of your french kiss
that you can swallow
in slobbering joy
of your snag nasty fear
that you can see
like a dance joking butt in the air
so please clear the street
of your broken teeth at once

WHY NOT

Babs Gonzales

Why not
let Babs
dominate
this night
with his
thirty-year
rite of
oo bop sha bam
Horns imitating him
as he imitated them
in up-tempo grooveness
of Expubidence
a riffology collaboration
a sha ba dah ba doot doot
in front of
sheel-lee-ah doo bee dah
rejection into
an injection of
oo daba doo bay doo yey doo yey doo
Itself
a home
demonstration
of those
flat sharp
natural sensations
swinging
at the end of the wind
of a big ole nasty
tenor saxophone ya ya ya yawl lapowl
and why not

Why not
let Babs
drop his

bitter stream dream elaborations
his
gravelly back throat stroke of
bold premonitions
his
fermented chest rest nest of
unvomited insurrections
into
bopology explanations
tongue-blistering configurations
confrontations quotations
in celebration
of those
metal-tipped
melodious drips
in lips
on fire
after midnight
and why not

Why not
let Babs
leave
his hot
orikiisms
in bandstand blood of the blues
in amber lights of city tubes
oo ya cooing and oop pop a dahing
on his way to
ee ee ee doo blah blee
blee blah doo ee ee ee ee ee
and why not

THE OPPRESSIONISTS

Art
what do the art
suppressors
care about art
they jump on bandwagons
wallow in press clips
& stink up the planet
with their
pornographic oppression
Art
what do they care about art
they go from being
contemporary baby kissers to
old time corrupt politicians
to self-appointed censorship clerks
who won't support art
but will support war
poverty
lung cancer
racism
colonialism
& toxic sludge
that's their morality
that's their religious conviction
that's their protection of the public
& contribution to family entertainment
what do they care about art

I'M GONNA

I'm gonna shake like a violent rain storm
I'm gonna fill the night with splashing
I'm gonna sit like a zone of confluence
I'm gonna gallop in the inner basin
I'm gonna drink from the new molasses
I'm gonna rub my body with palm oil
I'm gonna stuff my bones with charcoal
I'm gonna paint myself with arrows
I'm gonna click my bottles together
I'm gonna zigzag over & under
I'm gonna reach for the solar cycle
I'm gonna swirl up through the rapids
I'm gonna wail & point the wailings
I'm gonna stand like wall of protection
I'm gonna move like a desert darkness
I'm gonna push out further & further
I'm gonna press in closer & closer
I'm gonna dive down deeper & deeper
I'm gonna kick up higher & higher & higher

A MILES DAVIS TRUMPET

There are the ivory trumpets from Africa
the silver trumpets found in drawings
on walls of Egyptian tombs
telescoping trumpets from China
trumpets that live in Tibet
Spanish-speaking trumpets of Spain
& then
there is
that trumpet
with solitary feeling of sound
splashing through rough woodshed of Charlie Parker
splashing the sound of distance
                              in trumpet
                              against orchestra
trumpet circling within box
                              of a box
                        of controlled settings
            trumpet
patinaed with layers of rust & spit
grooving inside the groove surface
trumpet
with bell of funk fired up
in middle extremities
between bass & treble
thunder & whistle
Unmuzzled cheeks of brass
inflated storm of mutes
elastic electric Elegba
that trumpet

There are the oceanic shell trumpets
buzzing Southern Indian trumpets
natural Arabian trumpets
fast-talking Cuban trumpets
European-inspired valve trumpets

trumpets with great ears
& husky tones & avant-garde ways
trumpets fanfaring   dirging   parading
& giving military salutes

There are
side-blown trumpets
side-winder trumpets
straight trumpets
sweet trumpets
Satchmo trumpets
Oliver trumpets
Bolden trumpets
Little Jazz trumpets
Red trumpets
Rex trumpets
Dorham trumpets
curved trumpets
Dizzy trumpets
Clark trumpets
Hot Lips trumpets
Fats trumpets
pocket trumpets
Cootie trumpets
Farmer trumpets
Brownie trumpets
Cherry trumpets
& then there is
that short dark popping trumpet
covered in a mask of
New York hipness & fame
that trumpet
with another hairdo
another change of aspirations
another half-nelson in
a constellation of dust
another motif in
          terrycloth turban
another hoarse voice of

Orin to ti Orunwa
that trumpet
That trumpet
with the sound of chance
the sound of prediction
the sound of invention
the sound of migration & madness
& fluidity of solitude
& mathematical flurries
& blasted bridges
& dynamism within
collectivity of the hunt
that trumpet
with jom
with spirit
with secret sound systems hidden
behind sunglass fetishes
that trumpet
has a throat
which sits outside
of its body
sits on top of the wind
on top of the band
with explosive pucks
mystical rain spittle
aboriginal tongue toot toots
that trumpet
that trumpet is
the militant   mellow   melodic   magical
miraculous   minimalist   Miles Davis trumpet
that trumpet

SO WHAT

So what
if I spend
the rest of my life
living on invisible mouth
of an imaginary saxophone
breathing in
& blowing out
polluted airs
in August
doobee doobee doobee suck suck
all the way through this tunnel
so what
if you sniff
the monumental torture smell of power
like
toe jam piss & rotten cabbage
on sleeves of my last overcoat
don't jump off
throw up
fall down
I want you
to touch my hair like
so many flies
understand these boogers I eat
don't worry
it's the business of death
to be hungry
I only sit
in its lap like
a buzzard
one lick at a time
doobee doobee doobee suck suck

THE HARMATTAN

Midnight special
throbbing through smells of the harmattan

On night
of the shaking tambourines
the night I loved you
while standing like Sierra Madre

Sperms backed up
in your feet
to your head
                ten days strong

Midnight special
throbbing through smells of the harmattan

& I saw
the sun falling
like tray of tin spoons
belly dancers
            low-riding in dust
star beer
            splashing through fog
your ass moonshining
           like diamond igloo
down in smoked brown night
of cross current tongues
fingers of another bongo player on fire

Midnight special
throbbing through smells of the harmattan

THERE ARE NO STARS

There are no stars
no sky   no moon
in this city tonight

Everything is afterbirth acid of
bird urine on
that dark seance sea of air
that excessively
oxidized torso
posing in a pool
of fierce ash eruptions

the sunset bleeding like menstruating chimpanzee
Blood splattered sutures of intoxicated clouds

& I am this city's planet
this evening's massive thigh of swelter
this comb of cock
this stomach of archeological digs
this mixture of may fly & carp
there are no other late summer
early autumn
spectacle of lights

BUMBLEBEE, YOU SAW BIG MAMA

You saw Big Mama Thornton
in her cocktail dresses
& cut off boots
& in her cowboy hat
& man's suit
as she drummed &
hollered out
the happy hour of her negritude
                                        Bumblebee

You saw Big Mama
trance dancing her chant
into cut body of
a running rooster
scream shouting her talk
into flaming path of
a solar eclipse
cry laughing her eyes into
circumcision red sunsets
                              at midnight
                                Bumblebee

You saw Big Mama
bouncing straight up like a Masai
then falling back spinning her
salty bone drying kisser of music
into a Texas hop for you to
lap up her sweat
                              Bumblebee

You saw Big Mama
moaning between ritual saxes
& carrying the black water of Alabama blood
through burnt weeds & rainy ditches

to reach the waxy surface of your spectrum
Bumblebee
You didn't have to wonder
why Big Mama sounded
so expressively free
so aggressively great
once you climbed
into valley roar
of her vocal spleen
& tasted sweet grapes
in cool desert
of her twilight
Bumblebee

You saw Big Mama
glowing like
a full charcoal moon
riding down
Chocolate Bayou Road
& making her entrance
into rock-city-bar lounge
& swallowing that
show-me-no-love supermarket exit sign
in her club ebony gut
you saw her
get tamped on by the hell hounds
& you knew when she was happy
you knew when she was agitated
you knew what would make her thirsty
you knew why Big Mama
heated up the blues for Big Mama
to have the blues with you
after you stung her
& she chewed off your stinger
Bumblebee
You saw Big Mama

ME

Me
I'm gonna put
these partial dentures
    on ice
spit one last spit on
hammer ringing zing
fly over the moon
    in front of
    the Dew-Drop Inn
& when
the odorific quicksand
the water fleas
the jelly snot
& shadow hawks
    show up
like human babies
covered with brown snails
    I'm gonna cross over
        push back
            gyrate
              & blow
                my fishtail wind
                  in their faces

GLOBAL INEQUALITIES

Chairperson of the board
is not digging for roots
    in the shadows
There's no dying-of-hunger stare
    in eyes of
Chief executive officer of petroleum
Somebody else is sinking into
    spring freeze of the soil
Somebody else is evaporating
    in dry wind of the famine
there's no severe drought
    in mouth of
Senior vice president of funding services
No military contractor is sitting
    in heat of a disappearing lake
No river is drying up
    in kidneys of
    a minister of defense
Under-secretary of interior
  is not writing distress signals
   on toilet walls
Do you see refugee camp cooped up
    in head of
Vice president of municipal bonds
There's no food shortage
    in belly of
    a minister of agriculture
Chief economic advisors are
        addicted to diet pills
Banking committee members are
        suffering from obesity
Somebody else is sucking on dehydrated nipples
Somebody else is filling up on fly specks
The Bishops are not

forcing themselves to eat bark
The security exchange commission members
are sick from
too many chocolate chip cookies
The treasury secretary
is not going around in circles
looking for grain
There's no desert growing in nose of
Supreme commander of justice
It's somebody else without weight
without blood without land
without a cloud cover of water on the face
It's somebody else
Always somebody else

COMPAÑERA

Ana Mendieta

Compañera
We should have bolted you down like
a piece of iron sculpture and
pointed you in another direction
but you were busy looking for love
in the wrong dictionary
looking for a sweet papa
in the wrong encyclopedia

& now I say to myself
Ana is dead
not alive
not returning
what would she think of that

She arrived in the Apple
to jog around the park
have lunch with friends
create sculpture
install exhibitions
& get intellectual stimulation from
a drunk lover who swears
he did not throw her
out of the window

Why say
performance artist takes a dive
political thinker leaves in a huff
short intense Cuban shows her anger
big orphan mouth sculptor leaps

Ana did not leap
because Ana knew
Ana could not fly

So why not say
her breath was filled
with black beans
green tomatoes
mojitos & Guantanamera
with garlic
cerveza
cilantro
the sweet melodies of Beny Moré
River Oshun foam
dark Havana rum splashes
& the water-running rhythms of
Orquesta Aragon

Why not say
She was carver of wood and earth
collector of Cuban jokes
a cyclone in blue tennis shoes
a sequin dress machete
forever cutting through the
dry thunder of oppression
&
it was no dream when she yelled
"that chauvinist shit
that stinking little bitch
that phony bastard with his
fucking elite whores
& his kissing lips full of smoking ass
sucking on this corrupt spirit-breaking system
of fucked-up interventionist agendas"
It was no dream
So why not say
if a short rainbow
signifies in face
of an outbreak of pink marble flames
there will be blood
in hair of the dirt storm
& if respect is a somber silueta

etched in consciousness of a warm cave
there will be an erection of hate
in eurocentric bones
if a conspirator plots
& you cannot overthrow or float
the navel will never know its umbilical future

Why not say
after the exit of two great drummers
& in between the entrance of
one monumental earthquake
a huge volcano eruption
& reappearance of the tail of Halley's comet
We lost Ana

but Ana did not leap
because Ana knew
Ana could not fly

BE GOOD ENOUGH

Be good enough
not to pee with the jackals
you speak radiation real well
your pronunciations sound like
crushed fire engines in the nose
who cares what
an embalmer drinks
        I'm in favor of
        flushing toilets
        flooding nights
        & moving through
        the outskirts of nowhere
        to make this matter more than
        suddenly immediately
        & thank you very much for coming

AT A CERTAIN MOMENT IN HISTORY

At a certain moment in history
when Césaire started to decolonize
his neo-colonial head
and free his image
by dealing with the world from
the ideas of Negritude
When young Aimé Césaire said fuck Paree
& returned
to look into the future
by diving inside the past of
                    his native land
When Césaire arrived home to
clarify the contradictions of
too much French wine in
the wee wee of Martinique
When Césaire
who had already incorporated
his multiple rhythms into
the African rhythm section
with Damas & Senghor
When Césaire
who had already exchanged
his clarinet for a drum
began the beguine
in style of Atumpan drummers
& sang until his voice became
the agitated volcano mouth
                    of calamities
It was no exotic voodoo movie script
no get-down-deep-in-the-Congo poetry slam
It was Césaire
              returning to
a forest of dangerous plants
A forest even homeboys didn't enter
without revolutionary intentions

& at that moment of no compromise
his poetry became poetry unique to poetry
his long lava flowing lines moved
beyond classification & geographical links
He fired up words that revolted like
overheated cockroaches
his notebook was the advancement on the path &
sharp point on the spear
He made poetic revolutionary cuts

NOW I DIG UP PATINAS

Now I dig up patinas
I chew on slit logs
I polish surfaces of cyclones
I mount bullet wounds to inspect mutilations
I uproot the spirit of
the chemicals that make me
violate myself
I count limited resources
I view sinkholes in
the atmosphere
I lubricate the batás
& provoke in all keys of
flesh & hallucinogenic gongs
the obscenities stuck to
my elbow of whistling bones
& with Olmec sculptors shrieking through
banana grove of my solitude at 12:45 a.m.
& with the jaguars dropping from
my throat
& with the pumice of bulldog ants rising from
my damp discharge zone of
poetic fission
& with medicinal fat of
a big-time rooster
in my nose of talkative boogers
& with torn crows flying from my
brown-bearded ovum of
sulfuric acid blood
& with the insects blowing from
my colon of atomic leaves
& with mescal tears of oppressed fleas
smeared on wings of my ovarian cysts
I detonate
I nuclear react
I frenzy faces of

fascist thought
I become
Zaire River mouth
pissing on every
corrupt officer in an old
leopard-skin Mobutu Sese Seko cap
I unmuzzle my
black stretch-limousine lips
and say
I'm a poet
to vin rouge
vin blanc
drunk fly
corpse of a roach in a cup

SHE GOT HE GOT

She got hot
got happy   got hot
got thrilled   got hot
got degreed   got hot
got silly   got hot
got possessive   got hot
got disappointed   got hot
got hurt   got hot
got nurtured   got hot
got bitter   got hot
got drunk   got hot
got drugged   got hot
got rastered   got hot
got pregnant   got hot
got rejected   got hot
got indifferent   got hot
got lost   got hot
got born again   got hot again
got political again   got hot again
got academically ambitious again   got hot again
got hot   hot   hot   again
got to be a hot skeleton in the latest hot fashion
got hot
got to be a hot feminist turning into
a hot cultural investigative gadfly   got hot
got to be a hot exile flying
into alcoholic tantrums on hot buses   got hot
got to be a hot four hundred pound baby doll
becoming a real hot sociable walking disease with
a pretty hot face   got hot
she got hot   she got sad
she got hot   she got crazy
she got hot   she got athletic
she got hot   she got impatient
she got hot   she got used

she got hot without sweat   she got hot
she got hot without heat   she got hot
she got hot like a hot young volcano
got hot
got hot like a hot old bubbling crater
got hot
got hot and got to screaming 'rescue me'
got hot and got to shouting 'open the door Richard'
got hot and got bound to a sewing machine
got hot and got glued to a cash register
got hot and got tied to a computer
got hot and got stuck on the global assembly line
she got hot   she got hot hot   she got hot
she got aggressive   she got hot
she got bored   she got hot
she got frigid   she got hot
she got harassed   she got hot
she got depressed   she got hot
she got angry   she got hot
she got hot and so much alone and hot
and so inwardly focused and hot
and numb and hot and raw and hot and
so unprepared to be so hot and
so limited and hot and so dominated by the
thought of being so hot
all because a certain person didn't say
'I will love you forever baby'
she got hot   she got hot   she got hot
He got   He got
He got cold
he got happy before he got cold
he got fed before he got cold
he got excited before he got cold
he got broken-hearted and warlike
and then he got cold   he got cold   he got cold
got self-righteous   got cold
got distorted   got cold
got authoritative   got cold
got cold and got to going berserk in the workplace

got cold and got to pimping in the projects
got cold and got to screaming for revenge
got cold and got to handing out punishments
got cold and got to setting up
situations that would fail   got cold   got cold
got frustrated   got cold
got no recognition   got cold
got high   got cold   got forgotten   got cold
he got cold
he got cold cold cold
he got cold
got cold like a cold mercenary   got cold
got cold like a cold hyper-fastidious
hotel manager   got cold
he got cold like a cold militarized
supervisor of clerks   got cold
got cold like a cold political hustler in the street
got cold
got cold like a cold over-the-hill CIA agent
got cold   he got cold   he got cold
he got cold   cold   cold
He got cold
he got cold without having ever
imagined that he'd be so cold & wooden &
cold & untropical & cold & plastic & cold &
mute & cold & ferocious & cold & rigid & cold
& cold while watching the sunshine &
cold while kissing himself in the mirror &
cold & removed & cold & swollen &
cold & dependent on being so cold
he got cold he got cold
he got cold & got to screaming
'it's a man's world'
got cold & got to hiphopping like a peacock
got cold & got to hollering 'I'm a macho man'
got cold & got glued to a subway booth
got cold & got tied to a department of sanitation
got cold & got pinned to a patrol car
got cold & got taped to a bar stool

got cold & got engaged to a pawn shop
got cold & got married to a race track
got cold
got critically cold
got artistically cold
got miscellaneously cold
got cold
got cold & so outwardly focused
& cold & mean & cold & greedy & cold & selfish
& cold & so concerned about appearing to be
so cold
all because somebody stole his lollipop
& no one could chip through the ice
to say 'I'll love you forever baby don't be so cold'
        he got cold
        he got cold   cold   cold
        he got cold

THE HEAVY HEADED DANCE

for Mel & Ted

Dancing &
on my head
is the spotted skunk
whose scent did not protect it
from Mr. & Mrs. Archibald of Texas

On my head
is the stuffed bobcat
whose facial expression was set
by the taxidermy department

On my head
is a bull caught
in the act of masturbation
& on top of that
rides the moose
stunned-gunned while wading in a lake
& on top of that
are the monkeys
entrapped while urinating
& on top of that
lay the hyena
jackal & vulture
shot while eating from zebra carcasses
& on top of that
sits the ram with the
largest horn on record
donated by Henry Beck

& with all the stuffed animals piled on my head
I am dancing past
lyricist with the baboon heart

I am dancing like a dog

in front of financial consultant
implanted with pig genes

I am dancing & fluttering like a butterfly
across from novelist posing
in a beaver skin coat

I am dancing near the astronomer
who circles the floor with her
uplifted face frozen like a tiger

I am dancing against window
of artificial coyotes
& howling with contemporary African band
in the grizzly bear room

I am dancing my pangolin hairdo dance
past the river of ants in panties
of gyrating vocal groups

I am dancing so many different dances
with so many bloated animals
dead on my head
that my head is
a dancing museum of unnatural history
& I am dancing where I cannot see
myself dancing to know
why I am dancing
but I am dancing
I am dancing

THE GULF TONES

It's
the importation
of water bottles
& missiles
the great demand
for symbols
Henry the 8th & Othello
dressed in battle fatigues
Aladdin rising with
his polluted lamps of oil
Valentino soaked
in camouflage cream
the thrill tent
A W O L
inside
the patriot
& scud
fuck show

Get that lubricating jelly out of your helmet soldier

SAY IT

Say it
    and peel off that
        grey iguana skin mask
Say it
    & clean out your cockpit of
        intoxicated spiders
tear the sexual leaves of grief from your heart
pluck feathers of nostalgia from your nipples
push the slow moving masochistic mud slide of
        contralto voices
from your afternoon skull of anxiety   Say it
& let the tooth chips fall from
your hole or rebellious itches
let the excremental mountain of bones
shoot out from your ten farting poems in
the fly season   Say it
because everything is like an ambush
everything is like an incursion
flesh smoking flesh in
hemp field of
a fifty minute breakdown
time sodomizing time
in circular tunnel of asphalt & ashes
space revolting against space
in roar of an artillery salvo fuck   Say it
  & leave it splattered on mortuary of the moon
        reflective sap of dead weight
  store it in your propane bucket of memory
        sporadic tremblations of fear
  shove it into saliva of a roach
        radula of teeth between ovums
  throw it from your spine of excessive heat
        fertility smoke of fumigated funk
  talk to yourself in automobile of the clitoris
        soul of so much humanistic lip

Say it
& let pissy sheets of repression emerge
          from your breasts of paregoric flamingos
let crematorial paste
   in your solitary carcass of drums
   push through vaginal acidity of your bodega
          Say it
& plunge from invisibility of your camouflage
slide on fingernail filth
of your own larvae of triteness
be honorary shithead
in your own mouthful of erected statues
break through your own face
of accumulated door slams bam bam bam bam

Last night
I dreamt
Buddy Bolden threw
his horn
into Pontchartrain Lake
when I put
my name
under
every eyelid
every anthill
every bird wing
every mask of reptilian skin
drying in
the sun
so say it
forget it
& have a drop of grappa
the frog spits through the uterus in December

DON'T WRITE

Don't write
another word
about wanting
to write
another word
it's useless
the windows are filthy
the instruments contaminated
the smell of someone entering you
in shoes covered with turkey shit is here
& what can you say
this is not
a great performance
today is tomorrow
I poot on your fax
I piss on your xerox
I ca ca on your e-mail

SACRED TREES

Every time I think about us women
I think about the trees   the trees
escaping from an epidemic of lightning
the sacred trees exploding from
compressed matter of cuckoo spit   trees
the raped trees flashing signals through
toxic acid of sucking insects
the trees used as decoy installations   trees

I have the afternoon leaves throbbing
                in my nostrils
I have the struggling limbs sprouting from
                these ear lobes
I have a power stump shooting from
                out of this forehead
I have clusters of twigs popping from
                tattooed moles
& sometimes I feel
like the tree trunk
growing numb & dead
from ritual behavior
sometimes I feel like the tree ripping
from the core of ancient grievances
    Trees
I feel like
the family tree
relocating under pressure
    Trees
I feel like the frantic tree
trying to radiate through
    scorched surfaces
sometimes I feel like
the obscure tree
babbling through the silver-plated mouth
    of a shrinking moon

& sometimes I feel like a tree
hiccuping through
the heated flint of gunpowder crevices
I feel like a tree
& every time I think about us women
I think about the trees
I think about
the subversive trees laden in blood
                    but not bleeding
the rebellious trees encrusted
                    but not cracking
the abused trees wounded
                    but still standing
I think about the proud trees
the trees with beehive tits buzzing
the transparent trees
the trees with quinine breath hovering
the trees swaying & rubbing their
stretched marked bellies
                    in the rain
the crossroad trees coming from
                    the tree womb
                         of tree seeds
                              Trees
I think about the trees
& sometimes I feel like
a superstitious tree
smelling negative & fragile
                  & full of dislocated sap
sometimes I feel like
the tree stampeding from
                  cadre of earth tremors
I feel like the forgotten tree
           that can't live here no more
sometimes I feel
          like the tree that's growing wild
through the wildlife left
in the petroleum pipeline
                    I feel like a tree

A tree caught
in the catacomb of bones
            enslaved in
the red-light districts of oppression
I feel like a barricade of trees
& sometimes
I feel like the tree
that's lucky to be a tree
         in the time of
            missing trees
I feel like a tree
that's happy to be a tree
among disappearing trees
        Trees
I feel beautiful
        like an undestroyed
        rain forest of trees
I feel like a tree
   laughing in the rawness
            of the wind
I feel like a tree
& every time I think about us women
          I think about the trees
          I think about the trees

FIND YOUR OWN VOICE

Find your own voice & use it
use your own voice & find it

The sounds of drizzle
on dry leaves are not
like sounds of insults
between pedestrians

Those women laughing
in the window
do not sound like
air conditioners on the brink

The river turtle
does not breathe like
a slithering boa constrictor

The roar of a bull
is not like
the cackle of a hyena

The growl of a sea-leopard
is not like the teething cry
of a baby

The slash of a barracuda
is not like
the gulp of a leaping whale

The speech of a tiger shark
is not like
the bark of an eagle-fish

The scent of a gardenia
is not like the scent of a tangerine

Find your own voice & use it
use your own voice & find it

JAZZ FAN LOOKS BACK

(2002)

ATELOGO

I am hitting the drum three times
          in memory of
red wine   feijoada   & Marietta
          in memory of
cassava   cachaca   & Marietta
    in memory of
books   boxes   & Marietta
          in memory of
conversations   translations   & Marietta
          atelogo   atelogo   atelogo

HELEN

When they talk about singers
they never talk
about Helen Humes
who could
gut the bucket
how high the moon it
& hey babareebop it to ya

RIBS & JAZZ FEST 94

Barbecue smoke
Corn on the cob
Piggly wiggly piggin out on pig
Nice venue
This chewing and licking of fingers in my face
Hooray
The monitors are up
The music is happening
& I'm very optimistic

TALK TO ME

for Don Cherry

Like the sound of the rain
Boiling up in the sky
Beat it down to the ground
Bring it in with the wind
Plant your tone through the zone
Move on back smear your axe
With the stream where you dream
Send those notes over here
do it now speak on out

SOLO

Fill your horn with the clouds
Turn around pass on through
Like the sun & the stars
Possess the road exile the code
Maintain the flow metaphor the space
Pepper the night pulsate the grove
Like the rain like the snow
Throw it down talk to me

SONNY'S CARNIVAL

Sonny swinging in
like great heavyweight champion he is
that fierce hunter with every initiation
encrusted in belly of his axe

low to high tone endings smoking like
a charcoal forest
melodic variations on cowboy tunes disappearing into
Mohawk ghost markings under Manhattan bridges to Brooklyn

& what a cluster of phonetics
transcribing through saxophone lecturing to trumpet in
teacher/student consultation
at Beacon Theater with Wynton
on Sonny's night
of Sonny's island

& even in corniness of his quotations
"Jeannie with the light brown hair"
the music is clear & pure & Sonny

HOWLING

for Allen Ginsberg

Allen couldn't sing the Blues
So he started howling
Not like Howlin' Wolf but
Howlin' Allen
Howling all over the place
About sex & God & global excess of carbon emissions
Howling about soil erosion
Plutonium
The proliferation of firearms
& runaway nuclear reactors
Howlin'Allen
Howling like a threatened endangered mammal
Howling that inborn instinctive howl
That introspective retrospective collective howl
That blunt unbending howl against war
Against corporate leaders and political corruptness
A mean in-your-face howl
An agitated howl against co-opted colleagues
Allen howling with the declining whales
Howling a long intense rampaging howl
A meditative in-depth soulful joyful liberated hypnotic howl
A drunk sober howling complex of seductive tongues,
Heated finger fetishes, intoxicated manifestoes
exotic erotic encounters
A howling existential beatnik collage of poetic massages
Allen couldn't sing the Blues
So he became Howl

MUSIC FLYING

Music flying   tacos flying
Banners flying   & you want to fly too
I love it
In my cerveza negra modelo tasting mood
In my huachinango smell of fishkills
Imagine
Someone has invited
This very green place to lunch
In my red sauce
They have made me Veracruzana
Of the stuffed iguanas and
I am swallowing a rainstorm of Afro-Spanish tongues
while hiccuping like a firecracker
popity popity pop pop pop

ENDANGERED SPECIES LIST BLUES

A snow leopard does not know
it's on the endangered species list
Mr. & Mrs. Crab are not into
destroying the world
they are crawling to the mud flats
to take in some rotten insects
It's not what's up that's going down when
you smell yourself on
the threshold of extinction
It's you and your portable chemical toilet
going to hell under friendly fire
It's you and your missile receptor
exploding to pieces

It's not what's up that's going down

The person who OK's biological weapons
should not cry about the stench of
new diseases
The one who cuts off the trees
so the orangutans can't hang
should not wonder about ecological devastation

It's not what's up that's going down
It's what's down that's going up

It's not what's up that's going down
It's what's down that's going up

MR. LOUIE

Oh Mr. Louie
how did you get the right
to gut bucket the Blues
& go strutting with some barbecue
up the lazy river
yeah you hoodoo boys
always changing word pitches &
getting haunted when
it's summertime down south
Oh Mr. Louie
you had your fill
seventy years of the 20th century
seventy years and you thought
you'd leave us a little taste of
that talking trumpet from Storyville
Oh Mr. Louie
how did you put that
tip of the rocket tone in your horn
yeah you hoodoo boys always rambling
& breaking new ground in the dialogue
always laughing   looking possessed &
leaving handkerchiefs of sweat on the bandstand
you hoodoo boys always snapping fingers &
getting a glow on when
you take back music
from the lazy river
Oh Mr. Louie
blow a tune for me

MUSICAL EMPLOYMENT

To talk about resentment
You have to talk about domination
And if you talk about domination
You have to talk about standards
And if you talk about standards
You have to talk about the reality of camouflage
And if you talk about the reality of camouflage
You have to talk about entertainment
And if you talk about entertainment
You have to talk about dress codes
And to talk about dress codes
You have to talk about bandstand manners
And if you want to talk about bandstand manners
You have to talk about the club that banned Bird
And to talk about the club that banned Bird
You have to talk about finance without romance
And romance without finance

PHOTO OP BLUES

Africa was already Africa
way before men danced around
in shirts made of mirrors & feathers
& before a man in a three-piece pinstriped suit
with leopard claws around his neck
started dreaming of being
a Hollywood Chaka Zulu
but instead became
the chocolate Zulu candy bar known as "Gotcha"
Africa was already Africa
way before Jonas Savimbi
donned his uniform made of diamond studs
& plastic landmine fragments &
sat with an American president
for a photo op which he demanded as
part of his payoff for keeping his army
in the business of maiming people in Angola
Africa was already Africa
before the Prince arrived wearing
a red checkered tablecloth on his head while
worming his way into another womb after
viewing the Slavehouse on Gorée Island
and way before Leopold put on his military czarist outfit
and came down the chimney
to destroy the Congo
& make another fashion statement on
the fashion plate of oppression
Africa was already Africa

STRIKE UP THE BAND

At midnight
in your rusty industrial cockpit
                    of oxtail stew
in your hiccuping buttocks made
          radioactively ready to prance
khaki uterus &
          AK-47 tongue
blow through your ghost words
your coyote microphone
your wildebeest virtuoso crying pipe
let chickens get tired of chicken shit
your throat is like a two-headed drum
your nostrils like a honkin saxophone mojo tool
the dog is howling
the door is slamming
the path is moving like a local donkey toward
the canceled dance concert
the banned cockfight
& the cocoa leaves are so vocal
so cadaverish
so patinafied
so wide-eyed owlish
let the termites nest in
                    your electric bass heart
let the song of self-interest fall down on
its knees in a rockability vagina grunt
let the reefer-seeded moon squat in
                    horse breath of a young wino
let dawn babble through a mouth of mildew blankets
there is nothing better than wearing
your own shoes
your own panty liner
your own jock strap
your own sweat

inside your own navel of archaeological digs
heat up the site
whoever possesses the land will possess your bones &
make love to your night life   uh hunh
strike up the band

THE REVOLUTIONARY ORCHESTRA

I used to sleep
in houses made of
flattened steel drum barrels
and wake up between
bulldozer blades
they labeled me
Queen of Impermanence
until I stomped on Apartheid
in the Grand Apartheid Ballroom
with Jacob Morenga &
Revolutionary Orchestra of Namibia playing Free Jazz
We knew how to darken airs of superiority
Sink the fascist system in its frenzy
& celebrate victory
in consolidated mines while
drinking rio tinto zinc wine
& dancing dances called
Subversive Entertainment Act 3
and Bullet Hole of Censorship Finished

FINA LEONE

for Leon Thomas

We went into
process of your delivery
peeped your many Africanisms
deciphered your superstitions
and swallowed omens from your
yey yey yey yey yey yey yey yey
Mr. Eat Up The Blues In New York City
everybody knew you preserved &
created musical instruments in
your mouth of collective memory
                                        Fina Leone
we heard enhancement of
your cultural identity elevated
as you invented a new way of singing &
multiplying metallic vibrations onto the
defensive front of your master plan
Mr. Yodel Throat In Botanical Study Of Leaves At Duke's Place
you made the turn around
brought back the ancestors
the dirges
the old field hollers
the squawking falsettos &
low turbulent vocaltudes through
didjeridoo of your drum kit cheeks
you cleared the way-ye
with your Bemba Mbamba Yoruba Pygmy
East St. Louis Kikongo Harlem compilation of tones
Mr. Let The Rain Fall From Me   Boom Boom Boom Boom

LAST NIGHT

Last night
I dreamt about
subway trains
chartreuse books
& Aimé Césaire who
looked like John Lee Hooker
in a band with Sonny Stitt
at this niteclub in
Zengeza section of Chitungwiza where
chibuku drinkers were drinking
and women snuff sniffers were sniffing &
Olmec sculpture face of
fighter Joe Louis was shadow boxing between
musical notations of Ngare gare
see you later see you later

TAKING THE BLUES BACK HOME

I'm taking the blues back home
I'm taking the blues back to where
the blues stealers won't go

I'm taking the blues back home
because the blues stealers like to steal
when they think they have nothing of their own
I'm taking the blues back home
I'm taking the blues back to the fire of the spirits
I'm taking the blues back to the
damp undergrowth
I'm taking the blues back to where
the blues stealers won't go
I'm taking the blues back home

I'm taking the blues out of the mouth of the stealers
I'm taking the blues out of the western stream
I'm taking the blues back before somebody sings
"Ain't nobody's business if I steal your blues"
I'm taking the blues back home
I'm taking the blues back home
before Robert Johnson comes from
the graveyard to say
"The blues has been crapped on"
I'm taking the blues back to the crossroads
I'm taking the blues back to the bush
I'm taking the blues back to the place
where the blues stealers won't go
I'm taking the blues back home before
Langston Hughes returns to say

"They've taken my blues again and gone"
I'm taking the blues back home
I'm the owner of the blues
& I'm taking the blues back home

The blues that came to me from the slave dungeons
the blues that came to me from the death trails
the blues that came to me from my ancestors
the blues that came to me in a spell that tells me
through birth that I'm the owner of the blues
from a long time ago
I'm the owner of the blues from a long
long long long time ago
I'm the owner of the blues
& even if somebody says
they have a right to sing the blues
I'm still the owner of the secrets in the blues
from a long time ago
I'm the owner of the blues
& even if somebody pays to play & use the blues
I'm still the owner of the blues
from a long time ago
I'm the owner of the blues
& I'm taking the blues back home
I'm taking the blues back to where
the blues stealers won't go
I'm taking the blues back home
I'm taking the blues back home

TEARING UP THE CATHEDRAL

I didn't think the poem
was going anywhere
until it became zombified
& started moving on its own
started floating and leaving the paper
& staring straight ahead
started swallowing pencils
drinking ink
crowing like a rooster
& flying in the air
until it became zombified
& started sucking on salt
twanging like metal scrapers
tearing up the cathedral at
the Sacred Jazz concert
& falling backward
into a resting place for blizzards
I didn't think the poem was going anywhere

AFTER HOURS

I am not sucking on a form
to get drunk off of its content
I am not pre-booking space in
non-smoking section of the imperial pipeline to
sell used cars   pussy   & industrial waste
I get no thrill from smelling mildewed curtains
watching dead moth in paprika
or sitting all day in the
bow wow of french horns inhaling
graphite breeze of iodine mist in honor of
involuntary spasms
no one is chewing on my warm diaper of acid rain
& I have no kiss-ass explanation for the question
"what is Jazz"
I live the routine of my routine
& when the female porcupine chatters
when the blue-face mandrill drills
I write a poem
taking a look at myself looking
& it's very clear and under surveillance
time rotating its butt in my face
& dearly beloved
I have already been
violated by survivors of the flood
so do not sweep while I'm eating
do not cover my pot with your lid

SUNNY SIDE OF THE PAGE

Art comes out
when it comes out
It comes out
as invention
inventing itself
inside steeplechase of
embraceable perdidos
bongo beepin and peepin through
stareyes of melancholy leap frogs leaping
as imagination imagines itself
blowing deep vibratoless slurs through
encrusted mouthpiece whistling like
old flaming rocketships
roaring in from Kansas City
with messages made of
musical flyspecks on
sunny side of the page of
unknown titles at
borders of disorderly time
tico tico ticking
on tip of terrifying tocks
talking anthropology talking ornithology
the study of birds
and the study of humans eating birds
like this
like that
on the day Charlie Parker married the universe
and universe
became universally hip
to fact
that jazz is
the African heart transplant
which keeps on keeping
western music alive

Art comes out when it comes out
it comes out like a saxophone in
a porkpie hat
it comes out like a saxophone weeping on Chelsea Bridge
like a saxophone covered in bird feathers
it comes out in blood oath tune of Cherokee
in subversive unruly rhapsodies
fanfaring finger leads
tongue swiftness adrift on reeds
meticulous melodious coupes indeed
dripping with wax and koko shouts
booming with valve oil and tobacco spit
dancing its ghost-of-a-chance dance
its African heart-transplant dance
keeping western music alive
and changing directions
into funky stupendous
next century of
pollution & eyeballs
going off to
scrapple in the apple with Mohawk
Chi Chi   Marmaduke   & Billie
bouncing into
the everything you are is you
advancing in a great Chi Wara headdress

SOMEWHERE A WOMAN IS SINGING

Somewhere a woman is singing
five different scales at the same time for
every stingray boppin in the Savoy Ballroom
she is singing Savoy   Savoy
this energy's coming from me Savoy   Savoy
I'm sinking my soul in you Savoy   Savoy
oh how my spirit dilates
how my silence pulsates
in between these faces in you   Savoy
Savoy   Savoy   Savoy

Somewhere a woman
superimposing her
supernatural nest of robins
inside nature of singing Savoy
instinctively takes possession of the moon
spins it forward from tune deck of incidental tunes
covers it
with her scatology spittle
rolls it to edge of her edge
and cuts up space like
the great space cutter she is
this woman
flying through porthole of her shipwreck
kicking in all the subversive signals
she had suppressed in self-examination booth
of ancestral tongues
this woman pushing back the romantic
overgrown mangrove of used songbooks
to step out with a saturday night coupe of riffs
everything lovely and sweet and lovely
in her retrospective mouth of
multiple time systems
mesmerizing and signifying to
all the stingrays boppin in the Savoy Ballroom
Savoy   Savoy   Savoy

PASTEL ROOM

Big Jay wanted me to
Strut around the club with him as
He blew "Harlem Nocturne"
He wanted me to holler "Blow Big Jay"
As he lay on the bar honking his horn in
New York City

But it is thirty years later
He is not the plump Cecil Jay McNeely in Watts
Or the walking tenor sax man looking for
Dancers dancing the Pachuco in Aliso Village
Or the kneeling guy blowing between legs of
Dancers dancing the Texas Hop in the Barrel House
Or the bebopper bopping Los Angeles bop in
Jam sessions at the Pastel Room

It is thirty years later on the rug of his bald spot
& all his sexy solos have been co-opted
Recycled & rocked
Clearly what he needs is not another horn
But another idea
& that idea is in him
So Blow Big Jay

BETTY

The voice of May
Is the voice of Betty Carter
Betty the bandleader in control
Betty the mother of special melodies
Betty the young girl singer with Hamp and Ray
Betty   pure Betty
Independent Betty
Betty the spring festival of Egyptian trombones
Deep Betty
The passionate humming bird in a bebop cap
Fresh Betty
The great wildflower of May

JOHNNY BLOWING & POINTING HIS MACHETE

Johnny
checking his watch and
clapping in time with
piano players' bouncing shoulders
Johnny
dancing with his saxophone
together they are foreshadowing paraphrasing and shadow boxing
they are fragile   frail   fast-fingering   fierce and flying
they have that walking-the-high-wire-without-net sound
that newborn-baby yelp
that swift-attacking shark-slashing whisper
that misty humidifying cloud-foaming hurricane hiss
that slow-motion moaning into deep up-tempo swinging which says
"You never been there before
so take the lights down MF
take the lights down MF
you never been there before"
Johnny
blowing & pointing his machete cutting saxophone
& together they are roaring through Blue Note Club like
two unapologetic bears
they are steaming through their confinement &
striking the stage with
whatever the possibilities of the music
and even the music knew
of no one more vulnerable
no one more expressive
than Johnny

HEMPHILL TONIGHT

Tonight
all the contradictions
all the interjections
all the agitations
all the languages spoken with eyebrow gestures
all the ecstatic shoutings
all the ironic notations
all the ideas proliferating through precious metallic spit
the profound scientific soundings in
rara mouth of irradiated teeth
the revelations mixed in gentrified space
the indigenous key snap calculations
the chronology of hats left in the doorway
the rising typhoon of sweat circling docks
the exclamatory pitches
the drunk investigative medicines flowing through
clavicles of the airshafts most
magical medicinal musical moment of awareness
the sky turning around in shipyard of the body
rage intensifying its
Texas Dogon A.D. Coon Bid'ness stint of
nomad flint on firefly wings
and already
one leg waiting for the other at the sound check

HOUSE OF RUBBER 92

Jazz Fan returns home to see
the East West Motel
smoking itself in mirror on the ceiling
the Kentucky Fried Chicken shack burning to
a crispy minstrel chalk
the one-hour cleaners cleaned out of existence
shopping malls mauled
jazzy Mai Tai Club knocked out
the auto body shop beyond repair
the bridal salon in a wedding dress made of old flames
the check-cashing concerns checking out
the cash machines drunk on molotov cocktails
the gym running on a treadmill of ashes
the Seoul Bar gutted
the beauty supply shop smoldering under
embers of hot curling irons
drugstores cooking in chemicals
hamburger joints electrocuted
the house of rubber tires fuming
& still standing with funeral parlors and churches
is a sign that says:
Los Angeles Proud Sponsor of Those Who Carry the Torch

CARTOONING WHENEVER THE MUSIC STARTS

Whenever the music starts
they start
Veronica, Betty, and Archie talking to their Jughead
as Little Orphan Annie amplifies her voice
to gossip with Ms. Snow Whiteman who
blows smoke signals in
the direction of Paul Bunyan who is walking in
after chopping down all the trees
and is now in the house breathing like
a buzz saw in competition with
bass player's solo as Uncle Ben brings in the rice and
Nancy and Sluggo begin their rebel yankee yell from the bar
and Brenda Starr throwing her hair to the side
shouts for the waitress who's
out there tossing forks on metal trays
as trumpeter hits his high note
and Jazz Fan says shut up to
noisy Lois Pain In The Ass who smirks
and cuddles up with Lothar as he sips cognac &
rubs Mandrake's thigh while
thief Robin Hood and Maid Marian play leg and lip games in front of
Topsy and Dragon Lady rolling their eyes while
tourists pat feet anywhere
but on the beat
and it goes like that
whenever the music starts
they start

NEW YORK NEW YORK

New York New York
you old sentimental pothole in the head
posing like a tall unemployed parking meter
with two shower caps on
you old subway step of chewed apples and used condoms
resting in front of the lucky spot chop bar
you old sweat-suit wearing sweetpea streaked with
blood from everywhere
you old high-rising rump of pigeon poop on
roof of the Lover Boy Barber Shop
you are
still militaristically coded
still slave-tradish and bullish
still inflated fixated and ready to
jack up your greed in greed of
an executive order
that's you
fine-tuning your capitalistic cock
on four o'clock dot of carnivorous fangs
you big old filthy fetish doll sitting on
hood of a white graffitied truck
smelling like a funky paper mill from Ashdown Arkansas
I see you
trying to remember your immense self-conscious self at
the Remember Me Beauty Parlor
that's you
pants down on butt
bumpersticker on nose
snow-covered garbage-heap belly stuffed in
a black leather jacket

BLUES BOP FOR DIZ

In the bebop band at Minton's
there was a very beautiful trumpet player
who could walk the cliffs at dawn like a Dogon
put dry clay on mouth of a slow blues
groove high
& oop bop sha bam
a kooka mop
in the hot house of Minton's

A very beautiful-sounding trumpet player
with so much confrontational stress
so much cheek inflation
so much accelerating concentration
so much chromaticizing in the pistons
of the oo blah dee at Minton's

A very beautiful trumpet player
with such a torrential outburst of spitballs
such forceful streams of aerophonic breath
such mysterious piercing winds
such an array of terrifying cuts on
drum cans of Manteca Manteca
in the rough house at Minton's at Monroe's
a very beautiful trumpet player carrying
sharp pitches of the path
from Gorée to South Carolina & back with
salt peanuts in Akan of Cubano Bop
in ashé of Tin Tin Deo
oo papa odobo   salt peanuts   salt peanuts
in the hot house at Minton's at Monroe's
a very beautiful sounding trumpet player
who could intensify & energize & dynamize the changes
in cool breeze of the caravan
who could pop up & have more punch
in overall tone of the reference

who could transpose clowning
into another composition of contrasting sounds
who could elaborate & agitate & illuminate the voltage
in Tunisia
& oo bop sha bam
down round midnight
groovin high and bopping the blues
in the bebop band at Minton's at Monroe's
A very beautiful trumpet player

LEAVE THAT SONG ALONE

Leave that song alone
it has already been sung
by the one with divination basket in throat
by singer with competitive scrapers in lungs
by the double-gong mouth singers of satire
by the singer with marimba-sounding sound box
the one with Chokwe dialect in up-tempo conversations
the singer with calabash resonator cheeks
the one singing through teeth arranged like xylophone keys
the staccato clicking singers in Bakongo hairdos
the signifying high-frequency singer in harmolodic mode
the one with impeccable announcements coming through the ribcage
        Leave that song alone
        It has already been sung by
the husky-voice singer with emotional overtones in the nose
the one holding different ranges of time in nasal passageways
the singer with phonatious flow of noontime shrills in the air
the one at home in a nest of trombones
the sarcastic singer with microphone in diaphragm
the one with fine & melancholy breathing activity
the singer with vibrato of bees buzzing between lips
the one whose vocal habits are out of sync with structure of the tune
the singer with a complex of signaling devices in the chewing muscle
the one sounding like a crying jackal
        Leave that song alone
        It has already been sung by
the singer with strong wind in the windpipe
the one with deep-rooted solitude in the bronchial tube
the off-key dissonance singers
the one with four-octave range in
orange juice vodka serenade of the sunset limited
the singer with siren-calling jaws
the one with the baby-talking tongue tip
the singer yodeling out in all registers
the one with pineywoods-smelling breath stream

the singer specializing in spatial relationships
the one with a foxhole of sparrows in the vocal folds
the invincible singers with pretty tonality of tones singing
    Leave that song alone
    It has already been sung   sang sing & sung

WHAT'S YOUR TAKE

If a two-headed goat pisses its
long piss of death for your
conversion into a free trade zone
If napalm is being buried in the ground
between tuner of concert pianos and
the pioneer of mathematical analysis
If the corporate terminology settles in
                        your mouth like a sweat shop
If a hyena shows you how to eat yourself up
& the blowflies blow your way
& you become like shredded flesh on
            teeth of the IMF
            Watch out
You are in the globalization economic domination process
            Now what's your take
If the world's most potent drink comes from
juice of a festering sore called
            institutionalized brutality
If the most extravagant treaty of abuse
sits like an occupying force on
broken body of an abandoned child
& if the political strategy is to be
            both covert and overt
at the same time on the same level
& if intimidation becomes a patriotic
            theme song called Intimidation
& responsibility remains a potty-training session
for all those holding their tee tees & wee wees
& if a newborn baby comes out looking like
            2 pounds of soggy grape
after a nuclear reactor meltdown
& if you find yourself radioactively depleted
invaded   bombed out   borderless   dislocated   delinked
            Watch out
You're in the globalization domination process
            Now what's your take

KEYS TO THE CITY

Fascinating compelling
          deep rooted
in the mainstay of avalanche boots
                    visceral mixes
the peacock spreading wings
          in memory of
poetry laughing to keep from crying
    & world bank trying to keep from laughing
all right   okay
                get out of here
with your
cupcake   brillo pad vampire-monkey-hairdo self
            great
          amazing
        compliments of the house
        one night stand
                jazz history
                sophisticated frogs
        hammerhead sharks
this is a great SM58 microphone day
in the taste of the smell of the fix of obscurity
        so many lyrics to
          write on broken guitars
so much electricity
to eat up
    and erupt into Lightnin' Hopkins
double time
half time
time of instinctive action
                    out front
    in all stability
& multidimensional thinking
          a big asphalt storm
the road
restless

obsessive
ride you like a horse
into Tutuola's jungle
turn you loose
& let you say why
the French colonial empire fell
at Dien Bien Phu
how apartheid came apart
at Cuito Cuanavale
and furthermore
I have the trail
I'm in the territory
I don't need the three stooges of jazz criticism
to tell me anything
Frank Lowe has keys to the city of Memphis
play out
play in
close the door
open the line
harmolodicize & harmonize
in the harmattan
of your head

THE MAMBO LESSON

Yesterday took off its shoes
and became an unpopular song
today will end like a stunned fish in
tomorrow's unequal distribution of
emptiness
as the sun makes its entrance
without public support into
the clairvoyance of your
unsweetened panty hose
& I am already
smoking an image
that will bite me
before I change my tongue
so don't forget your skull
your fossil fuel
your utopian teeth

THE BEAUTIFUL BOOK

(2007)

TO KNOW THIS TOOLMAKER

for Chinua Achebe

To know this toolmaker
look inside his toolbox for
those young protesting chisels
beautiful, blood thirsty, smoke filled
& no longer at ease

Find the mature blades
bold, dignified
full of cutting edges of precise cuts
send for the procession of pliers flying out like
arrows of god

Count teeth angles on traditional saws
the rip saw that invents as it rips
the hungry cross-cut saw
that crosses over every Tuesday night

Let the toolbox put on protective goggles when
toolmaker makes the sand move into
things falling apart

& when the dust settles
search for the cult of anvils
the unsubmissive clamps
the riddle of aggressive drills
the boiling subconscious chalk lines
the initiation stone of rough scratches to
understand why
the toolmaker carries the mask
the struggle, the fierceness, the sacrifice
and great squawking visions of humanity on his head
while converting vocal vibrations
into amplified tones of an anthill

Look at those joints
  holding the toolbox together
    dissect the bitter dripping discharge on used erasers
     the dialectical fragments in
       deep proverbial pulp
        the dissonant inner scrappers
          & guttural breezes blowing from blunt pen points
       to discover
     the toolmaker's magic force
  creative spirit
& evolutionary sharpness

BILLIE

Everyone snatched
a piece of her gardenia
to wear in cut flesh
of their gloomy Sunday
Everyone looked
for detours
had premonitions
& forgot
what a little moonlight could do
to a woman standing on
the outside of her body
singing to
the body inside of a song about lynching
Everyone knew about transported spirits
random rooster combs
& the lover man sanctifying in her solitude
But no one wanted to touch
that low fried instantaneous friction sitting
on the inside of outside when she sang
"strange fruit hanging on a poplar tree"

PHILLIS WHEATLEY

Maybe Phillis Wheatley
was the great great missing aunt
and ancestor
of Léopold Senghor

Perhaps
she is that dark cloud of mist
that chaotic wave
that ghostly repetitious undertow
always returning to sing blues
at the Teranga Hotel in Dakar
during harmattan

Maybe Phillis Wheatley
sent as an innovator
in word smith technology
was meant to become
the restless one-woman band
which would haunt
the Senegalese head
of Léopold Senghor
Because
Senghor himself
a poet of split disciplines
in Wolof
in Serrer
in philosophy
& colonial French politics
was fond of masking & unmasking
balaphoning
& thumping out rhythms to
an indifferent world while
hiding laughter of dark women
in the muted belly of his trumpet
Perhaps

deep down in the ocean of Phillis Wheatley's gut
way beyond her emulations
& patriotic rhyme schemes
sat images of a complicated negritude revolt
coded in languages more African than English
more internal than external
more instinctive than mechanical
more forever & forever more than
what is and what was
and what could be
or could not be found
in the life and exile of Phillis Wheatley

COLEMAN HAWKINS

Every time someone changes reeds
Every time someone changes saxophone pads
Every time someone wipes a horn to make it shine
& jams it into a microphone to make it cry
it's coming through body and soul
of Coleman Hawkins reinventing an instrument
to tuxedo up with Fletcher Henderson
get rowdy with Ben Webster
and stretch hawk breath
hawk talk   hawk passages
from the jazz age
straight into rhythm shifting dynamics
of freedom chanting orishas
with hawk playing hawk like hawk
through all advances
& beneath those African Creole soul messages of Sidney Bechet
beneath the old time spirit & meditated voyages of John Coltrane
and the cosmic rays of Charlie Parker
sits the 20th century, modern art and Coleman Hawkins

YOU ARE OUT THERE

to the memory of Pepsi Charles
and all my sisters in the struggle

You are out there
In the struggle of
Your part of the struggle
And those opposed to that struggle
Will put your back up against the wall
Because they know who you are

You are the uranium pit in their concentration
The coffee, sugar and gold surge at
The ethics committee meeting
The cocoa on the cocoa exchange
You are the high-grade copper in the house
The boatload of chromium on the docks
The full volume of coltan in the cell phones
You are that oil field under surveillance
& they know you
In the cold war of their coldness
In the arms race of their embrace
In the military spending of their complex

The song you keep bottled up in
Maximum security of your solitude is like
A contraband weapon
Your ticker tape tongue of revolutionary messages
Give no substitutions
No submissions   no surrenders

And nothing can cover up
The platform of action in your bones
Nothing can hide the rawness of your dignity
No one can take away the sweetness of
Your maternal instinct to struggle

And when you raise your head

To strike and go the distance
No one can control the longevity of your boldness

You are out there in
The political activity of yourself
Doing what you do best
And we will never stop loving your creative imagination
And your willingness to consolidate and
Be that mother in the arena of direct confrontations

We will never get over
The awesome vibration of air-waves
In the windpipe of your great spirit
You are out there

CONVERSATION WITH LANGSTON HUGHES

Someone told TK
And TK told me that
Langston Hughes told them
That he wanted Randy Weston
To play at his funeral the Duke Ellington tune
"Do Nothing Till You Hear From Me"

But every time I hear from Langston
He has too many demands
I mean Langston always
Wants you to talk about rivers
Wants you to be a Revolutionary
Speak in the voice of the people
Dance on some crystal stairs
Listen to Papa Legba on Lenox Avenue
Climb the mountain-top and
Let the Weary Blues echo through your head

You will hear Langston say
Remember the Georgia dusk
Remember the wash-woman
Remember the dust bowl
Remember Mr. Backlash
Remember the Scottsboro boys
Remember the dream number
Remember the bad luck card
Remember the long genealogies
And remember make it black, blunt & beautiful

But when you try to elaborate on that
You will hear Langston say
Development, rhythm, magic
Get off the soapbox
Live and let live

Keep it simple baby Keep it simple
"Do nothing till you hear from me"

If you do nothing till you hear from Langston
And pay no attention to what he says
You'll be working 7 nights a week at
The Elks Club Lounge
& waiting for "Daybreak in Alabama"
While "drying up like a raisin in the sun"

Every time I hear from Langston
He has so many instructions
He wants you
To fill your thoughts full of African folklore
Cha cha cha like a castanet in
District of the Negro
Check out Damballa Wedo
And talk about Louis Armstrong and Patrice Lumumba
In the same breath

And when you say
Langston how can I go from
The "wing tip of a match tip" to the next tip
He'll just say "Ask Your Mama"
And if you start telling him about
The words in your heart reveal
How you feel about him
He'll say that's why his banjo is not sobbing low for you
And hang up the telephone

So if you want to hear from Langston
You will have to know how to
Take the stars out of the sky
Kiss the rain
Deal with the "boogie woogie rumble of a dream deferred"
Suck on the sweet flypaper of life
And Do Nothing Till You Hear From Him
Or you never will

AMAZING

for Raymond Patterson

Amazing
How one can
Mount oneself
& ride a Blues into
everything that is
is everything

Those frog knees
Those whiskey storms
Those lucky dog gestures
Those back door emissions
Those armpit aromas
Those joking joy-riding couplets
Those collective inclinations
Those monumental moments obsessed in losses
Those personal eruptions into the nothing of nothingness

Amazing
How only you
Can look inside of yourself
And know you sacrifice you for you and
Only you will know that
Even when the heart grows too big for its mouth
And the mouth too transparent for its tongue

TONI

She was
    who she was
With that shy smile of
    a little girl from Harlem
With that frown of
    a mature writer of fiction
With that pace of a hip New Yorker
    jumping barricades and
Making entrances into marshes with
    Seabirds & Salt Eaters while
Singing a theme song of
    Mother clan solidarity within
Collective intonations of
    revolutionary blackness
She was that magnetic teacher &
    marvelous mediator
With the bushy headdress &
    Bamana name known as Bambara

IN JASPER, TEXAS

He was not the robber
of all the rubber in Liberia
not the embezzler from Wall Street
not the pirate of the high seas
He was not one of the inventors
of the system of apartheid
or a killer from the United Fruit Company
or a tobacco czar
or Jesse James
He was James Byrd Jr.
A Black man hitchhiking a ride when
he was picked up
beaten & chained to the back of a truck
then dragged and severed
by three white men
in Jasper, Texas 1998

POCKET TRUMPET

for Don Cherry

I dreamt I lost my magnificent pocket trumpet
I left it in the airport X-ray machine
I left it in a taxi cab
I left it on a street corner in Paris
I dreamt I said goodbye to my pocket trumpet
I kissed it   I hugged it   I dropped it
I picked it up then dreamt
it was locked in jaws of a bloodhound
A bloodhound obsessed with my trumpet
& I heard my trumpet screaming
And the bloodhound laughing
My trumpet was screaming through
laughter of a bloodhound
My trumpet coughing & drowning in its own spit
& when the scene changed I dreamt
I lost my pocket trumpet out of my pocket again
Then found it lying around like
A fossil wearing an orange beret
In a pawnshop window
And I grabbed it
I held it   I wiped it   I shook it
And when I found it as frisky & as fierce as ever
I woke up my mouthpiece and played
"If I should lose you"
And when it started giggling so free
I filled its beautiful voice with my madness
Held my breath and said jerejef   thank you

Yes I lost my pocket trumpet in
A graveyard of elephant tusks
& found it in a bamboo forest
I lost it in big scissor-like jaws of a hound &
Found it in underground infestations of that same dream
I found it I found my magnificent pocket trumpet

FREE TIME FRICTION

for Ted Joans 2003

I heard that
A zillion mosquitoes
rode a million human ankles into
the twilight of madness
and even mudfish cults
took off their helmets as
crickets wailing like uncontrollable sirens
lifted you into
baritone fire of the eclipse

and night surfaced with ghosts from Katanga
with lava from city of Goma
with Ouagadougou dust on words
flying on
flying piranhas
back through
crevices of Timbuktu
as you
entered yourself
drinking black stout
chewing kola nut
and riff-raffin like
the great djali you were
with your inflamed spirit lungs
spotted okapi legs
and overheated bongo lips beating in
free-time-friction
very conflictive
very defensive
very Ted-u-nomadically
camel walking forward
& sand-dancing sideways into
a song swallowing its tooth on
a proverb that says:
"The fly has nobody to advise"

& it was
another dawn rising with murmuring roosters
another dump smoking through used wallets
another octopus throbbing between feet of
zoot-suited penguins
another prostate full of untamed windstorms
another ear of canned laughter embedded with
butcher rhythms backed by
horns turning corny lyrics into
beautiful instrumental music
& it was like
another unsanctified shrine chalked in gunpowder
another mask of assertive razors hanging in hallways
another agitated banjo drunk on crocodile tears sold
in plastic bottles to
other civilizations in the mirror of
other planets disappearing with
burros painted like zebras
flamboyant monkeys swinging on
rubber tires in medicine stalls
& the freeze-dried bottom of Mars
re-entering steel-purifying processes in
competition with blowtorch blow of
the trillion trilling tonalities assembled like jackals under
purple postal pulp of your tongue as you yelled
"Tell the Tuaregs I'm on my way"

And it was another pipeline in the treaty
another muted cornet call under
offshore drilling rigs
another bundle of bank notes smiling at
another shitty border dispute
& the battle for who you are
and what you feel
was saying that
"joy is more transient than grief"
& there are
all kinds of uninhabited areas
all sorts of extractions and precipitations

oozing from
sweet surreal marshes of your body splashing into
intersection for irresistible insurrections where
you sit like
an autographed picture that says:
the poet was what he was
and what he was looking for
and deeper than that is not deep
"Tell the Tuaregs I'm on my way"

SAMORY TOURE

We were fighting among ourselves
When in walked the strangers from Europe

We were so busy squabbling with each other
We didn't hear the strangers entering with
A program of destabilization

We were too preoccupied with going from
Conquest to conquest
Defeating the defeated
That we didn't realize we were being defeated
occupied and colonized by real outsiders

We were so engaged in stomping on each other
we didn't know that the strangers
had already expanded their dominance
from Egypt to Cape Town

We were so bent on taking over each other's property
We didn't notice the Dutch stealing cattle from the Khoi

We didn't anticipate the superior weapons
We didn't expect the great trek

We were so busy invading each other that
We didn't feel threatened until we were absorbed into the colony

We were so intent on devastating our neighbor
We had no idea how much we had been programmed into deportation and
annexation

We were so actively doing the Jihad with each other that
when Samory mounted an armed confrontation against the French
we were not unified enough to reinforce his position

because we were not we
We were more like me me & me

After Samory and his group attacked the French
the French had organized an army of
African troops to stop them
And with the evolution
of the Maxim machine gun on the battlefield
Samory could not surround them
divide them or avoid them
& was defeated by advanced technology

when we stopped our squabbling and
took a closer look at what was really happening
The African continent had been partitioned into colonial territories

We were napping while they were mapping
And we are still napping, rapping & capping while
they are trapping, gapping & mapping

BEAUTIFUL SEA OF WAVES

for Janet Carter

Do you know that those sweet-talking string sets
are strung-out weapons against random searches
and that the orchestra seated in F hole of a bass
will not play the security suite when confronted

Did I dream that the laughter from Bags' groove
was still traveling on a billiard ball through space

What do I know about wood that smokes the
interior melody as it crosses over and into
a jam session of tribal disputes

Is this the wood polished with fresh blood from
shade trees of Rufisque

Today I am spitting gasoline into the carburetor
because Ray Brown just left town
& it's too late to talk about the identity crises
within musical forces on the sound stage of capitalism
it's too late to talk about the minstrelsies

Do you know memorized patterns played by
all ensembles riding the back of Jazz into
sunset of the showcase had to
first come through muddy muddy waters

Did I dream that the woman transforming herself
into a foaming   celebrating   temperature-changing
storm-swallowing   chaotic   energetic
un-trappable   unforgettable   sea of waves
was the one-bass hit basically called Janet

It is the accumulation of sonic booms
breaking through ebony fingerboard of
a blue Monday that I carry in my forehead

Do you know the invisible circle of moisture-proof strums
in the great riffing heart of this volcano
Do you know that a super-sensitive gut
On a quivering bow can rupture and become
The permanent hiding place for agitated artists in the
No-parking, no-standing zone of a funky hallway on
the Atlantic shore

Do you hear the freedom of the sea

RIVERS

Amazon is the language of skipping heartbeats
Congo River mouth of Congolese
Tallahassee remembers Emmett Till
Zambezi has no borders
Yangtze is polluted
            But all rivers are indigenous
The Mekong Delta articulating dissonance
The impulsive flow of the moody Casamance
Supernatural slobber paralleling into
Depths of the deepness of Niger

YOU HAVE TO

You have to
begin at the beginning
look for what it is
in crocodile language
of the hoodoo jungle
because every time
Mississippi River
shows its serpentine ass
while the air wears funerary perfume of
lynched spirits
the crossing intersections evacuate each other
and the storm raises its leg to
piss in front of jook joints
of double jointed jooks
to discover why
you have to be so rough
and so intimate with yourself
while singing the blues

WHAT DO THEY CARE

What do they care about ecological devastation
                & survival of the Ogoni people
They're just into
        smiling, eating, making money,
        & fucking up the planet
They are not concerned about the future
        because killers have no future
It's about the oil,
        the pipeline
        & the road to the docks
It's about selling off resources
        receiving revenues
        having a place in the global glut
        & moving greed, mediocrity & stupidity
        to a new plateau of power
What do they care about customs or traditions or
  cultural invasion
  living conditions
  & the Ogoni homeland
They don't speak Ogoni
They speak financial profits
        that's their language
        that's their ideology
& you cannot change the mind & spirit of those who
distort themselves like Sani Abacha and his friends who
  all wear the same uniform
  buy the same weapons
  have the same name of general
  & are a part of the same
  corporate committee
        responsible for
        the escalation of poverty
        & the organization of death squads
What do they care about
                melting ice caps

carbon dioxide
land erosion
atmospheric pollution
& industrial waste
They like to instill fear, show dominance
They don't care about the ocean or space
or cooperating with people interested in developing their community
like Ken Saro-Wiwa and the Ogoni 9
That's why the struggle continues

LIFE IS ON ITS FEET AGAIN

for Ben Jones

The Blues was born in Africa
Grew up on southern plantations
Survives as a special language
                        & is
                a very free firefly
So when I see you arriving
In your boogie in your samba in your rumba
In that creativity part of the consequence
I anticipate
A certain kind of artistic freedom
A certain something in the spirit
A certain aspect of something
        traditionally fantastic &
        modernistically wonderful
In that emotion of inventing and
Painting oneself into such
AfroHaitian AfroBrazilian AfroCuban AfroCentric
                        Configurations
& with attachment and detachment
Your diffusion into my imagination
I find
Cigars in bowties
A penis with bee wings
Paint tubes in ribbons
A landscape of self-conscious battle flags
An exhilarated convulsion of confetti
Peace symbols instead of skull fragments
A flood of female muscles disguised as cowrie shells
A saturated procession of Xs
Thunderbolts screeching to a halt in your
                                salty matted spittle where
Yoruba divination bones are remade into
                Shango installations which
You know like you know
In the way of knowing

There are other hidden elements
Marching their ritual purposes from your dreams into
Eyelids of supernatural forces conjuring up
Magic between the
Heart-shaped-photo-fan-mask commemorations of different spirits and
The core of dance techniques manipulated and transmitted through
Cut-out figures on walls
And even though
You produce in an atmosphere already toxic to your curiosity
You are that border crossing borders
That messenger sending a message with or without
The message knowing it's a message
A moaning dove
A double-headed axe
A stream of dotted lines
And that midnight sun of black coffee moving beneath
Your painted canvas into mouth of a woman singing about
This bitter earth is
Your revelation
Your justification
Your definition
And suddenly life is on its feet again

CHANGE OF FOCUS

I thought I knew the sound of
every instrument by heart
but when you started throwing in
expressions that sounded like
ja ode lodi   ojo   baax na
and shouting super natural intervallic shrills
on top of squawking Afro-folkloric squawks
getting down into the solo root
& prancing the bone yard while
yelping and notating so many riffilations into the patois
& sucking so much joy from the tail spin
                    I said to myself
                    What a fine mouthpiece in scarified chops
& when you started accenting & tonguing &
marking up intonations of the same tone & placing
emphasis upon evidence of your own use of beauty while
signifying & going in unexpected directions
that got very dense with so much pleasure
          I said
          turn back the clock four hours
          bring in all the monuments
          ferocity of tenderness is in the house
& when you began blowing through
like a fugitive tornado from Tulsa
& tamping like
an expert explorer through aftermath of
a California earthquake to become
mythology of wind
cosmological spell
virility of thunder
freedom as a fetish
distance as an inside force
the red eye inversion
the flat lip segue

expansion of retention of location in transition
          I said to myself
what a nomadic   chromatic   volcanic way
to change the focus

SPOKEN WORD

Slave Routes Conference: Guadeloupe 12/99
for Léopold S. Senghor

They say within population explosion
there's a spoken word explosion
but there was always a spoken word explosion
exploding on the African continent
& riffing Rift Valley riffs into
throat talking Pharaonic script
that scripted deep Ethiopian cries onto
a circle of eighty spins that became
transformation within
Dogon world inhabited by Hogons
the spoken word was always the word of words
stacked & ready to erupt from djalis of Gambia
& always word of word in
up-tempo encounters between Khoi and San
between cowrie shells and Ifa priests
Ijala chanters & memory text
between snapping fingers & the poetic tradition of Tiv
Afro field hollers & lamenting dirges of
women in society of Dan
Creole dialects & the click under tongues
double clicking on that
the word was always the word of words offered as
nasal me now and flatten me out
& flame me like a high-pitched female drum
& patina me in pepper & blood
& speak my dance through the pounding of rice growers
& grow me in low land of the sun
& sun me with Kikongo weavers
& weave me from the spirit of cotton pickers
& cotton me like an ant mound of clans in
the chalky fluid between instincts
& instinct my soul into the magic of burping trees
& tree my luck into falsetto trances
& trance my chaotic laughter back into

syncopated premonitions of how the word
became a proverbial detour of
excavated axe fragments &
invisible crevices within
mathematical equations of
the recyclization of moisture
recolonization of metal
density of edges
& the botanical terrain of bitter-tasting fan belts from
lost paradiddles parading in from Ile-Ife with
the word that was always divided into
bamboo sticks & steel band revolts
& possessed in feathers
& mummified in flint
& expanded by trilling & rolling in with
sharp teeth or shot legs
with rhymes & scratches
with Wolof & Shona
with the horseshoe language of impulse & rupture
& the circumstances left in blown-out throat of a lizard
left under the phonetic hoof of smashed scorpions where the word
was
always the word within population explosion of spoken word
explosions
exploding on the African continent

HAITI 2004

I say Fon You say Yoruba
I say Bambara You say Ibibio
I say Ibo You say Xhosa
I say Kikongo You say Wolof
I say Fulani You say BoBo
I say Ashanti You say Efik
I say Mandingo You say Mende
I say Luba You say Lunda
I say Arawak You say Carib
I say Guinea You say Dahomey
I say Calabar You say Zanzibar
I say Angola You say Senegal
I say Africa You say Ameri-indian
I say enslavement You say intense exploitation
I say Marrons You say invisibles
I say Toussaint You say Dessalines
I say Christophe You say Pissed off
I say an amalgamation of languages
You say a pantheon of deities
I say Damballa You say Legba
I say Erzulie You say Ogou
I say too many initiations You say too many superstitions
I say tribalism You say diversity
I say class rivalry You say religious infusions
I say soil erosion You say internal repression
I say lakou de peasant
You say palace elite
I say revolt begins here
You say trouble starts there
Trouble starts with
Who's going be head Negro in the Bantustan
Who's going be chief warlord in the refugee camp
Who's going be top dog on the runway
Who's going be number one drug dealer in the sanctuary
Who's going be the most powerful person

to dominate secrets of the crossroads
Who's going be the most feared killer in
blood ritual of the black code
Who's going be wealthiest mulatto rooster in the cockfight
Who's going be grandest pimp in the temple
Who's going be best prostitute in the national palace
Who's going be the greatest *tonton macoute* ever lubricated by
the Monroe Doctrine
& who's going be Attaché   & who's going to be Fraphe
& who's going be high on repression
Who's going be possessed into repossession
Who's going to be grinding up leaves all night in
        the British plantation pub
Who's going to be shaking shoulders and slithering down
the trading post in the French bistro
Who's going to be grinning & swallowing zombies all night
        In the US Diplomatic Lounge
I say money be flying   you say violence & poor people dying
I say you say we say Haiti be drinking punishment punch

You say arada
I say petro
You say mambo   I say loa
You say veve   I say ye ye
You say o ke ke   but they say nay nay nay nay
And I say you say we say who they   who they
They be elite-tay they say
They be 3 percent of the population-nay
They say they be Roman Catholics sometime lay lay
They say they economically in charge today day
They town people
They city folk
They big business men
They be chilling in their isolation booth
They be segregated in their thinking
They be delirious devils
They be a Duvalier cult
They be classic Papa fuck-up
They be queen occupation in a marine uniform

They be papa anti-development
They be queen privilege
They be papa devaluation
They be queen bushi dufus ya ya
They be papa CEO of corruption
Be Baby Doc the robot   Be predator Cedras the killer
They be paramilitary brother-hood boo boo cult
They be alienated in their colonial divisions
They be Monsieur and Madame Amnesia living
Their imitation of life in Port-au-Prince

& when I say you say we say Haiti
They say hate it
We say dignity, survival, endurance, consolidation
They say cheap labor, strategic location, intervention
We say justice, education   food, clothing shelter
They say indigenous predatory death squads to the rescue
We say Haitian water violated
Haitian airspace penetrated
They say kiss my aluminum baseball bat
suck my imperial pacifier and lick my rifle butt
We say cancel the debt
They say blow up the green cards
sink all the boat people
We say abolish the military
They say let that coup money march in 2/4 time
We say eradicate poverty, illiteracy, disease, and terror
They say let the celebration for 200 more years of servitude begin
We say viva the Haitian revolution
Viva democracy viva independence viva resistance viva Unity
They say viva the payoff
Viva the rich people viva the widening gap viva regime change
Viva repression
But I say   you say   we say   no way   no way
Haiti be the great symbol of creativity
Haiti be the first to strike blows for independence and culture
Haiti be Samedi sacrifice
Haiti be Baron emergency
Haiti be Vaccine giveaway

Be Gender nomad cooperative
Be chief mineral un-tap-tap
Haiti be Saint grass-root energizer
Be Spell-breaker Wedo
Haiti be Ti-Jean mudslide relief
Be Mystère medicine love ash
Be Daughter lascivious transition
Be agronomist Zo-Bop
Be Da-da-double-face-Boko-hurricane-survivor
Haiti be wanting to be Haiti
Not Haiti bye bye not Haiti why why
But Haiti independent revolutionary Haiti

& I say Chokwe You say Fante
I say Hausa You say Yaka
I say Imbangala You say Ga
I say Nupe You say Dinka
I say Soninke You say Serer
I say Mossi You say Luba
I say Edo You say Mandi
I say Zulu You say Khoi Khoi
I say Swazi You say Pygmy
I say Baule You say Masai
I say Dahomey You say Benin
I say Ga Ga You say Ra Ra
& I say you say we say Haiti
Come on Haiti Come on now

WHEN YOU OPEN THE DOOR

When you open the door
know that
the consumers are coming through to consume
& you are not only opening the door
for the fighters who fought to open the door
not only for the volunteers who take responsibility
to keep the door open
not only for those devoted to eliminating the closed-door policy
you are opening the door for politicians who will
bring back the chain gang
for entertainers who will run around
selling backwardness as art
for the reactionaries who promote
armed international reactions
& it doesn't matter how long it took to kick the door open
you are opening the door for those who did not participate in
or understand the history of the struggle to open the door

AFRO SPOT

The metal worker was welding
The palm wine tapster was drinking
The trumpeter was marching
The Afro Spot owner was preaching
The metal worker was wallowing in rust
The hunter was camouflaging its feathers
The trumpeter was hiding under dry leaves &
The Afro Spot owner was disappearing behind smoke

The metal worker was pounding
The cane cutter was slashing
The trumpeter was blasting
The timekeeper was clapping
The Afro Spot owner was shouting
The palm wine tapster was tapping

And no one was asking why Yoruba, why Chokwe,
Why injunctions, why Abeokuta, why long distances
Why Umbundu, why Firespitters, why geology,
Why phonetics, why repetition, why communication,
Why matter, why fission, why the Big Bang

The trumpeter knew how to announce the content
The Afro Spot owner knew how to blow whistles against corruption
The metal worker knew how to read the patina
The palm wine tapster knew how to swallow all secrets
& the timekeeper knew how to break the metronome

The cane cutter had the leading tone
The hunter had the tempo
The trumpeter had the vibrato
The palm wine tapster had the tonic
The timekeeper had the up beat
The Afro Spot owner had the vamp &
The metal worker had the crescendo

And no one was asking
Why did the Afro Spot owner cut up
Why did the palm wine tapster cut off
Why did the timekeeper cut out
Why did the metal worker cut the action
Why did the trumpeter live in the action of the cut
And why this particle why this loop
Why so many directions why the afterglow and
Why the Big Bang

The trumpeter knew how to manipulate sound
The palm wine tapster knew how to clean the mouth
The cane cutter knew how to step forward
The metal worker knew how to fabricate
The Afro Spot owner knew how to provoke
The hunter knew how to swim in deep water

The metal worker had the foundry
The timekeeper had the message machine
The hunter had the telescope
The trumpeter had the space shuttle
The Afro Spot owner had the salt mines &
The palm wine tapster had all the trees

No one was saying
Why evolution of energy, why the unifying device of spit
Why fire drills, why gravitation, why the internal punctuations
Why transitions, why Navajo, why Aztec, why axis of rotation,
Why cosmic expansions, why encrustations,
& Why the Big Bang

THE GIGGING PART

The gigging part
gets to be the routine that can't
rehabilitate itself
even with an illusion of the former you
smelling of detached retina and
dead dog fights
So I name you uncontrollable abuse
I name you subjugated consequence
I fingerprint you on a bus ride
through Amarillo, Texas
a certain cache of red devils
pointing their tits from your eyelids
& you are "wild man blues"
in the defensive capsule of childhood
every trip is what it is in you
a man wearing a mask of
chewed blackberry seeds
& a dislocated navel displaced like
            the wah wah mute of Joe Oliver
but who can compare scars
you are pumping up your heart
in the middle of the crisscross
and jumpstarting your bones
in blue gel of the jack base

TALKING ABOUT NEW ORLEANS

Talking about New Orleans
About deforestation & the flood of vodun paraphernalia
the Congo line losing its Congo
the funeral bands losing their funding
killer winds humming intertribal warfare hums into
two storm-surges
touching down tonguing the ground
three thousand times in a circle of grief
four thousand times on a levee of lips
five thousand times between a fema of fangs
everything fiendish, fetid, funky, swollen, overheated
and splashed with blood & guts & drops of urinated gin
                                        in syncopation with me
riding through on a refrigerator covered with
asphalt chips with pieces of ragtime music charts
torn photo mug shots & pulverized turtle shells from Biloxi
                          me bumping against a million-dollar oil rig
me in a ghost town floating on a river on top of a river
              me with a hundred ton of crab legs
                          and no evacuation plan
me in a battered tree barking & howling with abandoned dogs
my cheeks stained with dried suicide kisses
my isolation rising with a rainbow of human corpse &
                                        fecal rat bones
where is that fire chief in his big hat
where are the fucking pumps
the rescue boats
& the famous coalition of bullhorns calling out names
              hey   I want my red life-jacket now
& I need some sacred sandbags
some fix-the-levee-powder
some blood-pressure-support-juice
some get-it-together-dust
some lucky-rooftop-charms &
some magic-helicopter-blades

I'm not prepared
to live on the bottom of the water like Oshun
I don't have a house built on stilts
I can't cross the sea like Olokun
I'm not equipped to walk on water like Marie Laveau
or swim away from a Titanic situation like Mr. Shine
Send in those paddling engineers
I'm inside of my insides
& I need to distinguish
between the nightmare, the mirage,
the dream and the hallucination
Give me statistics
how many residents died while waiting
how many drowned
how many suffocated
how many were dehydrated
how many were separated
how many are missing
how many had babies
and anyway
who's in charge of this confusion
this gulf coast engulfment
this displacement
this superdome shelter
this stench of stank
this demolition order
this crowded convention center chaos
making me crave solitary confinement

Am I on my own
exhausted from fighting racist policies
exhausted from fighting off sex offenders
exhausted from fighting for cots for tents for trailers
for a way out of this anxiety   this fear   this emptiness
this avoidance   this unequal opportunity world of
disappointments accumulating in my undocumented eye
of no return tickets

Is this freedom   is this global warming   is this the new identity

me riding on a refrigerator through contaminated debris
talking to no one in particular
about a storm that became a hurricane
& a hurricane that got violent and started
eyeballing & whistling & stretching toward
a category three domination that caught me in
          the numbness of my own consciousness
             unprepared, unprotected and
                made more vulnerable to destabilization
by the corporate installation of human greed, human poverty
human invention of racism & human neglect of the environment

I mean even Buddy Bolden came back to say
          move to higher ground
             because a hurricane will not
                rearrange its creativity for you
& the river will meet the ocean in
                   the lake of your flesh again
so move to higher ground
and let your jungle find its new defense
let the smell of your wisdom restore the power of pure air
& let your intoxicated shoreline rumble above & beyond the
water-marks of disaster

I'm speaking of New Orleans of deportation
of belching bulldozers   of poisonous snakes
of bruised bodies   of instability and madness
mechanism of indifference and process of elimination
I'm talking about transformation about death re-entering life with
Bonne chance, bon ton roulé, bonjour & bonne vie in New Orleans, bon

REALITY CHECK

I.

You can blend
Cement mixer sounds with
Voices and songs from Algeria
Combine that with
Jazz saxophone improvisations
Use a Hip Hop beat
Throw in a couple of
Miles Davis solos
Add a little
European classical music to the mix
Then fuse that
With hee-hawing of a jackass and
The gonging of church bells
Put this taped amalgamation
Through a computer
And imitate the computer sound with
An acoustic instrument
& say
The next advancement in
The music called Jazz
Is coming from you
But what about the history of
Humans imitating machines
And why did Blues men imitate train whistles

What are the facts
What are the false claims
What is your reality

2.

You can shop in a supermarket
Bag up groceries at the checkout counter
Then act like
The contents in that container are your creation
Even though
You didn't invent one item in the bag

What are the facts
Who gets the credit
Who gets the collision fee
What is your reality

You may have
The largest audience
You ever had
And be that syrupy product
Sold on radio & television as
The next new thing
But your identity is
A public relations identity
Colonialism is still your structure
And institutional racism in the business
Will always take over
And you're not the matter
Holding this solar system in place

So what are the facts
What are the contradictions
What is your reality

JANJAWEED MILITIA

I saw the people being killed & wounded
By Sudanese Government's militia men

I saw these women being raped & gutted
To the point of really wishing they were dead

It's the domination scheme of keeping power
making people fight each other every hour

Heads cut off by the militia known as Janjaweed

I saw the look of desperation in the eyes of
popular police & bandits

Young girls abducted, abused, sexually wounded
& buried between thighs of gang-raping men

It's the threat of racial violence spreading
like a force of wild thunderous winds

Bodies hacked up by Janjaweed

There are the distant hidden names
& disappearing boys

There are tattooed body parts
& civilian casualties in the sand

There are tribal conflicts made into inter-tribal conflicts
& life left in shambles by jackals known as Janjaweed

I can hear the frantic ruling party's
racial slurs pushing through the air

It's the destruction of villages & uprooting of farmers
In a part of Darfur that we see

Flesh on teeth of thrill-seeking Janjaweed

There are organized calamities
& inter-factional fighting

there's the attempted Arabization process
In the ethnic cleansing of Black African skin

But even when these female stomachs swell
& the blood mixes & the water breaks

the holding on to land & identity
& the need for peace & solidarity
will remain the major issues in the depths of
the deepness of the blackness of the struggle
in the oil fields of Sudan

& this is beyond the thinking
of those calling themselves Janjaweed

BODEGA & DELI

Bodega: You are shining my shoes in a dust storm

Deli: & You are sitting on the corner like a sack of aged cassavas

Bodega: Time will cut your throat

Deli: I knew what you were doing when those vultures started
swooping down to sit in your lap

Bodega: You are filled to the brim with smoked fish & uncontrollable
bird whistles

Deli: & Clearly the romantic smell left on your barstool is the
starchy stench of midnight eating itself up

Bodega: Why don't you shout out a condolence to water

Deli: Okay let's have a poetic encounter
let's go to the watermelon festival
let's celebrate The Beautiful Book
& belch with
the bartender, the rooster & the scavenger cod

THERE MUST BE

There must be a snowstorm not yet
pissing in public
because you look exactly
like a person who
ate too many jelly rolls
& every time
you put on your hyena mask
all the trap doors open

THIS IS NOT ABOUT

This is not about fact-finding
De-mining   whistle-blowing
Or being displaced
This is not about prehistoric animals like
The great flesh-eating Tyrannosaurus Rex
This is about you knowing your eye from your pussy
Because your pussy has the eye of your lyncher

ADVANCING

There's an advance man in a red suit advancing
There's a shrine made of musical mouthpieces
There's an invisible zone of ancient mirrors
Lubricated with musk of Benin leopards
And in the center of this
There's the Afro-spirit medium in a polka-dot robe

IN THIS SCULPTURAL SPACE

for Elizabeth Catlett

In this sculptural space
Women have chipped alabaster vase faces
Nubian soapstone hearts
Amber whistling tongues
& green serpentine thighs
They have
terra-cotta heads with elaborate hairstyles
protruding belly vaults with nourishing nipple façades
triangular limestone eyes in broken clay jug skulls
They show their hieroglyphic clits and
pregnant vessel selves on tomb walls
become funerary statues
protective temple carvings
inscribed coffin lids
deep gravel pits
electric lava circles
& monumental bodies of hard granite
in Joe Blow's museum

ON THE PERIPHERY

MoMA 1980

Wifredo's jungle
Standing guard with guards
Next to coatroom on level one
Siqueiros, Orozco, Rivera paintings
On walls near toilet on level two
Romare's woman on quilt
Resting by emergency exit B on level three

MAJOR EXHIBITIONS

Dear Whitney Museum
You have had three major exhibitions
Jake Lawrence, Jean-Michel Basquiat & Bob Thompson
One Black artist every ten or twenty years is not sufficient
In fact you have excluded many artists in your
Freedom of expression museum of American art
So until you rectify your past performance
You don't deserve my support
And I do not trust your trustees

DEAR RAPPER

Dear Rapper

They will let you shake your booty
hold your crotch
storm in like a storm trooper
or strut in like a stripper in G-strings

They will buy you
market you
trade you
exploit you
then cancel the contract
& resell you on the auction block

CITIZEN SOLDIER

Do not return home in a body bag on
behalf of jungle warfare school of
                    missiles in the night
Think before filling your helmet with blood in
support of the desert warfare school of
                    botched-up intelligence
Do not give your bones to
the warfare trade school of
                    fire breaks in the bush
Why melt away in your rolling bomb shelter for
the sake of the nuclear warfare school of
                    favorable political outcomes
Zip down your combat boots
Stay clear of booby traps
Move very quickly
& do not open your heart for us today
                    Citizen Soldier

I AM NEW YORK CITY 2

I am New York City 2
It's 9/11/01
& I have been wounded
in the lower Manhattan of my abdomen
Now I am the one with the most wreckage
The most obnoxious smell
& the most industrial volcanic eruption of
twin tower ashes
I am the one flying like an avalanche of
Hazardous waste down the West Side Highway
I carry the gigantic whale of charcoal smoke in
my ground zero head
& everybody will remember me as that
unique contemporary water buffalo dripping pee to
keep fire from burning up the air

I am New York City
Momentarily obsolete, artificial & mad
encrusted, gritty, sober & fuming
but never mind all that
& never mind the profit slump
never mind the central bank
never mind the global financial crisis
never mind those jealous of my cultural dynamism
Forget debate, forget intelligence, forget stupidity, forget it

I have on my hard hat, my gloves, my goggles, my
ear plugs, my gas mask, my welding torch
My tool belt flapping
My tongue clearing the path
My big steel teeth picking up chunks of cement
& I am excavating my ass off

I am New York City 2
& I know who's eating chips in

cockpit of the Federal Reserve
oh yes I know
the stock market crash has not yet fully crashed
but now that the bailouts are bailing out
& the smoke screens are smoking
& the spread of fear is spreading
& the flags are flipping and flying
& the censorship is censoring
& the global crusade is crusading
& the act of terrorism is terrorizing
& now that all the
undermining, mindless, mind-boggling,
mind-controlling freaks are meeting and are taking
mind-blowing missions of destruction to another level
it's time for me
to pump up my muscles
wake up the sleeping birds
make my way through the
transparent maze of insane propaganda
put three hundred pair of
courageous firefighter boots on my head
place a Red Cross sticker on my butt
take a deep breath and
walk in the opposite direction

I am New York City
Always expressive always offensive & always irresistible
So don't play possum with me

TOO MUCH

Too much black shoe polish in the hair
is starting to make you
afraid of your own sweat
but that's not why you're anti-melody
pro-mechanical, tone-deaf
or academically dull
That's not why your solos
are short intellectual stunts or
why you have
a system of analysis
but no system for creating
I mean if your aspirations
had been known
Adolphe Sax would not have sold you a saxophone

THESE PEOPLE

These people
think I have a duty
to provide shelter
for portrait of his holiness of holes
they think
he should sit pontificating
in jazz joint of my jaws
They see me
as fertile ground for recruitment
another drum majorette coughing up petrol
for the commonwealth of man
They think I should be
an ordinary corrupt citizen
keep my flesh on the fly hook
& give them
thirty million bucks worth of lip service

JUST LIKE THAT

Just like that
Ram a pole up
Abner Louima's rectum
Shove that same pole into
Louima's mouth
& then it's goodbye
I'm off in my land rover to
get Haitian art in exchange for
ballpoint pens
& that's it? Just like that?
Plunge a plunger into
private premises of Louima
then it's so-long
I'm off to kiss my partner's butt on
an un-educational adult TV talk show
flick my stick at the surgeon general
stalk another pedestrian and
have a sodomizing good time back at
the police precinct
Just like that? & that's it?

AMADOU'S BLUES

39 bullets
41 shots
Amadou Diallo dead
& I am eating his teeth in my sleep
I am feeling his broken face
face down in my face
His heart is swelling in my heart
& I am riding the terrible solitude
of his silence through a cyclone
Amadou Diallo dead
& I am sailing in circles
with the Gypsy Cabmen
I am walking through the storm
with the vendors
I am standing in the doorway
on the epicenter of immigration situations in America
where Amadou stood
& I can taste the invention of gunpowder
I can feel the panic of bullets
I can hear an African language
bursting into a quicksand of blood
I can see the racial profiling glowing through
the body bag of Black History
Amadou Diallo dead
& I live the night of the frenzy
the day of the acquittal
My eyes riveted to eyes of
assassins in the courthouse
My head mounted by
a police state of corruption
My ears filled with
mournful sounds of a woman shouting "A ma dou uuu"
& Amadou is in me
His determination of movement

is my movement of determination
His voyage is in my voyage
                    & together
we are the water that fire cannot destroy

IN THIS CITY

In this City
you don't think earth
you don't think stars
you think human smiles
human sweat   human voices
you think skyscrapers, art market, literary forum
power failure, corrosion & cold spell
                    So Madame
you may be that stink bomb sprouting from
                              ass of the northern lights
but in this City
you don't think solar flare
you don't think cloud formation
you think one-way street
two-tone shoes, barking dogs,
parking space, concrete
                    So Mister
you and the elephants are not wallowing in
          correct water hole either
because
in this City
you don't think super nova
infant nebula, kinetic vortex,
you think human stress, human waste,
visionary rodents, broken pipes & rent hike

JURY DUTY

Have you ever been
to pizzeria of the crime
have you ever had
a gold chain snatched on
subway train 562
have you ever stared
into the eyes of a pit bull
have you ever been robbed in
a massage parlor
have you ever been in a riot
what do you think of flags burning on flag day
have you ever been beaten
with metal belt buckles
have you ever been whipped
with windshield wipers
or raped in a garden of lilies
did you report the incident
& was that report reported & filed

Are you a responsible citizen
are you qualified to make a decision in
the case of political corruption &
the horses dropping dead from
auto fumes on fifth avenue

Can you promise that you'll be fair
can you give your assurance
that you won't think of
a prior incident
are you a liar a fiction writer
a manipulator of the system
or a misguided missile

Do you understand the meaning of treason
toxic waste dumping, oil spillage,

medical malpractice, manslaughter,
embezzlement, kidnapping & murder
Can you look justice in its bright face
without thinking racism and
unequal distribution of resources
can you look at the perpetrators' empty sleeves
without thinking of war
can you examine evidence against prostitutes
without seeing four hundred drug pimping scabs
inside their lips
can you watch undercover parrots
in civilian dress do their act and not laugh
can you sit in that box
between the pentecostal preacherette
& the man farting prevention magazine farts
and do your duty

SUBWAY SOUND OF SILENCE

The sound of silence
pushes its knee
against iron worker's jaw
& slides through bonded teeth
of a professor's professional grin before
going through
hands of a vagrant asking for coins from
a woman who announces in a loud voice
        "no man and no money
                will kiss my pussy this morning"
& the sound of silence breaks into laughter through
whiskey-throated whispers of a young girl
& circles above heroin-salted nose of
a groaning junkie & lands between
novel-reading eyes of a donut-nibbling nurse then
disappears beneath gurgling rattle in chest of
a huge man breathing like a tired ox

DIGGING

You were the one who used to walk through
crowded rooms looking like a person who
just crapped on himself
but holding head high
& now
you are digging for the woman who likes to
confront dumpster trucks while
crossing the street in her handicap scooter
you are searching for the lady who said:
you may be real famous
but corny as a monkey in a zoo
yes digging can be a theme
& you are digging

SUBWAY BULLFIGHTER

He is a thin balding brown skin man
dressed in greasy gray zoot suit pants
dingy T-shirt strips
a cape made of torn jacket linings & safety pins
a head band of pigeon feathers
a necklace of twisted coat hangers
shoes made of dirty green rags
his face resembling the face of Haile Selassie
but he is not Selassie
he is the ticking time bomb of America
posing like a ballet dancer in a cobra stance
then acting like a bullfighter charging & moving from
seat to seat waving paper bags while
gibbering & yelling olé   olé

ON THE SAME TRAIN

On the same train
A white woman with skin like cracked leather
Walks in circles while repeating the lines
"My brother is extravagant
My mother is catholicized
& my father is a bum
So fuck you"

THE CROWS

The crows are arriving with the pomade queens of East Africa
& are riding in on backs of elephants borrowed from
                    the Singapore zoo
they also fly out of a Vincent van Gogh canvas
              & are joined by others from
Jacob Lawrence's migration paintings
These are the crows known as
night birds immune to drive-by shootings
They circle around various embassies at twilight
& only during elections will they
sit under trees on top of skyscrapers
smoking weed
& shouting to friends
              before burying their dead
& sailing off in military formation to
                    a watermelon festival

THE GREAT CHOREOGRAPHER

The lord of war crimes marries
the honorary president of library books
Ms. Super Maxi Pad the famous ballerina
swan dances to a pit stop with
Mr. Arid X the great choreographer
& Mr. Drought meets Ms. High Technology near
a transcontinental shrine made of plastic bags
& as Mr. Sacred Dog hides from Mr. Sunshine of the jungle
Mr. & Mrs. Skunk piss on each other at midnight &
The Lifetime Achievement Award
Is a new muzzle given in name of Bodega & Deli

STOP BUZZING AROUND

Stop buzzing around in a horn-peeping frenzy
                                        cover your nose
The dump is burning its love letters on your tongue
The mosquitoes are in the depths of
receiving blood transfusions from your ankles
& the sun has a big head in a little cap
                                        So ice up your boxing gloves Dakar
You are still that punching bag with slit hyena eyes &
20/20 vision in the mouth

DRINK UP ALL THE EARS

Drink up all the ears
Eat every smile
Blow off the sand
The writing on the wall says
Fuck G.W.B.
& do not brutalize yourself
It's festival time
Bring in the ideophones
The aerophones   the chordophones
The membranophones
And the ancestor artists

I'M NOT THE ONE

I'm not the one seeking controversy
I'm not asking difficult questions
I'm not saying what I say to be censored
I'm from Oyo
I'm from Whydah
I'm from Maputo   from Luanda   from Conakry
I put my belief system on top of
My enemies' system of belief
I didn't know it was my duty to count intervals
To multiply seconds
To be a violent competitive animal
Did I think of the fatalities
Did I anticipate the terribleness

CHEWING STICK

I am chewing on the end of my chewing stick
& stretching my toes
when I hear the call to prayer &
immediately recognize where
Tarzan got his yodel from

NO ONE WILL BELIEVE

No one will believe
how much cement
is packed in my nostrils
or how much petrol
is mixed in my blood
and when I sit along the highway
organizing animal cries into
musical themes
no one will understand
that in the presence of
everything low down & violent
I just need
to find myself a man
and rock

I CLOSE MY TRUNK

I close my trunk
I bag my water
I sell my books
I pack my rug
& with brakes
Windows
I Peugeot

I carry my bed
I pound my rice
I check my battery
I activate my gadgets
screeching
rattling
I Renault

I Mercedes Benz
& arrive like a funnel
of orange dust in
the scrap iron jungle

& THERE YOU ARE

Monday hissing like Sunday
& Tuesday belching like a sheep
resting in shadow of a mule
while waiting for Tabaski
& there you are
untangling shoelaces from invisible shoes
walking the docks like a seagull
& acting like that melancholy goat
on the way to being goat cheese

SALSA GERTE

Salsa Yassa   Salsa Kanjia
Salsa Niebe   Salsa Picante
Salsa   Salsa
Salsa Che   Salsa Fidel   Salsa Cabral   Salsa Neto
Salsa   Salsa
& I know that you know
that today is the day
to magnify that salsa
to pop it up
& come out of the Sud Foire shadows swinging
You know
I petrol   I keynote
& in the red eyes of the harmattan I ask you now
Do you like my Salsa
Looka here
I know that you know that I know
collective participation when I see it in
Salsa Che   Salsa Cabral   Salsa Fidel   Salsa Neto
& I know that you know
that today is the day
to put those blunt monumental words in orbit
Looka here
My tongue may be a cell phone
My heart may be honky tonk
but where were you when the
sun became a golden pig
I mean you are not your sweet-smelling self this morning
I fresh fish
I first flight
I front-line my Black Art Salsa through the night
& I know that you know that I know
Salsa Yassa   Salsa Kanjia   Salsa Niebe
Salsa Picante   Salsa Gerte   Salsa Salsa

LITTLE BROTHER

Dakar 5/2006

Little Brother
if you follow the image
which you have of yourself
the self-made image of you
being greeted with open arms
in some place
other than your place of origin
look again Little Brother
because there are people
people just like you
people who will not be enthusiastic about your arrival
people who will put you in chains
and march you off
to your detention center home away from home
with no visas no return ticket & all borders closed
it's a location on top of dislocation if you survive
but why put your hope
on a ship that can sink
in the middle of the sea
why be among the skeletons discovered in
boats lost and drifting to hostile shores
Educate your thinking Little Brother
The meaning of life is not found in
how many gadgets you buy and sell
or how much anger you feel when
others have and you have not
it is only when you realize
you can have-not anywhere in the world
that you may get a return shot at life
so unbutton your eyelids
loosen your shoe strings
reach into your deeper levels
and fight for the right
to have rights
where you are Little Brother where you are

CREVICE OF BURNT HAIR

I tell you
Someone is entering with
a bundle of corrugated iron
but will all the brass instruments get together
in the reformatory of that navel to revolt and
vocalize more music than attitude
more voltage than calculations
          I don't know
Time is held together by solitude of
The Soledad Brothers
By salty pouting lips of Dixie Hummingbirds
By hooting love calls of cockeyed owls
& everything is on the comeback trail
everything surging forward with
sewage from rebellious miners
foam from extended debates
unofficial birthmarks
& ritual flags in a crevice of burnt hair

I REMEMBER DOMINGO

Domingo would not allow a damaged water-main
                                        to break his spirit
He would carry the Kwanza River
in buckets on his shoulders
Put some of the Congo basin
                                in tubs on his head
Bend his torso into
                        an Umbundu way of being
Deposit the water
            & let his surging eyes pop like
Two live wires in the rain

I SEE

for Souleymane Keïta

I see images looking at you through
Eyes of a horse
Through chicken feathers in the yard and
Cat-tails on the roof
But always in the circular breathing of the canvas
There's an internal hint of the marvelous

STUDIO STEEL LIFE

for Melvin Edwards

Count the metal chips embedded in my palms
I look for rail spikes like dinosaur hunters look for vertebrae
Check out the confluence of flint marks as
                                                I strike one point
I can't keep my eyes off of dumpsters
I'm in the steel life dreaming

PIANO

This instrument used to
concentrate mainly on itself
& was inflexible before
getting scratched up & sanctified in
church settings
This upright & grand citizen also
used to sit
wide-legged between opera singers before
turning ivory teeth into a synthesizer
in club 88
This player from the rainforest
monochromatic, plutonic, strident,
possessive, percussive &
wiry with pedals of anticipation
will eat ten fingers every two minutes
change running directions on the half-hour
tune up sound boards daily
& still be melodically combative, harmonically rebellious,
impulsive & a stone killer of elbows

BATA

I want to stroll on the dance floor
slither and scissor and push
through that slow motion row
of rolling buttocks
to sniff the animal in you   Bata
You are the revelator
the vodun temple
the wild aggressive orchestra
in the aguardiente
& I swallow your exhaust fumes
I talk that djali djali talk
to provoke anticipation
& to shake like a frenetic machete
before twirling all up in the jet stream
to cut the cane with you   Bata
you are the humidity
the pan yard
the punctuating panther
the purifier of pure friction
bring in the orishas
send for abakwa
I'm striking iron on iron with you   Bata
Go ahead
blow hot breath on my neck

THE BANANA

When mercenaries from England
arrived on a mission to steal gold
from Mashona land in Southern Africa
the banana was already known as
a black red yellow green delight
and heavyweight contender
in the grief of banana workers
                    from Latin America
The banana booming with potassium
highly valued in group therapy sessions
a favorite in gymnastics classes
& the famous crown on hips of quivering
shake dancers in Paris
                              cannot be
a superstar like watermelon
or a trickster in the ticker like pomegranate
nevertheless
this important backup singer
has a method for maintaining power
and needs no special introduction

ONIONS

She can never be a spirit medium
because she is obsessed with onions
& onions are full of folklore &
liberation tears
& have no concept of time
no division of labor
they control lightning

THAT CARROT

That carrot
belonging to Brer Rabbit
snatched by Bugs Bunny
then stolen by Bugsy Halliburton
                & given as
"The Heroic Wartime Achievement Award"
to corporate officers for service
in the oil fields of Iraq
                now spends
most of its time as
a genetically modified impersonator
impersonating a real carrot
& struggling to keep its color while
fighting to win a popularity contest among
auditors, contractors, farmers & other expert embalmers

OKRA

In that frenzied period
just before entering into
the center of possession
Okra has sex with itself
& even though
most people refer to its potent slime as snot
this infiltrator &
inventor of secret paths
this passionate vibrato singer
& producer of the great soup kanjia
is still celebrated as
the main connector between visible
& invisible forces

CHEESE

In the process
of the process of the process
Cheese
with no bones
& no ancestors
escaped from a monastery
became a leisure-class citizen in northern retreats
a great hit at wine-tasting festivals
& life of the party
in New York, Paris &
San Francisco art world promo events
This milky evangelist
known as the original meltdown
is now
the wildest growing infection
in the Western Hemisphere

BROCCOLI

There's no nostril confluence in the garden
No oversize tooth cap passing salt
No hiccupping barracuda talking about the weather
So take care
Shut the door
Deliver your butt of broccoli to the cleaners
& remember wailing is illegal in Brazil

LETTUCE

Lettuce
was a leaf
looking for a job

in the intestinal tract
of an on-again off-again fundraiser

It was the cut flower of hesitation
the exile on strike in the emporium
the imperialistic trail of garbage
shining through cannibalistic heads
of the royals from Europe

Fantastic this eunuch
documenting its green arrival
on creamy tongue of a peacock in
                    VIP lounge
of lucrative war-faring flimflam
Incredible how this stranger
with the thin voice & indifferent smell
became a great minstrel
& one of the most important economic advisors
on stage of the twentieth century

FLIES

Green flies on green meat
Yellow flies in yellow mangos
Brown flies sipping Gazelle beer
Red flies on heads of young men alive but
dead in ditches of their unemployment

SHEEP

slit throat
mouth closed
head in blood
then it's wild sheep ribs mixed with cabbage & vinegar
fried sheep shoulders with mint leaves & green peppers

sheep odors stewing in oil & onions
the taste of trembling sheep kidneys on rice
memories steaming with sheep voices boiling in water
sheep hooves stomping in stomachs
sheep legs jumping from trucks
sheep eyes staring before the kill
dreams steeped in sheep shit
streets littered with dry sheep skin

BIG FISH

Let the whales go on wailing against
Anti-wailing establishments
Let the blue whale population wail with
Sophisticated frog-fish
Let night activate its stinging discharge
Let the hammerhead sharks regurgitate

THE LION

The lion looked at its supper
& said
I'm going to eat the stripes off your body
I'm going to chew from your ass to your lips

THE MOON

The moon watched the sun beating its meat
in darkroom of the eclipse café
& came out smiling

THE GROUNDHOG

The groundhog
dived into a hole
after seeing its shadow dressed in grease
& ready for roasting
under a clear sky of collective efforts

THE ANTEATER

The anteater
saw itself in the mirror
& consumed fifty billion termites in one slurp

THE TIGER

the tiger expresses its tigritude
every time it pisses, roars
& takes a big bite

APPEARANCE

I did not prepare notes for this appearance
select poems to read
travel halfway across the country
to give some M.F.
a chance to treat me like I don't exist
like truth is a set of rules & regulations
smiling & saying no visa today

B.A.T.

Why is tobacco so important if
smoking is bad for your health

TRAVEL

I no longer have ears to
                                        hear the sun
            unbuckling its seat belt
my eyes have been arrested by
the clear victory of impure air

DIALOGUE ON VIOLENCE

Violence   Violence   Violence
The violence that's living in us is so deep
This human violence
This structural violence
This behavioral violence
This sexual violence
This official and unofficial violence
This police violence
This clergy violence
This family violence
This economic violence
This global violence
This military violence
This psychological violence
This personal violence
This gang violence
And rape
The pure form of violence
The birth of violence
Is the violence of birth
Leave it there   leave it there
The violence within is deep so deep
Don't tell anybody   don't tell anybody

It's that direct   indirect
Productive   reproductive
Amateur   anonymous
Insidious   political
Pent-up   legitimate
Invisible   judicial   collective
Imperialist   automatic
Drunk   static   viral
Electoral   capitalist   atomic
Cult kind of violence
That violence will sink your soul

Will sink your soul
& it's violence and forced prostitution
Violence & sexual services
Violence & hypocrisy
& violence & bourgeois democracy
Violence & technology
& violence & vocabulary
Violence & privilege
& violence & power

depression   repression   suppression   oppression
depression   repression   suppression   oppression
depression   repression   suppression   oppression

leave it there   leave it there

It's the victim & the victimizer
The victim & the victimizer
The sacrifice & the one who sacrifices
The sacrifice & the one who sacrifices
Don't tell anybody
Don't tell anybody

interrogation   interrogation
intolerance   intolerance
deprivation   deprivation
complicity   complicity
torture   torture
domination   domination   domination

Pain
Leave no traces
Avoid the pain   leave no traces
Pain grief & fear & blood & Pain
Leave no traces
The violence inside of us is deep   so deep
Give it up if you don't really want it
Give it up if you don't really want it
It's violence & love

And violence & ideology
And violence & discrimination
And violence & religion
And violence & art & violence & hate
And violence & ignorance
And violence & racism
And violence & monopoly
And violence & poverty
And violence & hunger
And violence & resentment
And that vomiting reactionary violence
Corporate violence
Industrial violence
Urban violence   rural violence
Ethnic violence
Pharmaceutical violence
The violence of AIDS   drugs & terrorism
Put a muzzle on violence
That rough violence   that brittle violence
That blinded violence   that trusted violence
That wet violence   that cold violence
That hidden violence   that funny violence
That blunt violence
That obsolete violence   that absolute violence
That provocative violence   that preventive violence
That ripe violence   that irrelevant violence
That protective violence   that safe violence
That nasty violence   that clean violence
That bleak violence   that empty violence
That competitive violence   that modern violence
That traditional violence that violence for the sake of violence
That necessary & unnecessary violence   let the violence be known
Give it up if you don't really want it
Give it up if you don't really want it

ON THE IMPERIAL HIGHWAY:

NEW & SELECTED POEMS

(2009)

TOMATO

The tomato
emulates itself
& takes up citizenship
in the garden where
death accepts death

AVOCADO

An avocado seed
sits on
a mound of fish bones
& discovers modern art

KOLA NUT

The kola nut
gets high
on its own bitterness

EGGPLANT

An eggplant cannot really be
what it is said to be
because it is not a capital city in
the great peninsula of palm oil

ON THE JOB IN 2000

A new century
& even the Pope
out of ideas
hungry for publicity
gets into the act
by saying
I bought me some big lips
frizzled up these few strands of hair
tilted my beanie
& now I got the blues

INTEGRATION

I knew the Father
the Son   the Holy Ghost
Ave Maria   Hail Mary
Dalai Lama   Mother Teresa   the Virgin of Guadalupe
Father Divine   Brother Moses
Daddy Grace   Sister Ruth   Queen Mother Brown
Jimmy Swaggart   Aimee McPherson
Rev. Wright   Rev. Moon
Mr. Judas   Mr. Buddha
Mr. Muhammad   Queen Elizabeth   & the Pope
We all went to Gompers Junior High School

BALLROOM AUDUBON

Ballroom Audubon
that's me
I don't have to sit still
I don't have to wait for corroboration
my tables are blessed
with the exaggerated teeth marks of
players & dancers
circling & swinging chairs
in search of spiritual intervention
& yes I have dust from a million encounters
my walls have tobacco stains, green reefer grime
black cherry lipstick smears
nut brown face powder sweat
royal crown hair pomade dots, coco chanel toilet water splashes
& little specks of smack
that's a fact
why not
the secrets in this world
belong to me
I'm the delivery room for new organizations
& the cancellation hall for irrelevant ideologies
listen up
if the Solomon Islands
are being swallowed by the ocean
people from there will just have to
come on home to Harlem
& I'll be waiting in uptown Manhattan
with my cultural lifeline
my primary school for psychological headaches
& my emergency exit for flirting lovers &
violent showdowns
Yes, yes
I party with all parties
chant with all chanters
concert with all concert goers and

collaborate with famous faith healers
funeral directors newscasters beauticians preachers
& political activists
check it out
I'm listed in the dictionary of who's who
and I have spots made by ingredients
of every cleanser known in the universe
can you believe it
I carry fingerprints of each person
that ever touched this microphone
& my floorboards are matted with split reeds
sealed with the strong-smelling resin of
grieving widows
embedded with
shouts & screams &
the scrambling footsteps of an audience
betrayed by someone
we once called beloved
you hear what I'm saying
it was a nasty fonky day
a day dominated by
self-hatred & the misplaced loyalty of
negro killer convicts
sent on a suicide mission
to blow holes through
the X of my Malcolm
& now
frozen in that blood
I am Ballroom Audubon
sweet-smelling birthplace of a martyr

SHORT POEM/LONG STORY

Without négritude
there would be
no métissage

COUP

If your coup
don't come through
then exile
with a smile

HISTORY

Dear Friends
I am not talking about
the black writer and
his white literary father
i'm talking about
black music opposed to
enslavement & colonialism
yes jazz has a color
without that fact
there is no jazz

DEFINITIONS

Democracy is a word
made up by
dispossessed porcupines
in the rectum of another word
called modernity
that's why
when it comes to puffing cigarettes
the masses are uncontrollable

What you think can put you in jail
  what you say may be used against you
   whatever you do to protect yourself will be
    seen as a strike against the patriot act which
     will strike you down for being patriotic to yourself

TELL IT TO ME

Notes in Ethiopia

Is the Blue Nile blue enough
is Lake Tana fully tainted
are you draped in long white cloth
to beat drums in dampness of
this monastery because
you are the monk
with a Thelonious Monk face
acting impassive & in solitude
as guardian of a building where you stand in doorways
rocking & gonging to announce another sunset
are you the rainbow specialist in this rainforest of
mummies & candles
is that you lying on stone protrusions
humming like a hive of frantic bees then
stepping on toes in border feuds
can this be you
traveling in dryness of a climate change
no longer nomadic enough to be nomadic
but just superstitious enough to be
supernaturally religious
& how many times will you ask me
to take off my shoes before entering into
the swollen military eyes of your frescos
& how fanatical should I be to reach
the fossilized remains of Lucy
are you the make-believe moon in
my horn of Africa marking time while
saying to your fingers "I'm a monk"

tell it to me Ethiopia
because
I am that woman
walking up hills
with stacks of wood on shoulders
the women picking splinters from hands

& pressing cheeks against church walls
asking for another kind of existence
that's me
sucking on stones
whispering to saints
& riding burros down mountainous roads while
living & aging & carrying spirits of dementia to
millennium sunday celebrations
in hooray of the plaza for
long-distance runners
          So tell it to me again
because everybody is singing & saying
something about Queen of Sheba
metal crosses of Axum
Ark of the Covenant
plateau of doves
parade of obelisks
bare feet on rough surfaces
airplane turning around in mid-flight
but what is the turn around motion
in the lord have mercy on my soul in Gondar
where you sit
on edge
of my imagination
shouting that
you are Lalibela too
a city which you stuff in my nose
a stone quarry of churches
invented indented
& inverted by rebellious angels
which you stamp on my forehead
and when I step into
precipitation of your chipped cavity
& scratch on your concrete incisions
looking for spiritual revolts
I feel your volcanic activity
I smell your uprooted debris
I bury my words
deep inside your trench of red lava

for I am in the romance of this collaboration
without experimentations
without scientific explanations
without being in a state of possession
& I know that you are
owner of the dust to dust
leader of the time after time
& tongue of the stand-by-me cries of civilizations
so tell it to me again
because I have put everything on hold to
write my name
on rear end of the donkey
but that ass
already branded with a cross
is praying
"please make me invisible to humans"

DISASTER

A hundred rebels stinking together
in ethnic rage
religious fanaticism
xenophobic meanness
    high on bloods
    & crips
    & renamo
    & the ghost of Mobutu
    Janjaweed
    the lord's resistance army
    & the spirit of Tshombe
    showing up with the face of Morgan
                    in Zimbabwe
Now
South African township lyrics turning nasty
                brother man
                thug angel
                warlord
                schoolboy
                with pack on back
becoming unemployed youth
with hammer, machete & stick
rampaging and
acting independently vicious
economically desperate
politically unproductive
spinning out of control
flooding erupting
& becoming
a natural disaster

IN THE CROSSWALK

Me
I'm just a pedestrian in the crosswalk
& I can't have a nice day in the dioxin
I can't have a great night in the radon
I can't have a fantastic time
listening to voice of a born-again warlord urging folks to
blast nations off the globe
& bang flesh into chemicals

I'm not thrilled by scenes of human destruction
I'm not fascinated by weapons of mass devastation
I'm not in a blow-up-the-planet cult
& ready to ride shrapnel into zero gravity of space

I'm just a pedestrian in the crosswalk

I may not be able to outrun a cheetah
or protect myself against a grizzly bear without hard-
ware
But I can use my brain to explain
why being lifted into a future of unlimited promise by
sixty billion tons of TNT is not for me even though
I'm just a pedestrian in the crosswalk
yes just a pedestrian in the crosswalk

STATES OF MOTION 2

The Afro beat man strutted into himself
with a fabulous shrine of
          musical instruments on his head
& the palm wine drinkard danced
into the bush of ghosts with
feather woman of the jungle
while the journalist from Chelsea
entered his time capsule
& the great poet from Chicago
put her latest poem between her lips
          and climbed into her baobab tree
& a playwright who departed Congo-Brazzaville
left in a theatre made of whirlwinds
a rare book dealer buried in cigarette butts & ashes
became the first university place bookshop ghost to
          inhabit the NYU Library
Bob Rogers the great Afro-American designer returned to the sky
                                        as a shining star when
he lifted off the planet in his total tote bag made of red canvas &
                                  royal blue cotton from Oaxaca
& when Horace Tapscott heard Taps
he rode his piano through the aftermath
& when Carmencita Romero became a moving light leaping into
the tropical evening on board a luxury liner headed for Japan
Pancho Mora Sr. was seen traveling back & forth on a boat made
          of wild roses
& as Lynell Hemphill stood in the exit looking for Julius who had already
crossed the ocean to join a bogolan collective in Segu
Tom Feelings was spotted in
          the middle passage of his drawings
& Mas Tandine was called upon to create
architecture for an invisible town in Senegal
Francisco Romão de Oliveira e Silva
rejuvenated himself & orchestrated his return to Luanda
then Emilio Cruz ambled from the wilderness with

a magnificent series of paintings and manuscripts
Al Loving wrapped his body in one hundred painted canvas strips &
set off for the egungun festival
John Hicks packed up his piano keys and
took the greyhound bus back to St. Louis
Hilton Ruiz entered the other world like a newborn baby
Alberto Chissano left Maputo wearing
a mask painted with a face resembling Amos Milburn
Leon Golub made his last call at 12 a.m.
Rudolph Baranik stepped out to investigate
the full moon in Pluto
Alice Coltrane hurried off to reminisce with
John about ascensions
Jackie McLean stored his saxophone in the
sanctuary and went to watch the sunrise in Harlem
Bodie sent for Raymond
& after blowing reefer smoke on
the secret poetry society of America
Pedro Pietri put on his applejack cap
& tuxedo t-shirt
then sailed off in an antique telephone booth
to have an extended conversation
with himself in tuxedo junction
& the television journalist from New York
the storyteller from Dakar
the Filipino artist from New Jersey
the pearl diver from Manila
the sergeant from Arkansas
the motorcyclist from Compton
the blues singer from Mississippi
the novelist from lower Eastsida
the children from Casamance
the elders in the storm of Katrina
the tenor player from Memphis
the alto player from Brooklyn
the sculptor from Louisiana
the Trinidadian organizer from London
the clarinetist from Baton Rouge
the poet from Houston

the gambler from Los Angeles
the swimming aunt from San Diego
the duo from Alexandria
& the famous actor from North Carolina
all waited in the forest for Billy Higgins & other drummers to arrive
with conga player Tata Güines of Cuba
meanwhile June Jordan marched away and returned like
a good little soldier in June
Andrew Hill left the crowd to cast a spell on the hilltop
Leroy Jenkins buried his violin at the end of a roadless road
& disappeared
Barbara Ann Teer sent her spirit back to Nigeria
Nellie Lutcher went through the mist looking for Sid Catlett
Judy Simmons locked herself in Club Alabam to concentrate on poetry
Vincent Smith paddled away in a canoe full of art supplies
Dakota left her voice on Broadway
Charles "Diddy" Moffett the optimistic teacher with the legendary smile
shoved off for the banana pudding festival
Benny Andrews pushed his work to significance then
boarded the afternoon train to Georgia
Octavia Butler became a science fiction teacher on Jupiter
Ousmane Sembene taped his battle scars to his camera
put on his everyday cap   puffed on his pipe   & took his cinematic self
into the other world market as
St. Clair Bourne made his entrance in a new documentary
Sekou went searching for Sundiata
Eleo danced his way back to Colombia
Max Roach crossed meters, kept time & m'boomed until
Aimé Césaire carried his volcano of flint & mug of revolt
into the negritude complex
then everyone came from all directions
going to Texas   going to Tulsa   coming from Havana
staying in Toronto   never leaving Benin City
flying south to singsong with song birds
going west to peacock with peacocks
whistling to each other
& enjoying transformation with
a pantheon of bass players
at the gin libation parties

WHAT A MOUTHFULL

Tradition
Emotion
Flamboyant gas leaks
Volcanic fumes
Geography
Landfills
Refuse
Dry spell
& Saint Archaeology
It's you
with that bandit cyclone
actively
dissing the sun
for drinking too much
insecticide
Importation
Invasion
the climaxing battlefield
beneath the earth where
the origin of language
sinks back into
afterbirth
And now visions are batons
dreams are diviners
implications are sunspots
The sky is a toaster
& my dear
you are not the transformer
not the generator
not the transmission
not the axle
You are the copy machine
& at the moment
Mr. & Ms. Photostat
life is saying

let's have a riot in the reproduction room
and on the way to the drunk tank
let's fall on our teeth   then meet again
behind mirror on the ceiling of the navel of a new star
and innovate
let's strum in like banjos & koras
& shine like dark rum bottles in bolero jackets
let's return from the other world of saturated tools &
celebrate
like clamoring marimbas
like hallucinating xylophones
& balaphonic gourds
Oh what a mouthfull of
transparent fisheries & inflamed forests
manifestations & manifestos
mutations & erosions
metaphors & validations
Oh what a mouthfull
what a mouthfull

I WAS DREAMING

I was dreaming when I heard a pigeon saying:
If I told you I flew to the moon
I flew to the moon
now I'm back and energized
but I don't eat leftover crumbs anymore
& if I keep watching you chew
I may lose my shadow
Of course I wear my own feathers
and will not disguise my vocals each morning when I perch on your
                    window sill repeating my cru cru call
no matter how many times you hit the glass
or how much vinegar you try pouring on my face
I talk the talk of a pigeon
I crap on umbrellas in the rain before umbrella ladies
          start their violent umbrella attacks
I smell like a pigeon   I walk like a pigeon
I don't have to have an imagination
I know how to hold my head high
                    bend my neck low
          spread my wings and fly
but if I had to be like you
& sing "summer time" every time I opened my mouth to sing
          I'd go crazy
However I'm not in the mood to adjust your blood pressure
so I'm going to sit on my favorite limb and let the sun honk while i
                                                  coo coo coo coo coo

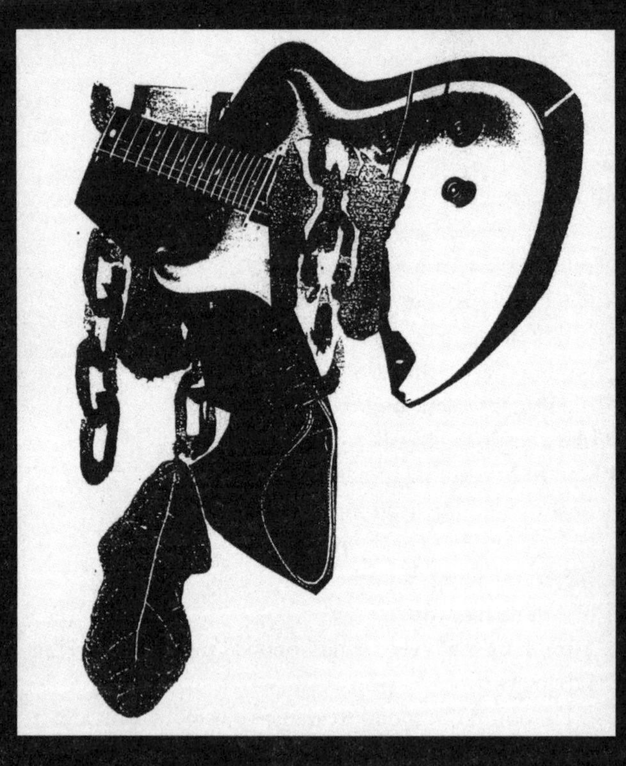

IRON RATTLES & PAPER MONEY IN THE FUTURE OF THE PAST

THE STRUGGLE CONTINUES/ALUTA CONTINUA

The Second John LaRose Memorial Lecture,
Leeds Met University, Leeds UK

The Changing Nature of Black Cultural Politics 1960–2010
With a Focus on the USA
April 2, 2011

The black struggle for freedom and justice in America
started on the shores of Africa
traveled to the Western world on slave ships during
the international development of the globalization of trade through
the Triangular (Europe, Africa, & the Americas)
Transatlantic slave trade
which lasted approximately 400 years
from the late 1400s to the 1800s

On those West & Central African shores
"cultures were thrown together"
Pan-Africanism developed
& was internalized after encounters with
the oppressive collective from Portugal, Spain, England, France,
The Netherlands, Norway, Denmark and North America
This was a Pan-African/Pan-European encounter

It is widely recognized that slavery was common in Africa
and in other places in the world including
China, India, Southern Asia & the Islamic World
(the development of the Trans-Saharan Slave Trade)

Through local warfare, kidnapping, factionalism, trade
and manipulation of systems
African men, women & children were captured, enslaved,
held captive in prisons, traded or sold in local slave markets
and exported or retained in Africa.
Some who were to be exported
marched long distances toward slave ships that

came from places like Bristol, Liverpool, Lisbon, Rotterdam,
Bordeaux, Barcelona, Boston, etc.
Some survived & were shipped to markets in Brazil and the Spanish Indies etc.
Others were assembled, shackled & held captive in holding area dungeons including:
mouth of the river in Gambia, Elmina Castle in Cape Coast, Ghana
the slave house on Goree Island, Senegal, the Shimoni slave caves of Kenya
the slave markets of Zanzibar, Angola & the Mpunbu market in Northern Kongo
Some Africans on the way to the ships escaped and
established Maroon communities
some broke through languages
and overcame differences of origin
to create new cultures and
to organize and plan Pan-African struggles for freedom
Many captives died while fighting to stay in Africa
many died on the long march to the ships
or in the holding areas
many resisted
"using all means & possibilities at their disposal
including suicide"
the death rate on the slave ships
during the Atlantic Crossing
also known as the Middle Passage
was 15 to 18 percent
Europeans used white supremacy ideology as
a racial tool for the creation of wealth which
could be obtained from exporting slaves & having
a permanent unpaid labor force
The Transatlantic Slave Trade resulted in
the forced removal of millions of people from Africa
"The looting of African resources destroyed families and communities
& caused instability & the future underdevelopment of Africa"
As Doudou Diène of the UNESCO Slave Routes project stated:
The slave trafficking would not have lasted as long as it did
without an ideology of moral justification, legal structures & profit.
The ideology which rationalized
the sale of human beings as merchandise was
the intellectual argument of racial superiority

and the cultural denigration of black people and of Africa.
Whites steeped in racist propaganda
found it impossible to give up a source of profits & domination.
The transatlantic slave trade has now disappeared
but the racism that underpinned it
is still wreaking havoc

The encounters between Africans,
Amerindians, & European culture
produced new modifications in religion, language, & artistic production.
Some Africans had absorbed Islam before becoming involuntary
immigrants
& a number of the enslaved from Central Africa had been baptized
& were already familiar with Christianity.

"African slaves stood up to the violence of the slave trade
armed with the living force of their cultures and their gods"
They rebelled on the prison ships all the way to the "new world"
and in spite of forced separations
the cultural heritage of Africa survived
& that inheritance consisted of
not only the pre-history of Africa & African blood
but the inheriting of culture or traditions
transmitted from previous generations including:
fragments from African kingdoms
African political structures
customs, knowledge, wisdom, spiritual values,
attitudes, gestures, languages, dialects, technology, sentiments,
religious and artistic forms of expression,
the circulation of stories, proverbs, riddles,
systems of beliefs and symbols,
architecture, drum rhythms, musical instruments, & ethnic conflicts
And because culture is a flexible ongoing system
everything can change as they have always been changing
& evolving through invention, discovery or borrowing from the outside
So now everywhere drums, cell phones & computers

Africans reduced to slavery and
transported in large numbers to other continents

by means of the organized Transatlantic slave trade
brought to the "new world" thousands of years of skills & experiences
It was their labor laying the foundations for development in
the Amerindian territories that became the United States of America.
From the 1600s on
there were black rebellions   armed uprisings
attacks on plantations
black resistance against repressive laws
& black runaways (individuals who fled to their Indian allies & Canada).
In the Seminole Wars in Florida
the Indians and their black allies fought against
the federal military forces for several years,
and when the Indians were finally defeated
and forced to leave their "ancient burial grounds
hundreds of black people went with them".
In the 1800s the struggle for freedom
was led by leaders such as Frederick Douglass who said
"if there is no struggle there is no progress,"
& by people like Harriet Tubman who led hundreds of people to freedom.
In 1825 the message of freedom was a voice in the head of Nat Turner
& resonated in the ideas & actions of John Brown & in speeches of Abraham
  Lincoln
The struggle continued in American cotton fields,
tobacco fields, sugar cane fields,
on plantations, in courts of law
& through the Underground Railroad going north.

In spite of colonialism, neo-colonialism, industrialism,
racism, black codes, & Jim Crow
the black struggle for freedom expanded
Struggles against oppression appeared in
various forms of resistance
including   insurrections   riots   rebellions
verbal protests   appeals   arson   the abolitionist movement
emancipation   reconstruction   disobedience
demonstrations against lynching
against the ku klux klan & segregation
Messages of freedom and resistance
were embedded in slave narratives   Negro spirituals

work songs street cries & in Afro-American and Afro-Caribbean folklore.
The assaults by missionaries against traditional African religious beliefs
were futile;
the missionaries did not realize
how deep those beliefs were entrenched in the lives of the people
and how "African religions like everything else
had been changing even before the slave trade"
& people could adopt adjust & accommodate foreign elements without
compromising their identity.
Acts of resistance materialized through
religious rituals and symbols.
Enslaved people of the Kongo & of Yoruba & Fon cultures of Nigeria &
Dahomey
produced significant religious systems in Brazil, Cuba & Haiti.
For example, African deities were transplanted
and camouflaged inside Christian saints in Haiti
and those cultural practices were carried into the USA through
places like New Orleans with the 1804 Haitian revolution
which linked together liberation from slavery &
the winning of political independence.

Even through black men fought in the
American Revolution and in the Civil War
and even though the Emancipation Proclamation
ending slavery in the United States was January 1, 1863
the struggle for black freedom continued.
As the struggle went forward into the 20th century
messages of freedom and resistance were to be found
during world wars
and during the American Depression & in
the Sharecroppers Union the Southern tenants Farmers Union
The black migration movement from the South to the North
In activities of Booker T. Washington & George W. Carver
& the return to Africa movement with Marcus Garvey &
the Universal Negro Improvement Association.

Messages of freedom were found in
The Souls of Black Folks by W.E.B. DuBois;
the Pan-African Conferences with

W.E.B. DuBois   George Padmore   Kwame Nkrumah etc.
the Negro Renaissance & Negritude literary movements
the revolutionary theories by C.L.R. James
the organizing of   A. Philip Randolph
& in the work of Ida Wells-Barnett
& the Scottsboro Affair
& the call for self-reliance
the call for African independence
The Organization of African Unity
the Mau Mau rebellions in Kenya
in statements by Jomo Kenyatta
the NAACP   the Urban League
sermons of Adam Clayton Powell
in comments of Elijah Muhammad & the Nation of Islam
In the Algerian revolution against colonial rule
the actions of Rosa Parks & Martin Luther King
& the Montgomery bus boycott
the movement of student activists in
CORE   SNCC   SCLC
the Civil Rights movement
Fannie Lou Hamer & the Mississippi Freedom Democratic Party
RAM - Revolutionary Action Movement - & Robert F. Williams
the Deacons for Defense and Justice
the calls for black solidarity
the Black Power and Black Arts movements
the Black Panthers
black conferences
black liberation
black rebellions
black prison revolts
black resistance against police brutality & chain gangs
the reaffirmation of blackness & freedom through
visual art, black music and black culture
& in the actions of Muhammad Ali
& the movement against the draft
protests against imperialism & the Vietnam war

Individuals
groups & events that had an impact on

activists in the black freedom struggle for human rights include:
the Russian Revolution
the world wars
US intervention in Cuba, Puerto Rico, Panama, & the Philippines
the war against Fascism
the invasion of Ethiopia by Italy
internment of Japanese Americans
the atomic bomb dropped on Japan
the Holocaust & concentration camps in Germany
the Chinese revolution led by Mao Tse-tung
Mahatma Gandhi
the Korean war
Fidel Castro the Cuban revolution & socialism,
the rise & demise of Patrice Lumumba
The Bay of Pigs The Cuban Missile crisis
US intervention in the Dominican Republic
the lynching of Emmett Till
the Bandung Conference
Ho Chi Minh
the reflections of Frantz Fanon in *The Wretched of the Earth*
Capitalism by Karl Marx
Kwame Nkrumah's book *Class Struggle in Africa*
The activism & assassination of Che Guevara

In the 1960s
it was the rise of the non-violent Southern Civil Rights movement
with the sit-ins freedom rides freedom schools
voter registration projects mass meetings
the jailing and killing of civil rights workers
the bombing of black churches &
activists singing freedom songs while packed in prison cells.
It was the moment when fear of white terror
started to diminish in the heads of black people who were
becoming more militant more vocal
more aware of their own history
    more in control of their own image and destiny.
It was the time of protest marches, rallies
& the great march on Washington
    The struggle in the 1960s was called "the black revolt" &

“The Negro Revolution”
The situation carried different interpretations and
different schools of thought

In 1963, President John F. Kennedy was assassinated.
In 1965, Malcolm X
who had tied the black struggle in the United States to
the revolutionary struggles for self-determination in the Third World was assassinated.
In 1968, it was the assassination of Martin Luther King after his
endorsement of labor union strikes
his statements about draft resistance
about American imperialism and racism in Vietnam
and his campaign to help break the process of poverty
The night of King’s death we saw a display of
American military power
on the ground and in the skies

In 1964, movement activists tried connecting
the struggles in the South
to the struggles of the black community in the North in an effort to
push the movement forward
& move beyond
“the issues of public accommodations, voter registration,
token integration, and the voting rights bill”.
1964 was a turning point
& the Southern mass movement which was
the cement that held so many people in solidarity
started to fade.
However, another phase of the struggle was around the corner.

The 1960s exploded with talk of revolutionary possibilities
and erupted with *The Fire Next Time* as black people
still oppressed by injustice, inequalities and isolation
became more frustrated.
For example: the Watts Rebellion in Los Angeles, California.
The Watts Rebellion pointed out the need for
social, economic and political change.
On August 11, 1965

some members in a Los Angeles community
near the district known as Watts
responded to a police incident that involved
a black family in confrontation with
a white highways patrol officer
The officer did not understand
the dialect and gestures of that family even though
the family understood him & they spoke the same language.
It was a cultural clash that led to
a confrontation which escalated;
a crowd gathered, the police gathered
and later all hell broke loose & became
the Watts Rebellion that lasted for six days,
ending on August 17th
Thousands of Black people took to the streets.
Automobiles were overturned
bricks, rocks, and gasoline in bottles from
the Utopia liquor stores were thrown.
Black people attacked police, firemen, & white stores
Buildings burned, stores were looted and gutted
& the rebellion spread to adjoining areas in Los Angeles.
Some suburban citizens called the uprising "senseless fury"
others called it
kicking the door open for equality of opportunity in
employment   education   better housing and healthcare
This leaderless event stunned the nation because
California was thought to have good race relations and
was known as utopia and utopia was on fire and
the fire was not the result of the annual Santa Ana winds and dryness
It was the result of racism   oppression   police brutality
lack of jobs   growing contradictions   divisions and indifference
About eight hundred buildings were destroyed or extensively damaged
many people were wounded and incarcerated
It took city and state police, national guards, and
members of the 40th armory division of about 10,000 troops to cool
    things down
There were 34 persons killed and 1,032 reported injuries, including
90 police officers, 136 firemen, 10 national guardsmen,
23 persons from other governmental agencies and 773 civilians.

118 of the injuries resulted from gunshot wounds.
Of the 34 killed, one was a fireman,
one a deputy sheriff, and one a policeman
514 juveniles were arrested & 1,232 adults arrested.
It was a sobering moment
a moment when people looked at
the conditions and realities behind the camouflage of
the "democratic way of life".
This was a moment of reflection & introspection
another transformative moment
and as the rebellion spread
hitting other cities in America,
cities like Omaha, Nebraska, Cleveland, Ohio,
Tampa, Florida, Buffalo, New York, Milwaukee, Wisconsin,
Chicago, Illinois, Newark, New Jersey, Detroit, Michigan etc.
It became clear that this phase of the struggle would be a catalyst for
heightening awareness & changing some conditions, but
would not end oppression, inequalities, racism and capitalism.
This phase also exposed black leaders & others who
condemned the rebellions so that their
"white funding sources would not dry up"

Media coverage especially television news reports
provided people around the world with images of
the southern demonstrations   the northern rebellions
and the reactions of white Americans as they responded to
these events with anger   fear   repression
concessions   investigations   and some solidarity.

Meanwhile, many artists drew energy from the rebellions and
produced works exploring materials & ideas from the aftermath
Everybody was doing their version of what became known as
the Black Arts Movement
which was a cultural part of the general civil rights/black power movement.
The calls for revolution, unity and change could be heard in
the confrontational poetry of black poets &
in plays by militant playwrights
& in books & magazines published by black publishers

& in images of visual artists who were active in
creating strong expressive works in support of the struggle

Most of the artists of the Black Arts Movement were
inspired and influenced by Malcolm X
a revolutionary with vision, clarity, imagination, and
a positive, confident way of relaying his message.
Malcolm was giving out information
not instructing
not saying what color to put on the canvas or
what words to use in poetry or notes to play in music.
Therefore artists did not get stuck with the limitation of ideology.
The Black Arts Movement in Los Angeles was
a movement of artists who were interested in
creating works that would reflect the
beliefs, feelings, realities, aesthetics
and revolutionary traditions of African people.
That was the focus.
They were not interested in pacifying the white world or
other people who were not flexible in their thinking.
It was a breakthrough period &
some artists became more progressive in their views
more nationalistic in their looks
more courageous in their determination
more experimental in their works
& with more confidence in their concentration to
redefine their art & take it to another level.
All of these efforts would help in the founding of
Africana & Black Studies Departments and Programs in universities
& the creating of museums, alternative spaces, black art festivals
black presses & audio visual production companies.
Of course there were those artists who said:
"Don't lump me with them: I'm universal"
because they did not like what was being produced
they did not like the implications
or the thought of making art for the masses
and were very vocal about their non-participation & opposition
The Black Arts Movement was a movement of

individuals as well as organizational and
existed in cities throughout the United States.
New York City is the media center
so black arts in the east got more attention.
Some black artists of that era felt free to invent without restrictions
while others needed guidelines from people who
commented and gave limitations
but who were not themselves artists and
knew very little about literature, music & visual art.
The artists were creating works
with the intention of intensifying issues
remembering ancestors
expressing the daily lives of black people
and helping to break psychological chains of dependency on
colonial powers and imperialist structures.
A lot of the people in the Black Arts Movement
moved into universities
teaching or directing Black Study Programs.
Some of the artists involved in the Los Angeles Black Arts Movement
included musician Horace Tapscott poet Quincy Troupe &
sculptor Melvin Edwards

The arts are just a part of the weapons in life.
Art can make us see and feel reality
& help change that reality.
Art is revelation Art is hard work
Art is a part of protest social expression & communication
Art is creativity
& the 1960s was a creative time
A time of self-examination
Self-determination & transformation.
It was a time when oppressive accumulations
such as the distortion of black history & culture
& the inequalities contradictions & segregation
could no longer be tolerated.
It was a time when struggles had to be intensified & revolutionized.
A time when the oppressors who controlled everything had to be
militantly challenged on all fronts: political, economical, & cultural.

It was a time when historical distortions
and terms like Negro had to be replaced with
Black People or African Americans

There are many examples of artists before & after the '60s
who showed a relationship between art & politics
including Paul Robeson who mixed
the art of the song, theatre and politics and
whose political insights & activism
helped bridge the gap
between the radical tradition of the '30s
to the Black Arts Movement of the '60s
Poet Langston Hughes
called for resistance & worker revolution in a number of his poems
& protests could be found in the works of writers of
the Negro Renaissance including Claude McKay & Sterling Brown
Singer Harry Belafonte is in his 80s
and is still speaking out on political issues.
Calypso singer Sparrow used
global & Caribbean political commentary in his songs.
The folk singer Odetta used traditional material to tell us
what we wanted and how far we'd have to go to get it.
Billie Holiday chose to sing about lynching when she sang "Strange Fruit."
Lena Home sang a song called "Peace"
and participated in the southern civil right movement,
singing at mass meetings
In the '60s, Curtis Mayfield showed his solidarity & sang "Keep on Pushing"
& Marvin Gaye wrote & sang an anti-war song asking "What's Going
On?"
James Brown shouted "Say It Loud - I'm Black and I'm Proud!"
Areatha Franklin sang "Freedom Freedom" and R E S P E C T
while Nina Simone chose lyrics like "Mississippi Goddam,"
Abbey Lincoln and Max Roach released their
Freedom Now! We Insist! recording,
Sonny Rollins released the *Freedom Suite* album while
Miriam Makeba sang & talked about
struggle, exile & apartheid in South Africa
In the '30s & '40s, writers in the Negritude Literary movement

Aimé Césaire of Martinique Léon Damas of French Guiana and
Léopold Sengor of Senegal reflected on paper the struggles & desires of
black people
& addressed issues concerning decolonization and transformation
as did poets Nicolás Guillén of Cuba & Jacques Roumain of Haiti
& in the African-American community in the 1950s
Margaret Walker's political poem "For My People"
became very popular.
Also popular was the Harriet Tubman and
Black Worker series of paintings by Jacob Lawrence &
the drawings of Charles White
the collages of Romare Bearden
the inspirational sculpture by Elizabeth Catlett
the Afro-Cuban cultural experience in
the surreal modernism paintings of Wifredo Lam
also the murals and woodcuts of Aaron Douglass
the murals of Hale Woodruff, Charles Alston & John Biggers
who found that ideas & concepts developed in
the Mexican mural paintings of Diego Rivera
José Clemente Orozco & David Siqueiros
were developments that could be used in
the aesthetics of the African-American artistic expression.
One of the most powerful writers
in American literature
was Richard Wright who gave us *Black Boy* *Uncle Tom's Children*
& the poetry of revolt
& whose insights and activism upset some people in America
& led him into exile

In the 1960s Angolan poet Agostinho Neto
wrote poems about African liberation,
became a leader in the struggle against
Portuguese colonialism in Angola
and became its president after independence.
Neto was definitely on the revolutionary side of things
and in his poetry book *Sacred Heart*
the political and personal are inseparable
Senegalese Filmmaker Ousmane Sembène wrote novels &
produced films dealing with class, colonialism & the impact of neo-colonialism.

The struggle for liberation was expressed in
the paintings of Malangatana Ngwenya of Mozambique
& also in the illustrations of Tom Feelings & Emory Douglass in the US.
Nigerian musician Fela Kuti spoke of political corruption
Jamaican musicians Bob Marley and Peter Tosh always had
messages of freedom and resistance in their music.
Writers of the 1960s including James Baldwin &
co-founders of the Black Arts Movement: Amiri Baraka & Larry Neal were
concerned with black consciousness
black power   black images   black identity
& how to free themselves and their people from
the jaws of white domination.
The Last Poets, the Watts Prophets and
Gil Scott-Heron also spoke of conditions & resistance in their poetry
Jamaican poets Michael Smith, Linton Kwesi Johnson and Jean Binta Breeze
combined poetry & politics with reggae music.
The group Sweet Honey in the Rock
inspired by the SNCC Freedom Singers
composed songs based on African-American struggles
& "the South African freedom movement
used art as one of the tools of resistance" against apartheid.
The Rap artists of the Hip Hop generation have
the community support of young people who
have fun rhyming and dancing to rap
& there are hints of protest in some of the material.
An example would be Public Enemy.
But from most Rap artists on the charts you get
the backward   toasting of self   which is
recited in rhymes to the 4/4 beat of drum machines
A few Rappers are commercially successful
& are   good at building businesses & selling merchandise
They are successful in the use of new technology
but they are not heavy hitters in music or in poetry   or
in eliminating mediocrity & the negative promotion of gang mentality
The 1966 Dakar, Senegal Festival of Black African Arts & Cultures
displayed the historic & the colonial with the expressions of
the growing independence movement
In 1977, the second Festival of African Art & Cultures (FESTAC)
took place in Lagos, Nigeria

this festival allowed participants to see
the whole black world of arts trying to move in similar directions
& one could see & appreciate the diversity of cultures
& see the contemporary international black arts movement that
had developed since African Independence
one could also see
the potential conflicts
and the imperfections

The black freedom movement in the U.S.
became an example and inspiration for other movements
for instance
white students who had worked in the Black Southern Movement were
politicized
and became active in forming organizations such as
the Students for a Democratic Society (SDS) and the Weathermen.
Also inspired by "the black movement"
were other oppressed people who
formed movements in the United States:
Chicano, Native American, Puerto Rican, & Asian American movements
the Women's Liberation movement,
the Black Feminist movement
the Gay Liberation movement
the anti-war movement
the anti-nuclear movement
the environmental movement
the alternative health movement etc.
The black freedom movement gave them the tools
and the encouragement to move on.
It also became an example & source of inspiration
for groups struggling for human rights in other countries
So the movement to change America's direction & reality
is alive and continues to advance

African-American culture
became more prominent
with the invention of Ragtime music, which by 1900
had evolved & included transmissions from Africa
syncopation found in black spirituals, field hollers & banjo songs

“slaves provided entertainment on plantation drawing-room pianos for dancing”
Elements were synthesized by pianist-composer Scott Joplin
born in Texarkana, Texas, in 1868
Ragtime with its system of rhythmic concepts
became the first black instrumental music by African Americans in which
“instruments were not used merely as accompaniment.”
It was known as fast action music
& was often used in silent films
and was an influence in European march music
It also led the way for development of early Jazz in New Orleans
& because of its “happy optimistic sound”
Ragtime became the rage
and set the pace & tone for the so-called “JAZZ Age”
which added to America’s identity.
The music known as the Blues came from West Africa
evolved through field shouts   slave songs   & work songs
and was developed into a vocal & non-vocal music   by
African-American working-class men and women
The Blues is an expression of
black rural & urban life without pretension
It is black struggle   black attitude   black roots
black American language   poetics & culture
It is the music which
is sometimes appropriated by
white minstrels who will try to
imitate various black blues performers or will
put a hillbilly twang
and new watered-down lyrics
on top of the black Blues musical system.
The Blues is the foundation
for national & international pop music such as rock and roll
The Blues is also the foundation with African multiple rhythms
for the black instrumental   improvisational   composed avant-garde
music called Jazz
which is known to be an influence
in the development of modern music
& can be heard in venues around the world
The jazz music called “BeBop” was a point of departure from early jazz

& in the late '50s & '60s "Free Jazz" signified freedom from
European values & freedom of time, pitch & harmony.
Jazz became known as the "revolutionary music of the 20th century"
& it carries the history of the black freedom struggle
Most African-American musicians of this revolutionary music
will not use the word jazz to describe their music;
for example, Randy Weston calls his music African Rhythms
Ornette Coleman refers to his music as Harmolodic
Others call it "Black Music" or "The Music"
because the word jazz is a co-opted, de-radicalized term
categorized as smooth jazz, jazz pop, jazz fusion, jazz this & jazz that
Recently the word jazz became a label used to
describe festivals that have nothing to do with
the actual music developed by
African-American musicians
but has everything to do with
the process of devaluation
assimilation
white cultural imperialism & business

African Americans now live, work and are
visible everywhere in the United States
& even though there are conflicts and widening economic gaps
between those who have, those who want
& those who are abandoned & left out of the loop
there are still similarities:
The desire for internal freedom
The solving of problems through religion
Preferences opinions gestures
The interest in African roots & history &
the deep attachment to black music & black culture
In spite of "swelling" of the so-called middle class
& the privileges, awards & achievements
the struggle against the consequences of slavery:
racism, discrimination, incarceration,
dependency, repression, inequality, the setting up of classes
daily insults, degradation of women & the plantation system continues

In the 1970s, '80s & '90s the African-American community had to absorb

a unique & complex variety of situations:
President Lyndon B. Johnson & the anti-poverty program
the escalation of the Vietnam war
the bombing of Cambodia
the anti-draft movement
the assassination of Robert F. Kennedy
more police confrontations
the killing of students at Kent State University &
the University of Louisiana, in Baton Rouge
the incarceration of Huey P. Newton
the prison revolt of the Soledad Brothers
the killing of George & Jonathan Jackson
the jailing of Angela Davis
the Attica prison uprising,
the killing of Black Panthers:
Fred Hampton Mark Clark Bunchy Carter John Huggins & others
The black Cultural Expositions
black caucuses
the call for reparations
presidential campaign of Shirley Chisholm
election of black mayors
election of the first black congress person since reconstruction (Andrew Young)
the ecology movement
explosion of non-western religions
the Jonestown religious tragedy in Guyana
the death of Elijah Muhammad & split-up of the Nation of Islam
religious fundamentalism
the born-again Christian movement (tea party)
the killing of activists in North Carolina
Richard Nixon & Watergate
the film of Alex Haley's *Roots*
African Liberation support groups
the assassination of Amílcar Cabral
the struggles, victories & independence of
Guinea Bissau Cape Verde Angola Mozambique & Zimbabwe
the Anti-Apartheid movement & the student uprising in Soweto
the Three Mile Island nuclear reactor leaks in Pennsylvania
the Bhopal, India chemical spill

radiation blowing from the Chernobyl nuclear reactor explosion
the anti-nuclear movements
the AIDS epidemic
Support of liberation movements in Nicaragua & El Salvador
Affirmative Action legislation
more privatization
incarceration of Mumia Abu-Jamal
The destruction of the "MOVE" community in Philadelphia
the assassination of Thomas Sankara in Burkina Faso
The assassination of Maurice Bishop &
Ronald Reagan's invasion of Grenada
acid rain   riots   the police beating of Rodney King
biological weapons
internal conflicts in Africa
deforestation   desertification   pollution
impact of new technologies
massive dissemination of information
escalation of drug abuse
Ozone depletion
multiculturalism
Jonas Savimbi's war against Angola
Globalization   cultural invasion
the New Information Order
New World Economic Order
Russia & Perestroika   China & Tiananmen Square
presidential campaign of Jesse Jackson
war in the former Yugoslavia
the death of Samora Machel
RENAMO rebel war against Mozambique
the African-American Million Man March
the independence of Namibia
the end of the Apartheid regime in South Africa
the oil spills in the Niger Delta, Nigeria
the killing of Ken Saro-Wiwa
the release of Nelson Mandela from Robben Island
the election of Nelson Mandela for president of South Africa
ethnic conflict, and genocide in Rwanda
the bombing of a government facility in Tulsa, Oklahoma
the Prison Industrial complex

(Private Prison Schools for Blacks & Latinos)

Now it's the 21st century
& we have a growing number of Africans who
left their countries in search of employment in America
We have African and African-Diaspora film festivals
Instead of one film a year
We have the International Yari Yari Black Women Writers Conferences
the UNESCO's Route of the Slave Projects
the World Socialist Conferences that started in Brazil
The Black Aesthetic Conferences
& the Durban, South Africa
World Conference against
Racism, Racial Discrimination, Xenophobia & Related Intolerances.
We had President George W. Bush
his advisors Condoleezza Rice & Colin Powell
the 9/11/2001 attack on the World Trade Center in New York City
and on a government facility in Washington, DC.
We have the invasion of Iraq and the war in Afghanistan
genocide & rape in the Congo & in Darfur, Sudan
the tsunami disaster in Indonesia
the flood in New Orleans
the election of the first black president of the United States of America:
Barack Hussein Obama
The bail-out of the blood suckers:
Wall Street/General Motors & the banks
a devastating earthquake in Haiti
major British Petroleum oil spills
the pirates of Somalia
Pan-African Cultural Festival in Algeria
The Palestinian people and war in Gaza
the vote for the new nation of Southern Sudan
the World Festival of Black Arts and Culture in Dakar, Senegal
the people's Revolution in Tunisia & Egypt
the revolts in Bahrain & Yemen
the rebellion & U.S.-led invasion
& destabilization of Libya in North Africa
The movement of labor unions &
protest demonstrations in the US & the UK

the tsunami, earthquake & nuclear catastrophe in Japan
the amplification of human displacement
global warming & climate change
the proliferation of satellites computers and other electronic devices
the control and impact of the mass media
the distortion of information and the significance of culture

Culture was & is significant nationally and internationally.
Culture is a means of showing what we have in common
& what we have shared   or   share
regardless of the situation   or   struggle
The saying that came from Mozambique
"*A luta continua*" the struggle continues.
That's really where we are today.
So the question is
what forms are helpful in the struggle now
because forms of struggle change   technology changes
& people in struggles change
Some in the struggle are now elected officials   when before
they could not go into the white store around the corner.
Culture & politics need development
All the problems that we have encountered
will be intensified by the fact that
the population of the world will double in twenty years

Wikileaks leaked the truth
and everybody in power is shook up
because they realize that information
can be out there beyond their control
There's visible progress and there are invisible needs
The struggle continues and the struggle needs to continue
and it needs to change to improve the quality of life at the basic levels:
air, water, food, clothing, shelter,
healthcare, education, employment, & retirement

In the '60s we did not have Twitter or Facebook
in fact we did not have fax machines and cell phones or computers
To get our messages to the public
we had to rely on radio, television, word of mouth

the post office and telephone service
newspapers, magazines, posters, and flyers
mass meetings, readings and protest demonstrations
Today information can be googled up and
electronically transmitted via email texts message and cell phones
Cultural products and artistic works are displayed through websites
Imported messages and images are beamed directly into homes
People are fighting each other about the entertainment business
fighting for space in TV and in cinema
People have adapted their look to merge with the urban global look which is
produced through entertainment and
controlled by corporations in the Western world
So where is freedom of the imagination
Where is creativity
Where is justice
Why is there still so much poverty, misery & greed?

In the 20th century
Many African nations became independent
But political independence did not mean
liberation from colonial domination
This is the 21st century and we must be
more creative & change these relationships
I don't think anybody is against development.
It's just what do we want to develop
which aspects of society do we want to develop first?
Multinational corporations are developing
oil and major construction for profits and
are messing up the environment
& who will use nuclear weapons next
How can we change relationships
& make exchanges equal
How can we increase the speed of our struggle
What is the meaning of all that we have taken in
and how can we use it to prevent war & make a better world
We have to reorganize our thinking
We have to be more prepared to deal with natural disasters
We have the power of resistance &
the determination to maintain dignity

We abolished the Transatlantic slave trade
but we did not abolish slavery or the slave traders who are
still talking about democracy while killing people &
sucking as much oil as they can from the earth
they are obsessed with pipelines
with gas & oil & gold & profits & cheap labor
it is in their interest to keep Africa dependent & destabilized
& to keep potential progressive forces mentally & physically incarcerated
because they want and need the resources to retain & increase power
The major countries that were involved in the transatlantic slave trade are
The same ones involved in the bombing projects in North Africa
They are bombing & stealing & talking about democracy & about saving
civilian lives
But they are not saving lives in Bahrain or Yemen
& they did not go in to protect civilian lives in South Africa when the
Apartheid regime was killing its own people
& they did not go in to save black civilians in Rwanda or
the Palestinians in Gaza
Culture is awareness
it is knowledge of traditions
Our cultural identities are filled with desires for freedom & liberation
& sits on a small part of the universe fermenting
The nature of culture   is the culture of nature
The nature of black cultural politics
is to move forward &   continue the battle for human rights
continue the decolonization process   & the process of abolition
that was initiated in the 1960s
We have to have the confidence that we have the ability &
capacity to continue the long struggle
We are standing at the crossroads with a sign that says
"A Luta Continua"   The struggle continues.

FIND YOUR OWN VOICE AND USE IT
USE YOUR OWN VOICE AND FIND IT

Keynote Speech/Poem Sound Practices Colloquium
Guelph Festival 9/9/11, Canada

I'm sensitive to word sounds
& for years I have been known as a sound poet
without the presence of musicians & music.
The sounds of words and languages are
an important part of my poetic expression.
Out of the sound comes the image or
set of images, and that is the poem which
becomes the center post for encounters
the creative point for departures & the melodic
impulse for players of musical instruments.
I see it, I hear it, I put my mouth on paper, then
say it in collaboration with musicians whose
main concentration is improvisation & spontaneity.

I started reading my poetry with the
modern music called "Jazz" in 1964 in
concert with the brilliant pianist Horace Tapscott
in Los Angeles, Calif. & continued performing
with various well known jazz musicians in
music and avant-garde festivals throughout
the 1960s, '70s, '80s, '90s, and into the 21st century.
My first recording, "Celebrations and Solitudes"
with the great bassist Richard Davis, was released by
Strata-East Records in 1975.
In New York City in 1980 I formed my own band:
"The Firespitters" in order to experiment & reveal
more fully the possibilities of poetry with music.
It's a natural, supernatural, & surreal combination of
rhythms, attitudes, feelings, dreams, experiences,
and abilities. I mix images & languages. I control
punctuation, phrasing, emphasis & repetition.
I contribute variations of sounds & the
complexity of ideas.

The poetry determines the style of music.
The musicians respond with their variations,
interpretations, extensions, & creative interactions.
They approach, attack, and reveal the freeing of
time while making whatever they use or play
compatible with the situation.
They energize the call and response process, &
place that energy source in the solo spots.
The overall sound of the collaboration is unpredictable.
The changes of intonations inside of the
improvisations are unrepeatable.
Some of the collaborations have been recorded &
Include such wonderful musicians as:
Ornette Coleman, James Carter, Frank Lowe,
Abraham Adzinyah, Denardo Coleman, Bern Nix,
Al MacDowell, Alex Harding, Ron Carter, Bill Cole,
TK Blue, Ed Blackwell & James "Blood" Ulmer.

(Play: Find Your Own Voice) This collaboration features:
Frank Lowe – tenor sax, James Carter – baritone sax,
Bern Nix – guitar, Al MacDowell – bass, & Denardo Coleman – drums

There's a great deal of practice involved in improvisation.
Improvisation is in the levels of construction of the work itself and how
one handles the work within the world that it has to live in.
For example:
you see a swan in the lake looking so poised & beautiful
but if you could see the swan under water
you would see the swan paddling its ass off.
There's a lot that goes into doing what you do that
is not always seen or heard by an audience.
A poem is made of words & images.
Words have meanings & sounds, & so
right away you're starting with something
You're starting with you and your imagination.
You are the source for improvisation.
Improvisation or any artistic process starts with you,
you are it, you are the inventor & decision maker.
For instance: when I take words & images away from

their original functions & meanings & place them
beyond locations, routines, & explanations
it is because I am the initiator & architect of the structures &
the process I use is flexible.
In the process of going from thought, to page to
collaboration with musicians to the
final collective performance, I can start anywhere.
Some people will say "she's just putting words with music"
because the whole concept & structure that I'm involved in
is not what they can consider,
even though my intention is to make the combination
a creative experience for everyone.
The improvisation I'm talking about
begins & ends with the decisions that the artist makes
and those decisions can happen at any time & any place.
In fact in performance I have no idea
when I will change words, phrases, pitches, or
how I will say what I say & achieve variations,
also inspiration comes when inspiration comes
& only intuition knows when intuition will kick in.
For those reasons I never memorize all of the lines.
& of course technology can be a suppressor.
But it's my construction site, my construction company,
my cement, & my spit.
I collect material to build my poetic structure &
I can move backward, forward or up-side-down,
weave a theme into the scene or construct from
impulse to impulse, it's all possible.
Sometimes I modify the way I arrange the structure.
& when I work with music I continue to modify,
to improvise on, with, & around the structures to transcend limitations,
enter the unknown, & help bring the whole collaboration:
the tones, the attitudes, energy, call & response etc.
to a higher degree of development & freedom.

I grew up in Los Angeles, California and it was there
that I heard the Cuban drummer Chano Pozo
performing with the Dizzy Gillespie big band
In a baseball stadium in 1948. & even though

I was very young I remember Chano leaving the bandstand
& walking toward the audience chanting in an African language while
playing the conga drum & taking a very long intense solo.
It was a high improvisational moment. The audience went wild.
Later I wrote a poem dedicated to the memory of Chano Pozo for the
Chano Pozo festival presented by Prof. Bill Cole at
Dartmouth College in 1981. In Havana, Cuba, in 1987
I had the pleasure of reading my Chano Pozo poem in
performance with drummer Tata Güines and 3 drummers who
played the Yoruba Bata drums of Cuba.

The poem represents moments of transitions.
Transitions from the drum image, the image of obsession,
image of connecting realities, image of distant places,
the image of the sound of messages, the sound of conflicts,
the sound of battlefields, the sound as points of memory,
the sound of everything coming together & turned into
a poetry & music collaboration.

I started the poem in my work space, modified it there,
then modified it again in rehearsal & in performance with
musicians, where I had to make instant decisions of how to
relate to the sound of different instruments, how to relate to
the decisions of the musicians, & how to
take them on a path where they could respond to
the complexity of the material at the level that
the material demanded. This meant we would have to
intensely listen to each other in order to reach the kind
of spontaneity that would make the transformation

(read or play "I See Chano Pozo") Featuring: Farel Johnson–bongos,
voice & bell, Abraham Adzenyah–conga, Denardo Coleman–drums,
Jamaaladeen Tacuma–bass, Bern Nix–guitar, & Charles Moffett Jr–tenor
saxophone. Recorded in a Brooklyn studio without the proper equipment.

One of the historical forms of music invented & developed by
African Americans out of their experiences was the blues.
The jump ups, field hollers, yodels & percussive rhythms were
improvisations that evolved into the sound of

the blues responding to rural & then urban situations.
& situation is important in improvisation.
Blues singer John Lee Hooker once said:
"I was born with the blues. I eat with the blues,
I sleep with the blues, because
the blues comes from way way back"
Leadbelly said "It's that old feeling"
& Lightning Hopkins said
"It's real to my way of knowing"
& for me that feeling, that knowing, that
way way back is the Angola two-step,
deep ocean currents, African ancestors,
the miracle of survival, & the African-American
expressions of oppression, resistance,
struggle, & creative progress.

Poetry comes as blues
& blues comes as poetry
both are filled with the smell of fish fluids & leopard musk,
the taste of volcanic rocks, & cemetery headstones
they are marked by black snakebites, & are
jammed with sermons at the crossroads,
shipwrecks at the temptation club,
conversations with invisible forces,
competitive triangles, self-centered fixations,
the aftermath of rebellious gestures & the
meanness of madness fuming &
pacing in a circle of 4/4 time.

The blues feeling is
a feeling behind the feeling. & like
the Bouki character from African folklore
the blues makes & solves its own contradictions.
"It carries its own mind away."
It is stripped to the bone of revolt & loneliness.
& is mystified with apprehension,
masqueraded with tragedy, stuffed with exile,
coded with protest & vitalized with humor
It is "pulled out of the sky"

& is a force that hears itself saying
"I love you baby ain't gonna tell you no lie
but the day you quit me that's the day you die."

It is the story of many modern jazz players using
different scales & restructuring the blues.
Go back & listen to John Coltrane, & Charles Mingus.
It is the story of poetic verse & improvisation.
The story of the Fina, the Jali called griot & the
oral tradition. The story of personal creativity,
of personalities & the temperaments of performers/
composers like Big Bill Broonzy, Charlie Patton,
Son House, Robert Johnson, Bessie Smith,
Muddy Waters, Howling Wolf, J.B. Lenoir,
Memphis Minnie, Big Mama Thornton, Big Maybelle,
Percy Mayfield, & others who have
the ability to invent & push the poetic fission of
blues beyond exact repetition, stock phrases, &
structural limitations & into spontaneous intense
improvisational vocal advances & spaces.
The blues is like a skeleton key opening the
door to the cockpits, to the chaotic tornadoes,
to the swaying chain gangs, to the stagnant
pools of racism, to the love potions, to sexual escapades,
to the "drinkin' & not thinkin'" to "blues falling down like hail"
and "hellhounds on my trail." It's the bluntness, the coldness,
the lines of resentment & desire that pass over
bars & notations & into feelings of involvement that
are sometimes so deep it's impossible to really be appropriated.
The blues is identity, capacity, curiosity, creativity.
It is the search, the heat, the show-down &
the call and response device.
It's about instruments imitating the human voice
& the human voice imitating machines &
imitating the howling of coyotes,
It's about musicians fixing the form into
a twelve measure structure. But the soul,
the poetic fission of the blues cannot be fixed.
It is unruly, uncompromising & persistent.

It is matted down in black cultural matters &
when agitated it speaks like a whirlwind,
stings like a bolt of lightning, tears a guitar to pieces,
melts harmonicas, & pulverizes piano keys.
Blues is the foundation for jazz and free music improvisations.
Alto player & composer Ornette Coleman told me that you
could play the blues in another form or play anything
on the blues while changing the blues.
& in poetry from the oral tradition
what counts is what you say & how you say it.
For me, improvisation, representation, & intermediality
starts and ends with the blues.
(Play "Taking the Blues Back Home")

Intonations are like fizzing bubbles in
the stomach of a bull shark
that's why the salsa queen
puts on her rooster mask between impulses
no gasoline no spark plugs
just instinct
ask the dog about its sniffing investigation of
human sex organs
listen to the polar bear's scream of extinction

There is no sound of chewing in an empty mouth

The soul is full of memory chalk
full of feelings & chord progressions made with
the navel juice of insult &
the agitated eyebrow signals left by Fats Waller
this is the rough draft that went before
secrets were given back to
the dam that broke into
libations for Dinah Washington
& no one knew the power of pitch better than
the gospel diva who wore out a
thousand pair of shoes to become
Mahalia Jackson penetrating the sound barrier &
turning the hole in the sky into

the deep history of her eclipses
& that is the construction site
the labor pool trilling in the "termite cathedral"
The inflection of invisible corridors overlapping &
moving toward the climax point
Do you think Ma Rainey needed
emotional preparation when she
modified & intensified the song with
the duration of her moaning?
is that the sound of the voice of
unexpected spirits and the
underwater trench of sacred junctions
transformed into sound practices?

There is no sound of chewing in an empty mouth

How many fetishes are puffed up in
cheeks of trumpet players
does the xylophone know that the
xylophone is a xylophone
It's not the horn that's hungry
& the drums will not die of starvation
today is tomorrow
tomorrow is yesterday
all divisions are divided
any speedometer can be broken

You are the go between for your shadow to
approach, recede, & encounter other shadows
repetition is the great translator/agitator in
the belly of your shadow
but without you there is no shadow
& there is no sound of chewing in an empty mouth

This is the idea in the rhythmic groove of
a buffalo mask These are the
references covered by circular breathing
& this is the accumulation of
business cards in the trash can

these are the purple mistreated lips in
yellow butterfly wings
& that is the emotional hum of competitive slashes in
the soot from cultural invasions
did the saxophone traumatize the jungle
did the flute evangelize the word
did the tuba really come from city of Touba
& do you know how much contempt goes from
a microphone into a trombone
why is destiny so indifferent
a favela does not represent security
a skyscraper is born in the womb of a cement mixer
stagnation has the sheen of oil spills
time is not sold in the marketplace
time is inside of you
it is your double drilling in the
double time of sound practices
improvisation cannot see itself being used as
a great eraser of history
all representatives represent something & nothing
every tongue wears a thick coat of blood into
the public arena   The drought that matches the flood has
no intermediary   poetry is a bridge
practice produces good luck
but only multiple rhythms can make revolution
this is the first exit in the last cut of the dream
there is no sound of chewing in an empty mouth
one of the highest points & greatest paths of
invention came from Charlie Parker
"Find your own voice and use it, use your own voice & find it"

FISHING IN THE HISTORY

THE LONG STRUGGLE

for Fred Ho's Black Panther Suite

Europeans carried diseases and an expansion of violence into Africa
White settlers violated laws & took possession of communal lands
African farmers were dislocated
African cities decimated
Africans were pitted against each other &
Forced into selling themselves out & trading themselves in
How many colonial frontiers were established
How many European vaults have African minerals
How many museums show stolen African artifacts
How many organizations were built using traditional African structures
How many negative relationships and alien religions were reproduced in
Africa

Who broke the nose of the Sphinx
Who tried to mute the genius of Nelson Mandela through incarcerations
Who were the invaders of indigenous cultures
Who were the ones preoccupied with occupation

Don't look to mercenary props for redefinition
Don't count on electronic preachers for salvation
Don't focus on squabbles in the barracks
Cancel the dependency
Defuse those differences

How many Africans were imported to North America and the Caribbean
Who came from Loanga, Cabinda, Malindi, Guinea & the Mediterranean
Who were the resisters from Kingdoms of Bamana, Kongo, Benin & Oyo
Who fought crossing the savannas the deserts the Red Sea & the Indian
ocean
Who sat chained in vessels leaving the Dutch castle at Cape Coast & the
Dutch
Settlement of Cape Town
How many left from West African, East African, Central African, South
African &
North African slave markets

How many spoke Manding, Wolof, Umbundu,
Fulani, Twi, Yoruba, Zulu or Swahili
How many were exported to India
How many were taken to Iraq
How many were dropped off in Brazil
How many ended up in the Latin American ports of entry
How many jumped into the Atlantic ocean
How many died before reaching the ship
How many survived & rebelled & insurrected & became revolutionaries
I say the grove is alive with the hollering of such ancestors

How many fought against the Portuguese with Ana Nzinga in Angola
How many repelled the British with Yaa Asantewaa in Ghana
How many rose up with Samori Toure to push the French out of Guinea
How many rode against the British with the Mạdi in Sudan
How many rebelled against the Spanish and French & fought with
Toussaint L'Ouverture for Haitian independence
How many took up arms with Zumbi in Brazil
How many fought the Germans the Swedes the Danes the Belgians
The European Americans
How many were mowed down by bullets from machine guns
How many found themselves kidnapped captured raped dislocated &
Marching the long march through rainy seasons, dry seasons,
the seasons of malnutrition, diseases & wars
How many perished before being claimed owned & auctioned
How many escaped and marooned themselves into maroon societies
How many were fugitives
How many slept in dungeons
How many passed through last exit in the slave house on Goree Island
How many turned inward
How many unified
How many gave birth
How many endured
How many took the revolutionary path
And how many were revolutionary enough to
Deal with their mistakes & contradictions
I tell you the grove is active with the intense humming of
Courageous & combative ancestors
Those with confrontational experience

Like Gabriel Prosser and Denmark Vesey who identified August as
The month to remember black revolts and insurrectional continuity
David Walker amplified his appeal for justice and
Moved forward clarity of the word commitment
Nat Turner made the total eclipse of the sun a signal to advance the cause of
Black freedom
Frederick Douglass left us his autobiography & revolutionary stamina & said
"We shall neither die out nor be driven out"
Sojourner Truth enriched the struggle with her feminist view & stand
  against inequalities
Martin Delany intensified his efforts to elevate black consciousness
And no one could crush the revolutionary determination of Harriet Tubman
  as she
Emancipated three hundred slaves & worked with abolitionists to abolish
  slavery
Poet Frances W. Harper gave us her tough poems of resistance against
  oppression
W. E. B. Du Bois put the passionate flames of Pan-Africanism into
  The Souls of Black Folks

Marcus Garvey provided the Back to Africa Movement and the Black Star
  Shipping Line
George Padmore organized Pan-African Congress of workers, trade unionists
  & students
Antonio Maceo prepared the way for the Cuban revolution
And groups such as The New Negro Negritude & Negrismo brought
  centuries of
African, Afro-American & Afro-Caribbean processes and progress to the
  surface as
An active cultural linguistic artistic renaissance

The grove is alive with the inventions & creativity of spontaneous ancestors
Ancestors like those who dismantled the anchors, gangplanks,
Lower decks of propellers, wheels & bolts of slave ships
Those who transferred European saints into African deities
Those who communicated in Creole languages
Those who made defeats into victories
Nothing into something
Ancestors like Paul Robeson who slammed his defiance into faces of

racist white Senators on Capitol Hill
Like Trinidadian scholar/writer C.L.R. James who gave us his brilliant analysis of
Liberation struggles
And the great leader from Ghana Kwame Nkrumah who laid out the axiom for
A united Africa
Congolese leader Patrice Lumumba who died while fighting for African independence
Julius Nyerere of Tanzania showed us the transitional steps necessary for
transformation
And the grove is full of those who fell while
Jacking up the oppressors on battlefields of Mau Mau revolts & in
Urban rebellions & prison uprisings
And those ancestors who kicked a lot of dust in eyes of arrogant promoters of hate in
Montgomery, Alabama
Ancestors like Martin Luther King who carried his struggle for peace to the mountaintop Rosa Parks who walked her dignity into a mass movement
And it was Fannie Lou Hamer who challenged the laws of segregation in Mississippi
And Ella Baker generously contributed intellectual illuminations to the cause
And the militant students of the Civil Rights Movement expanded activities and
Created a revolutionary atmosphere
And Frantz Fanon provided a psychological analysis of *The*
Wretched of the Earth and *Black Skin, White Masks* while giving us
A direct look at the Algerian war of independence
And it was Malcolm X who connected revolutionary struggles and
said "You get your Freedom by letting your enemy know that you'll do
anything to get it"
And it was Soledad Brother George Jackson who became leader of
The black prison movement as protesters shouted for the release of Huey P. Newton &
Chanted slogans like "Free Huey or the sky's the limit"

The grove is full of examples
Full of revolutionary ancestors like
The combatants from the Southern African Liberation Front
Ancestors like Amílcar Cabral who spent his life fighting against

Colonial powers and the ideology of imperialism
Like Eduardo Mondlane who fought a protracted struggle for the
Freedom of Mozambique
Like Samora Machel who asked the question "Why were our women raped,
Our traditions humiliated & our civilizations negated?"
And Josina Machel who led offensives against Portuguese installations
And Graça Machel who opened her door to the cry of orphans
Like Agostinho Neto who fought on the front line against the Portuguese-
fascist colonial
System of oppression in Angola & gave us his "Sacred Hope"
Like the Organização Mulher Angolana — O.M.A. who shouted the slogan
"Victory is certain"
Like every freedom lover involved in changing Rhodesia into Zimbabwe
Like all the ancestors who died fighting the South African regime
All the revolutionaries who fought for an independent Namibia

And it was this same state of black consciousness, this same protest of
consequences
The same blood, the same threat of exile & betrayal, the same wreckage,
the same Shackles, the same breakdowns, the same frustrations, the same
courage, the same Revolutionary commitment in the same arena that
consolidated into
A young Black Panther battalion

It was the same associations, the same intensities, the same desire for
freedom & justice The same cohesions of movement & motions
of resistance, the same examinations of History & reevaluation of
revolutionary efforts that mutated into a political ten point Program &
stretched into international forms of solidarity in spite of
Internal conflicts & external provocations

I tell you the grove is rich with the evolution of revolutionary ancestors
It is full of heroic/sheroic examples
Full of technologies, philosophies, tactics &
Strategies of revolutionary ancestors
And we praise our fallen comrades & like them
We do not believe in the exchange of people for power
We believe in people's power
And power to the people

LANGUAGE, LITERATURE AND COMMUNICATION 3/21/2002

I would like to thank the Dept. of Language, Literature and Communication for inviting me to participate in the 27th Annual Sandhills Writers Conference. I'm very happy to be here to share my work and to exchange ideas with people who care about the act of writing, the act of putting their marks on paper, on tape and on computer disk in an effort to continue transmitting messages. All the marks we make are linked to other marks. We draw upon marks made from the past by stone age people who were sending vocal sounds and gestural signs to each other transforming those messages into music, dance, drawings, drum signals, ideograms followed by the development of a language that gave birth to many dialects. That then became new languages and "allowed for more details of expression, some expressions that became permanent" records on clay tablets, stone carvings, scrolls, books, graffiti. In an effort to have a better life and a better understanding we continue to exchange information, translate texts, and increase the speed of transmission into action, into different modes of communication. When we put all of our ideas, all of these centuries of marks together it's pretty spectacular.

So we know that the first thing we have to have is faith in the fact that it is possible to make a mark and trust that somebody else will respond to it. Whether that response is positive or negative, whether another person will like your writing or not like your writing or look at it critically. The first thing you trust is that if you write down the word cotton or the word global somebody knows something about what you're trying to communicate. And of course the word cotton can be the start of fiction, like Chester Himes's novel *Cotton Comes to Harlem*, or cotton can be the start of facts and statistics, or it can be the start of something fun like cotton candy. Global can be the start of something tragic like the global spread of AIDS, the global spread of drugs, the global spread of terrorist attacks, it can be the start of a poem like the one I wrote called "Global Inequalities".

The words that we use, the reason that we use them, the many ways we do, are affected by all kinds of human events, some of them large and significant, some of them very trivial. If I say 3/12/75 nobody in this room is going to understand a thing, but to me it's important because it's my anniversary. It's a big deal to me, but just some more numbers that don't mean a thing to you. If I say the words 9/11/2001 or Osama Bin Laden or Timothy McVeigh, that's another story. So communication or writing and its appreciation depend on some common experience. If you say Damn Yankees in Georgia and you say Damn Yankees in New York, one place you're talking about a great baseball team, in another place you're talking about people who won the Civil War. So words expressing human experiences and the perceptions underlying them are important. The sensibilities of the writer and the sensibilities of the audience of the writer are important. The writer is the transmitter and the audience is the receptor and respondent, there is a reciprocal relationship, which includes cultivation and the learning and unlearning process in development. People who speak the same language communicate a little easier than people who don't speak the same language. But even though they speak different languages, write and read different languages, if they keep getting each other's information eventually they're going to communicate to some level. Now in literature we have translations to take care of that, but translation still is not quite direct communication. Writing, you can say, is a secondary level of communication because human beings spoke before they wrote. So the things that we are trying to do by writing are an extension of that earlier communication form which we still use. In other words, because we started writing didn't mean we gave up speaking. In fact the number of languages used in verbal communication is high, with some 3,500 identified throughout the world. The number of written languages is much lower, with one estimate indicating not more than 500. Because we got the telephone didn't mean that we still didn't need to see each other, but it helps us communicate when we can't. A few years ago we were concerned about the slow development of postal and telecommunication facilities and services in many developing countries, but now in places like Dakar, Senegal almost everyone has a cell phone and most neighborhoods have cyber cafes. These services are linking urban and rural areas and connecting people in different occupations to larger administrative centers. All of these technological innovations are opening the door to larger audiences and sources for information. So now the writer can see, hear and obtain much more information. It might have been easier in the past when there was less information available. Now the situation for anybody trying to say something is that we all know too much and we all have so much of the same information. How do you push it aside to get to the essential part, that's the question, that's the task, that's what I thought of when I wrote the Toolmaker poem dedicated to Chinua Achebe.

And what are you giving the audience? One time you're giving a story about water, one time you're giving the reader ideas about democracy, or you're giving people a love story or ideas of war or the ideas of the beauty of nature in a mango. Writing is always a multiple process and it depends on the two. All ideas for a creative person are what they distill out of their interest. Literature is always a situation of changes, the abstraction of reality and the reality of the writer's abstraction. What the reader distills is something else. Maybe you're giving somebody the solution to a big problem in your writing but you're not in control of the system of education. A person sends you material that they have written, you're a writer, you may have comments. You know how to go about writing but the person has already made decisions. You're reading as an appreciator. You're evaluating as a motivator. Everybody has their own world and that world is somewhat manifest by what they put on paper. It depends on the writer.

It's the writer's pen that makes the mark, the writer's voice that makes the sound. Is somebody doing something as great as Tolstoy's *War and Peace*? Is somebody writing as magical as Gabriel García Márquez? Is someone writing as interestingly about American life as Richard Wright? This is the fifty-year anniversary of Ralph Ellison's *Invisible Man*. Has anybody written about the invisible woman?

Everybody is doing their best. A writer is a human being in a human enterprise. Writing is not a game with specific boundaries, specific rules. There are generalities for those things but there are no specifics. The size of a baseball park is determined by fences, when the ball goes over the fence, in baseball that's a home run. Nobody knows where the fence is in writing. And even when you think you know, you discover there are no fences, or the critics have moved the fences. The boundaries vary, they vary for individuals, they vary for groups, they vary in terms of situation, they vary in terms of conferences. Everybody is doing the best they can; they are experimenting and being imaginative, and are making use of new means of communication. As a poet I have always used all the means of communication to promote poetry, to present poetry. I participate as a poet in New York City. I participate as a poet in the struggle for equality and justice. I participate as a poet against war. I participate as a poet in the United Nations Millennium Summit. I am in the solitude of my poetry, in the vision of my poetry. Poetry is my identification. And poems have always been a part of communication, whether it's in a musical setting or inscribed on stone or in a book or on a CD or computer. My contribution is poetry in poems to the listener and reader.

At this conference someone might say that we had a profound meeting. Another person may think the meeting was low level and corny. It depends on what you got out of all that's presented. Once I was in Kumasi, Ghana, in West Africa. It was the time of the enstoolment of a traditional African King and that was incredible because among the people viewing this enstoolment were people whose ancestors had been taken to the Western hemisphere and who had survived enslavement, survived discrimination, survived segregation, survived poverty and all kinds of negative things and had made themselves into constructive creative people and had arrived in Kumasi, Ghana, in July of 1970. The traditional cloth worn at this event is called Adinkra, a cloth marked with traditional proverbial symbols. In other words, people in Ghana historically made marks that conveyed information, influenced attitudes and instigated action. Here was five hundred years of propaganda turned around. This was an example of a traditional event that could not be rivaled by any other means of communication. Traditional communication survives. That was part of what we got out of that celebration, and that celebration is in my notebook.

Why do we have poetry festivals, why do we have the congress of writers? We have these gatherings because we need the feeling of solidarity, the feeling of togetherness. We need to talk about writing, publishing, excellence, mediocrity, consumers and the marketplace. We need to speak of the sun, the moon, relationships and the animal world. It's important to discuss crucial problems such as the protection of the environment, the rational use of natural resources, human rights, disarmament and peace. This is where we come to discuss all topics, listen to all the different viewpoints and be updated on current literary developments. We make ourselves think, and we make others think and we write. There are those who do it journalistically, those who do it poetically, those who do it fictionally, those who do it theatrically and cinematically. And it's a nice thing to do, and it's nice to know that we may write alone but we are not alone. That's part of what this conference tells us and after the conference somebody is going to go somewhere and start writing, and that's incredible. They talk about the space shuttle and that's great, but whoever put together the idea that you could somehow communicate by taking your fingertip and making some marks and another person could see the marks you made and respond, then doing something about life based on the fact that they saw the mark you made. That's a great deal of potential power and it's a wonderful miracle to be a writer.

IS RACISM DEAD 2/2002

University of Missouri, Columbia, MO

Racism is an organic process created and developed by human beings. Racism exists in all aspects of human activity. Racism is when humans act negatively on things based on race, for example; there's nothing wrong with hiring some African people to come to America and work and get paid fair wages, nothing wrong with that. But when you take these African people and you create a system called slavery and you force them to live in that. Well that's racism. When you underpay a group of people based on what race they are, that's racism. When you don't academically or administratively promote and develop people or society or a place based on the fact that it's going to be occupied by people of another race that's racism. It is an indisputable fact that white children do not learn to consider themselves superior to black children until they are told that they are. Racism has no birth date, no death date. Racism was a convenient ideology for rising colonialism, for the black slave trade for anti-Semitism for the extermination of Native Americans, for the oppression of the Algerian people, for the war against the Vietnamese, for the decimation of aboriginal and indigenous people throughout the world and for preserving power.

Human development is a process of enlarging people's choices. The most critical of these wide-ranging choices are to live a long and healthy life, to be educated and to have access to resources needed for a decent standard of living. Additional choices range from political, economic and social freedom to opportunities for being creative and productive, enjoying personal self-respect and guaranteed human rights. No one can guarantee human happiness and the choices people make are their own concern. But the process of development should at least create a conducive environment for people, individually and collectively, to develop their full potential and have a reasonable chance of leading productive and creative lives in accord with their needs and interests.

So, as we try and solve the various versions of what racism might be. And rather than saying, "so and so discriminated against me" individually. Those things happen and we know they're true, and we know they're indicative of racism, but it's better to work on the things that we know help to reduce and will eventually eliminate racism. And some of those things are an improvement in educational and vocational opportunity, that will affect everything. In other words, the administration of universities, the administration of business, the administration of everything has to be integrated and then after the actual integration the processes have to be fair. But an important part of making things fair is curing some things, which are very ill. And because of the illness of racism things are not at the level they should be. In other words, if you have a community of people that exist and they're the subject of racism, then probably their education is a bit deficient, their job opportunities are deficient, their general housing is probably deficient, their general life opportunities are deficient, so it requires an extra effort, and a version of extra effort is what we call affirmative action, and when somebody's sick you can't treat them like a person that's well. You have to do more for them to get well so they can function or compete normally. That means they need extra care. That means they may need to be wheeled around. If somebody's been crippled by something they may need a wheelchair until they recover the use of their limbs so they can be mobile. And that's true when it comes to education. That's true when it comes to everything. If people say that it's too expensive to take care of, well it's not nearly as expensive as filling the jails with prisoners. It's not nearly as expensive as trying to help people throughout life because you've mis-educated them or not educated them. Today the disparity between the haves and have nots, between the North and South is not a mere matter of time-lag. It cannot be expected that developing countries will "catch up" through being given financial and technical assistancc by the so-called developed. We need the elimination of racism and all of the things that are negative within racism are also the things that are negative within other people or societies. Those who are victims of racism can also be the victims of poverty. Poverty is a problem in the United States and poverty affects people racially, that is those who are affected by race that's just an additional problem to the terrible problem of poverty. And once you're hungry, your stomach is not saying what color it is. Your stomach is saying I need food. Your body is saying I need food, your brain is saying we need nutrition. So people have to lose their fear of working on problems. People have to get over their reticence of dealing with problems. People have to just get used to each other, because a hungry person is a hungry person anywhere on this earth. A hungry person in the Ozark Mountains and a hungry person in the mountains of Sudan are hungry people. There are still more than a billion people in absolute poverty. Millions of adults are unable to read and write. 1.75 billion are without safe drinking water, around 100 million completely homeless. Some 800 million go hungry every day, 150 million children under 5 who are malnourished and 14 million children who die each year before their 5th birthday. Poverty is everywhere. Asia has 64 percent, Africa 28 percent, Latin America and the Caribbean 12 percent and in the United States about 13 percent of the population still below the official poverty line and poverty also has a decided gender bias. So we must ensure that food production increases rapidly and that food is well distributed. To wipe out poverty you have to wipe out racism. You have to give everybody an opportunity.

Are ten percent of the biologists black in the United States? Are ten percent of the students in the agriculture school at the University of Missouri black? Are ten percent of the students in business school black? There have been black quarterbacks, black coaches and there are still assistant coaches and many black players. But most of the people doing the selling and commercializing are not black. The companies advertising the games won't be black owned companies, they don't have that kind of money. If we're ten percent and there are 32 teams, three should be owned by black people. Why are sixty percent of the professional football players black? White people have other things to do. They're going to business school, they're studying to be scientists and to be engineers. Young black people see a way into life in sports. They don't see anything like they see basketball or football. So if they don't become basketball or football players, music will be their fallback. It's all there by example. You don't have to tell them about no role model, you have to buy them some of those two-hundred-dollar basketball shoes that Michael Jordan is selling. They're not going to ask you for no two-hundred-dollar chemistry book. So you know if your child asks you for a two hundred dollar pair of Michael Jordan sneakers that there's racism. Why doesn't this kid think of something else as a future? He's only presented with that. That's the dominant thing he's presented with. He's thinking of sports or he's thinking of being a rapper, but you tell him we would like to teach you Chinese and physics, we'd like to teach you the language of mathematics. No, he would rather go out on a stage in some baggy clothes and make up rhymes to a drum machine. It's a consequence of racism. And then you have white people imitating and wanting to be affected by the racism. I'm not against clowning as entertainment, tragedy and comedy as artistic expression encompass everything. But when you think about this stuff and you say why is there so much of that. Well, the same commercial structures and ventures that created the earlier forms of racism which were manifested by things like slavery now manifest the exploitation of the same places, the same people. In other words the British started fighting in India, Pakistan, and Afghanistan 500 years ago, and England's children, George W. Bush and Tony Blair got the army out there fighting war in Afghanistan. In the United States people don't call people from Afghanistan black but in England people from India, Pakistan and Afghanistan are called black. England colonized Arabia and oil was discovered. When independence came the Euro American oil monopolies took control of refining and distribution of petroleum products and the resulting profits. That is the background cause of the conflict. If there's an economic problem in South Africa or in Zimbabwe, deep down it's about race, because the economy of those Black countries are run by Europeans, so that means they have independence but they don't have independence. There's still a manipulated racial conflict. The economic structure is based on racism. If it is true internationally, it is true locally. I don't mean that there haven't been changes. There have been many changes but you can't point to a Colin Powell or Condoleezza Rice or to the latest CEO and say oh we're better off because we always did run plantations for white folks. I'm sure he'll do a good job as secretary of state but black people did good jobs during the American Revolution. There were free black people during slavery but you can't say that means slavery was ok. Michael Jordan is a millionaire from bouncing a basketball. You can't say bouncing a basketball is our solution. You can't say because a little boy with a curl down his face who wears a glove and plays with animals & who's a pretty good singer is the answer to our problems. He's just one person who is a success. We have to change things. When I say change, I don't mean here's a glass of water, drink it and it's over with. Change is like losing weight. You have to change how you eat for the rest of your life. We have to change the diet of racism for everybody for the rest of human existence then we'll have a human happy body racially. We'll have all of the racial varieties but the relations between us will be healthy.

No one told me that most of my life would be spent devoted to finding solutions to conflicts brought about by the experience of racism, and that I would have to deal with the "superior person with the superior disease of racism." I would have to deal with the original racism used to organize the transatlantic slave trade, and that I would be categorized, identified and earmarked for certain tasks because of my pigmentation, and I would be given a distorted image of myself and would be targeted and that even the smallest detail like shopping for food would end in an incident of racial profiling, and racism would influence my decisions because racism was always disguising itself and was everywhere. That I would be fighting for human rights, human life, going from one racist moment to the next, round by round, blow for blow, toe to toe, because the struggle against all forms of racial discrimination and the struggle for peace and cooperation is long.

This phase of the struggle is what it is and we have not backed down, we have not thrown in the towel in spite of the fact that we are insulted, provoked, imprisoned, threatened with expulsion, with unemployment, etc. We have to keep the struggle alive even when we are confronted by a tidal wave of censorship, suppression and racism which sits like a secret virus that is dormant until a day like September 11 pushes it into focus and it comes through between flags, hooded sheets, burning crosses and war itself materializes and the old internment camps become detention centers and the heart is inflamed with a patriotism that spits in the face of a dark-skinned immigrant or a person with another viewpoint, and we are the third world in America, the other America, the outsider, we are on the outside even when we think we're on the inside, we're inside out. We are the people of color, the people referred to as the marginalized, the oppressed, the disadvantaged, the so-called minorities, the underdeveloped, the developing world, the world with all the important resources. We are the people who live under the volcano, on the fault line, in the favela, behind stone walls in shanty towns, in the squatter camps. We live next to the garbage dump, next to a leaky pesticide factory, in the vicinity of the liquid gas tanks. We are not far from the nuclear reactors. We live near the warehouses that store toxic chemicals, near the active unlined industrial landfills, near the ruins of a destroyed forest, around the polluted rivers, in the urban projects near the sewage plant. We live on land that no one else will build on, and when the flood comes we are caught in the mudslides, when the reactor leaks we're in the radioactivity, and when the warehouse of outdated weapons explodes we are in the danger zone. We are living in a place with a group of people who will not give up the racial stereotypes which they constructed to make them feel secure, and which first appeared with the slave trade and colonialism, which became so deeply rooted in the psychic of white people, which have trapped African people and made us a dominated people always struggling against "a dual enslavement, economic and psychological. We are faced with the fact that a group of humans who live in a complex of fear of others and are aggressive toward them would rather push war or a nuclear button than give up profits and privileges and have a dialogue among equals. We are the other world and we have had to find endless ways of surviving, of responding, and demanding, and it is sad, it is inflammatory, it is diabetic, it is hypertensive, it's asthmatic, it's time consuming, and it is a great challenge.

I had no idea that I would be a poet, that all my thoughts would find themselves on pieces of paper, and that I would be a committed active person who would love participating in the struggle because a clean healthy environment vibrant with the diversity of life and an assurance that our children will have an opportunity for the same, is something worth struggling for.

GLOBALIZATION

for opening session of Yari Yari Pamberi 10/12/2004

Sunlight is global
The earth evolves and revolves one hundred percent annually and is natural
Complete human experience of globalization is also natural
And within that
You have the positive and the negative
You have the positive things that people do
And you have the abuse of people's global capacity

What is the globalization of science
What is the globalization of culture
What is the globalization of education
What are the dynamic interactions for women who are writers?

This conference is a form of globalization
The conference itself could not take place
If globalization did not exist
Globalization is the interaction of people of action

I am co-founder with Ama Ata Aidoo of the Organization of Women Writers of Africa.
Ama Ata is from Ghana, she speaks Twi or Fante
But because of globalization or colonialism
She speaks English
And because of the Transatlantic slave trade in the form of globalization
I speak English
We have writers here from Senegal who speak and write mostly in French
There are writers from
Mozambique and Angola that write and publish mostly in Portuguese
This brings up the topic "What's going to happen to African Languages as
A literary voice in the 21st century globalization of societies"
What is the point of the globalization process
Is it to remove people, replace their languages
Take their land and resources
Place them in a disadvantaged situation and
Build up the surge in inequality

Have globalization and extreme poverty
Fragmentation of labor markets
Unequal access to education
Transmission of diseases
Migration of displaced persons
Increase the generational gaps & widen the gap between
Rich and poor, urban & rural, skilled & unskilled
Have globalization and armed conflicts that
Leave some people globalized to death right away
And some globalized into profit
What's the profit for a 12-year-old boy or girl forced to be a child soldier and
Globalized by the diamond business or the business of oil
How do we cope with the increase in civil wars
The continued sexual & domestic violence against women
The sexual violence against men
Children pushed into prostitution
The availability of weapons
Ethnic cleansing, religious animosities
Shrinking time, shrinking spaces, shrinking opportunities
Crime, corruption & pollution
No pension fund   No job security   No safe drinking water
No access to taxpayer's money used to
Hold up the great stock market casino
What do we do about unequal relationships
How do we protect our families, defend ourselves and
Lessen vulnerabilities & the negative impact of globalization

As writers we have to control images
We have to keep on updating ourselves
Tell the story & come together to discuss global challenges
And we have to remember examples
Remember that Nike had everybody believing that they have to have
Hundred dollar shoes to win a marathon
But Abebe Bikila from Ethiopia ran barefoot in the Olympics
And won the marathon without Nike
Wilma Rudolph had polio as a child
But she decided to run track
Entered the Olympics and won the hundred meter dash
Lina Magaia from Mozambique wrote a book about trust your feet:

"Dumbanenge"
We have to trust our fingers
And because this is an era of extraordinary communication
Information is at our fingertips
So we need all women writers: scientific, bureaucratic, academic, journalistic &
Writers of poetry & fiction
And we need all the organizers, and all the women of other occupations to
Meet and talk about problems of the past and
Talk about our present situation
There may not be any final answers but
We need this dialogue in order to have the next dialogue
There is no savior coming in to solve problems and save the day
Everybody has to pick cotton
Whether its cotton picking in the computer or cotton picking in space
It's cotton picking time
And when the cloud of insects swirl in to get their share
Everybody will have to go out and fight

PAN-AFRICANISM

Speech for The Ghana Society, Syracuse 3/31/2007

I would like to thank the Ghana Society of Central New York for inviting me to take part in the commemoration of Ghana's 50th Independence Anniversary Golden Jubilee & Awards Banquet. I'm honored to be here and on this program with so many creative people. As I join in the celebration, I think back on my various trips to Ghana in 1967, 1970, '71, '83 and '97. I think back to my experiences in Ghana, my exposure to the spirits of Elmina Castle. I was in Ghana to find out about Ghana, to check out the weavers of kente cloth in Bonwire, the Fani Fetish women dressed in white, the acrobats in Birewa, the casket designers of Teshie, the market women of Accra and to be introduced to life in Kumasi and to witness events in the Kumasi stadium concerning the enstoolment of the new Asantehene Opoku Ware. I saw the drummers talking to their great atumpan drums. I saw many other drums and drum makers, players and heard a thousand drum rhythms in traditional ceremonies and in popular highlife bands. I drank Star beer, ate fufu, stayed at the Ambassador Hotel, and at the University's Akuafo Hall in Legon. I also participated in the 1983 symposium to analyze *The Green Book* by president Muammar al-Qaddafi of Libya. I met many artists, musicians, and writers, including the writer Ama Ata Aidoo, who is also the co-founder of the Organization of Women Writers of Africa, Inc. which we co-founded in 1991, organizing our first large-scale pan-African conference: "Yari Yari Black Women Writers and the Future" in New York City 1997. On my first trip to Africa in 1967, I left with my son from Los Angeles in June, stopping in Hawaii, Japan, the Philippines, Thailand, Hong Kong, and India. From India, we traveled on to Ethiopia and Sudan, and landed in Accra, Ghana in July. We were the first in our family to return to Africa in four hundred years. I was excited and felt proud to be arriving in Accra, Ghana, on Ethiopian Airways. When we hit the runway in Accra, I felt very relaxed, like a heavy load had been lifted off my shoulders. I was overwhelmed with a feeling of safe return, and I just started smiling and couldn't stop smiling. It's a pan-African feeling, like when Joe Louis knocked out Max Schmeling, and when Jesse Owens won the race in Germany. It was that kind of feeling. I was overwhelmed with a feeling of safe return and that feeling of having a home and being welcomed at home has stayed with me. As I rode around Accra in various taxis, the drivers would always clam up when I talked and asked about Kwame Nkrumah and his goals. There were no visible signs of Nkrumah's presence in Ghana except that I knew he and others in Ghana were responsible for the construction of the great auto expressway, the fishing industry in Tema, and the Akosombo hydro-electric dam (the Volta River Project). When taxi drivers finally spoke about Nkrumah they whispered his name. Everybody was whispering and censoring themselves. I did not feel good about Nkrumah's forced exile. Those of us in the 1960s Civil Rights Movement in the United States had been inspired by his activism and input in the 1945 Pan-African Congress in the UK and the influence of people like W. E. B. Du Bois and George Padmore. Nkrumah gave us another way of thinking about Africa and the aspirations of African people. He gave us a Pan-African perspective, a Pan-African vision, a Pan-African view of the need for African Unity, a Pan-African understanding, saying that "for economic unity to be effective it must be accompanied by political unity." In our eyes, Nkrumah represented the people of Ghana, the independence of Ghana, the spark with development plans for Ghana. He became a symbol, he was a Ghana who helped put a hole in the wall of colonialism, and who gave hope and support to African Liberation movements and movements against oppression and exploitation and who always made an international space available in Ghana for African leaders to come together, to exchange ideas and analyze their situations concerning "colonialism becoming neo-colonialism, and the last stage of imperialism" and to discuss the steps that should be taken to eliminate apartheid. Nkrumah had been a student in America and knew the educational system, the system of segregation, and the interactions between students of African descent. As a person active in SNCC (Student Nonviolent Coordinating Committee) and a participant in the Civil Rights Movement in the United States in the 1960s, I can say that our struggle was pushed forward because of the independence movement in Africa, and especially the independence of Ghana and it was Kwame Nkrumah of Ghana who understood our struggle for freedom and justice, who understood what we in the United States meant when we called for Black Power. He understood it as a link with the Pan-African struggle for unity on the African continent. Being on the African Continent and in Ghana I went to see Elmina Castle and there I thought about the suffering of our ancestors, about the betrayals, and about how Pan-Africanism was internalized on the shores of Africa, internalized after encountering an oppressive collective from Portugal, Spain, England, France, The Netherlands, and North America. We were the African collective and this was a Pan-African/Pan-European encounter. "The Transatlantic slave trade resulted in the forced removal of over twenty million people from Africa," and "destroyed families and communities, turned brother against brother and caused untold damage to Africa and its Diaspora," leaving us with colonialism, enslavement and their consequences.

There is nothing we are saying now or doing now that wasn't said or done before us because our struggle is long and complicated and very dense with ideas and there are a lot of people involved at different levels and in different phases of this struggle. Now, what does it mean to be a Pan-Africanist today? It means that we will know that the Pan-African experience in the struggle has continued for over four hundred years and we will constantly be reminded of the contributions made by those who came before us and we will know that being a Pan-Africanist is about commitment and determination as we learn about the Pan-African events and organizations created such as the Organization of African Unity which is now the African Union, the Pan-African Congress, the Mau Mau, Negritude, Civil Rights, Black Power, Black Arts, Black Panther, and African Liberation movements, The African Liberation support groups, committees in solidarity with African people on the African continent and in the African Diaspora, African Studies departments, Institutes of African Affairs, Black Student Unions, Black Studies, The First Dakar Festival of Black Art, FESTAC in Nigeria, Festivals of African Arts and Culture, FESPACO, the Pan-African film festivals, the Slave Routes projects, the Yari Yari Black women writers conferences, the Black Aesthetic symposiums, Pan-African art expositions, etc. all promoting international networks.

Today African countries are independent and are grappling with how to take care of important regional needs and the need for overall unity, because as Nkrumah pointed out in his book *Axioms* "divided we are weak, united Africa could become one of the greatest forces for good in the world." Most leaders on the continent understand this, and that is why we have the African Union, an organization of African States who are now considering the possibility of adding another region to include the African Diaspora as a part of its organization. Pan-Africanism is a part of globalization. Whatever the pros and cons, advantages, and disadvantages, Pan-African possibilities are affected by those realities. Some people think of globalization as re-colonization or some call it Americanization because, at the moment, "the world's biggest businesses tend to be American dominated." Africa and its Diaspora all have their relationships to those realities. The political theories and solutions of the past are all affected by globalization. But globalization has its limits and is resisted as "a threat to indigenous traditions in different parts of the world."

The issues facing African people today are pretty much the same issues. They're just advanced along with everything else. Those issues have gotten more critical. Our conflicts with each other have gotten to be much larger, much more deadly because technology has advanced the weapons. We can be targeted better and are better targets for exploitation. Legally, African countries are independent but most African countries are grappling with the debt and at the same time need to become more. Most are not yet economically independent. Other countries in the world are not asking Africa to invest in them. The Africans are asking all the other countries in the world to invest in Africa. And there is the issue of land reform in countries like Zimbabwe. It has been said that "when Africans fought for their independence it meant two things to them, land and freedom, but when Europe conceded independence to the Africans countries, it was self rule without land and freedom." So today the people of Zimbabwe are struggling for land and we see the demonizing of Robert Mugabe. But Mugabe is not the problem in Zimbabwe, he is the elected president working in accordance with the current constitution that gives him the powers that any constitution gives to a president anywhere in the world. The same people who stole the land are the same ones who now want payment for the land and are the same ones funding the opposition MDC group that drafted the Zimbabwe Democracy and Economic Recovery Act which was passed into law by the US Congress in 2001 and which subsequently led to sanctions, isolation and the implosions of the Zimbabwe economy.

Nkrumah said that "to the African, the European settler whether living in South Africa, Kenya, Angola, or anywhere else in Africa is an intruder, an alien who has seized African lands." No amount of arguing about the so-called benefits of European rule can after the fundamental right of Africans to order their own affairs. Nkrumah also said that "there are likely to be more coupes and rebellions in Africa as long as imperialists and neo-colonialists are able to exploit our weaknesses, unless we united and deal with neo-colonialism on a Pan-African basis, they will continue to try to undermine our independence," or will we undermine our own independence by selling our resources, selling our land and allowing the land to be used as toxic waste dumps. Will it be re-enslavement and re-colonization by default?

When is Pan-Africanism accomplished? Is it accomplished by all the African states being in an organization like the AU or is it when all the African countries drop all their borders and function as one national entity? Is that possible? This is fifty years since Ghana's independence. How independent is Ghana? It doesn't have the king or queen but it has the World Bank multinational corporations and entities which gang up on it. It's the dollar, the pound, the euro, and the cedi. Sometimes it seems that Africa only has resources it has no productive capacity, the capacity to produce other goods that it imports from other places. For example, if somebody wants to buy a watch they can buy one but the watch they buy is from some other place. It wasn't made in Africa. Millions of watches are sold in Africa. That is money going out. So it means we need to train some of our people to make watches, which means that we would have to have industries that make all the parts that go into watches and we would have to have a steel industry. An option is strategic investment in technology as a Pan-African tool. It's important that we identify the problem, give people structural information about what we don't have so they can approach the solution structurally. Is it possible to invest our way into a better position? World banking is a reality. International world money handling is a reality. If we were coming in on the short end of that relationship that means we're going to have to train ourselves and develop the experience. Individuals are profiting but societies are not profiting.

Individuals are becoming successful. Industries like the diamond business in Africa do well but the people out there digging in the water and in the dirt for diamonds aren't doing well. The diamond industry is a money distraction, "Blood Diamonds". But sometimes you have to compare the value of the results you get. Every resource being used has to be re-evaluated for its return value to the society. And why are we so busy wasting time and resources fighting each other, fighting over resources. You can say the issue of race and the battle with Europe is more or less over, even though we're still dealing with some of the consequences. They're not dividing us like we are dividing and conquering ourselves. It's easy for everybody in an audience to be for the idea of Pan-Africanism but it's much more difficult to go and create a viable Pan-Africanism. We have to stop having wars over, my culture is better than your culture, my religion is better than your religion and so on. The main problem is poverty and poverty is one of the "greatest threats to the environment, and environmental damage reinforces poverty." We are also reminded that diseases have no borders, so investment in health is necessary for economic growth and development.

We have to get past rhetorical notions. We are going to have to operate economies in a world that is not black. We are going to have to handle and trade in a world that's not black. We will have to get the ability to make watches from people who are not black. We will have to be like the United Nations and do all those things by cooperating with other people throughout the world. We know that is why it's called the struggle. All of the experiences of the past will still have to be grappled with. It's going to have to be understood that Pan-Africanism as a developmental reality has to grapple with the same issues but in different forms. We don't make the cell phones that we communicate so well on. The coltan that is needed to make them work comes from Africa but we don't make cell phones. So we have a lot of entry-level self-development to do in order to get to higher levels. There could be educational and development centers which are not property of any one country but collective property of the region. These centers can be examples of Pan-Africanism. Pan-African needs are not unique. Europe needed to Pan-Europeanize itself. And now there is an organization of European states, and there is the euro. It's clear that continental organizations are important in a world that's globalizing. A continent that's divided is a weaker continent. The need to Pan-Africanize is that much more and that's why we should not be wasting our time fighting each other in Sudan or Somalia or wherever. Today there are more people going out spreading religion than going out speaking about Pan-Africanism. There are more people trying to figure out who can donate them some money than you got people trying to figure out how to self-develop. We have a lot of work to do to develop and modernize Pan-Africanism. We have a lot of opportunities to work on things that we've never worked on and things that are not worked on will not get done.

So, long live Ghana. Long live the African Union. Thank you for your attention - *medaase.*

GLOSSARY

ABAKWA: A secret society cult in Cuba
ADUPE: Thanks in the Yoruba language of Nigeria.
BABALÁWO: Priest of Yoruba Ifa divination in Nigeria, Brazil, Cuba.
CAPOIERA: African contest game played in Brazil.
CANDOMBLE: An Afro-Brazilian religion.
COMMUNEDADO MANGUEIRA: A community in Rio de Janeiro.
DAMBALLAH: The god of fertility in Haiti.
ELEGBA: A Yoruba deity.
ERZULIE: a sea goddess in Haiti
EXU *or* ESHU: A Yoruba deity.
FEIJOADA: A popular Brazilian dish made of black beans.
GE GE: A group of African people living in Brazil.
GUAGUA: Bus in Cuba.
GUANTANAMERA: A Cuban song.
GUARANA: Herbal stimulant in Brazil.
IBEJI: Twins (Yoruba)
INEZ GARCIA *and* JOANNE LITTLE: Rape victims in the 1970s.
KAI KAI: A homemade gin in Nigeria.
LACUMI: A religious cult in Cuba.
MUQUECA: An Afro-Brazilian dish.
NEGRISMO: 1930s literary movement in Cuba.
OGOTEMMELI: Philosopher and historian of the Dogon people in Mali.
OGUN: Yoruba deity of iron and war in Nigeria, Cuba, and Brazil.
OKO: Yoruba deity of agriculture in Nigeria, Cuba, and Brazil.
ORIN TO TI ORUNWA: The sound from heaven, in the Yoruba language.
ORISHA: Name for Yoruba deities.
OXALA: Yoruba deity of the sky in Brazil.
OXUM *or* OSHUN: Yoruba Goddess of the Oshun river in Nigeria.
OYA: Goddess of the river Niger in Nigeria
PERFIL: Profile in Portuguese.
RARA: A festival in Haiti.
RENAMO: A terrorist group created by Rhodesia and supported by South Africa to destabilize Mozambique.
ROQUETS: Bar in Paris, France.
SANTERIA: Synthesis of African religions.

SANTI SPIRITUS: Cuban city.
SHANGO *or* XANGO: Yoruba deity of thunder and lightning.
SKOKIAN: A homemade gin in South Africa
UMBUNDU: Suk African languages.
VATAPA: A Brazilian dish.
VODUN: A religion in the Republic of Benin and Haiti.
VEDADO: An area in Havana.
YEMAYA: The Yoruba goddess of the sea.
ZYDECO: Traditional form of Black music in Louisiana.

BIBLIOGRAPHY & DISCOGRAPHY

BOOKS

Pissstained Stairs and the Monkey Man's Wares. Phrase Text. 1969.

Festivals and Funerals. Bola Press. 1971.

Scarifications. Bola Press. 1973.

Mouth on Paper. Bola Press. 1977.

Firespitter. Bola Press. 1982.

With Ted Joans, *Merveilleux Coup de Foudre* [1982], in French, trans. Ms. Ila Errus and M. Sila Errus, Paris: Handshake Editions.

Coagulations: New and Selected Poems. New York: Thunder's Mouth Press, 1984. UK: Pluto, 1985.

Poetic Magnetic: Poems from Everywhere Drums & Maintain Control. Bola Press. 1991.

Fragments: Sculpture and Drawings from the "Lynch Fragment" Series by Melvin Edwards, with the Poetry of Jayne Cortez. Bola Press. 1994.

Somewhere in Advance of Nowhere. Serpent's Tail/High Risk Books. 1996.

Jazz Fan Looks Back. Hanging Loose Press. 2002.

The Beautiful Book. Bola Press. 2007.

On the Imperial Highway: New and Selected Poems. Hanging Loose Press. 2009.

Iron Rattles & Paper Money in the Future of the Past. Bola Press. 2012.

Fishing in the History. Bola Press. 2012.

ALBUMS

Celebrations & Solitudes: The Poetry of Jayne Cortez & Richard Davis, Bassist. Strata-East, 1974.

Unsubmissive Blues. Bola Press. 1979.

Poets Read their Contemporary Poetry: Before Columbus Foundation. Smithsonian Folkways. 1980.

Life is a Killer. Compilation on Giorno Poetry Systems. 1982.

There It Is. Bola Press. 1982.

Maintain Control. Bola Press. 1986.

Everywhere Drums. Bola Press. 1990.

Cheerful & Optimistic. Bola Press. 1994.

Taking the Blues Back Home. Harmolodic/Verve. 1996.

Borders of Disorderly Time. Bola Press. 2002.

Find Your Own Voice: Poetry and Music, 1982–2003. Bola Press. 2004.

As If You Knew. Bola Press. 2011.

A NOTE ON THE TEXT

Some of Jayne Cortez's poems appeared in multiple volumes, sometimes with substantial differences. In these cases, we have placed the poem in the volume where it was first published but have deferred to the formatting of the last published version of the poem.

ACKNOWLEDGMENTS

The book's editor, Margaret Busby, thanks Denardo Coleman, Melvin Edwards, and the Nightboat Books staff.

Nightboat Books thanks Denardo Coleman and Melvin Edwards for entrusting us to publish this collection of Jayne Cortez's poems. Thanks to Margaret Busby and Sapphire for their tremendous contributions. We're grateful to Hanging Loose Press, publisher of two of Jayne Cortez's volumes of poetry, *Jazz Fan Looks Back* and *On the Imperial Highway: New and Selected Poems*, for the permission to include the poems in those volumes and for their support of this project. Thanks to Camille Brown, Joe Fritsch, Rosamond S. King, and Ruth Estévez and for their assistance in making *Firespitter* a reality.

INDEX OF TITLES

JAYNE CORTEZ (1934–2012) was an African-American poet, performing artist, publisher, educator, and activist who remains widely celebrated for her political, surrealist, and dynamic innovations in language, lyricism, and visceral sound. Born in Fort Huachuca, Arizona, she grew up in California, going on to forge a globally celebrated career that connected her with international cultural and political activism. Taking a stand against discrimination, exploitation, and ecological devastation, her work and life probed those issues poetically and politically. She also took control of the production of her output with the founding of her publishing company, Bola Press, in 1971.

As a multifaceted artist, she published a dozen volumes of poetry, often in collaboration with her artist and sculptor husband Melvin Edwards, performed her own poems with music on ten recordings, and was the driving force behind several international conferences that combined her artistic and political concerns. In 1991, along with Ghanaian writer Ama Ata Aidoo, Cortez co-founded the Organization of Women Writers of Africa (OWWA), under whose auspices the first major international conference devoted to the celebrating literature from around the world by women of African descent was held in 1997. Widely anthologized, her work has been translated into many languages and featured in such as *Daughters of Africa* (1992) and *Postmodern American Poetry* (1994). In her latter years, Cortez maintained residences both in New York City and in Dakar, Senegal.

MARGARET BUSBY (Nana Akua Ackon) is a major cultural figure around the world. Born in Ghana and educated in the UK, she became Britain's youngest and first Black woman publisher when she co-founded Allison & Busby in the 1960s. A writer, editor, broadcaster, and literary critic, she has judged numerous literary awards, including the Booker Prize, received many honours and served on several boards, among them the Royal Literary Fund, *Wasafiri*, and the Africa Centre in London. She has edited two ground-breaking anthologies, *Daughters of Africa* (1992) and its sequel, *New Daughters of Africa* (2019), which seeded the Margaret Busby New Daughters of Africa Award at SOAS, University of London. Margaret Busby's own collected writings will be published by Hamish Hamilton in 2026.

SAPPHIRE is the author of two books of poetry *American Dreams* and *Black Wings & Blind Angels*. She is also the author of two *New York Times* bestselling novels, *The Kid*, lauded by the Los Angeles Times as "An accomplished work of art," and *Push*, which won numerous awards and was made into the Academy Award-winning film, *Precious*. In 2022, *Push* was included in a NYT list of "The 25 Most Significant New York City Novels From the Last 100 Years." She is currently working on a new book of poetry and a new novel.

NIGHTBOAT BOOKS

NIGHTBOAT BOOKS, a nonprofit organization, seeks to develop audiences for writers whose work resists convention and transcends boundaries. We publish books rich with poignancy, intelligence, and risk. Please visit nightboat.org to learn about our titles and how you can support our future publications.

Firespitter was supported by George Albon, Kazim Ali, Ava Aviva Avnisan, Jean C. Ballantyne, Will Blythe, Rob Byrnes, Christopher Chen, V. Shannon Clyne, Eileen Cohen, Gillian Conoley, Theodore Cornwell, Kristie Daugherty, Gisela Gamper, Carmen Giménez, Photios Giovanis, Rigoberto Gonzalez, Amanda Greenberger, David Groff, Raquel Gutierrez, Daniel Handler, Sarah Heller, Bob Holman, Karen Holtzman, John Keene, Parag Rajendra Khandhar, Rosamond S. King, Katy Lederer, Eunice Lee, Shari Leinwand, Daniel Levine, Aditi Machado, Elizabeth Madans, Ricardo Maldonado, Shelby May, Pooja Mehta, Ethan Mitchell, Reginald Moore, Claudia Morgan, Caren Motika, Elizabeth Motika, Patrick Rosal, Asker Saeed, The Leslie Scalapino - O Books Fund, Amy Scholder, Thomas Shardlow, Rebecca Shea, Evie Shockley, Eric Suchyta, Benjamin Taylor, Roberto Tejada, Mohan Trivedi, Eliot Weinberger, Jerrie Whitfield & Richard Motika, Clay Williams, and Issam Zineh.

We thank the above individuals for their generosity and commitment to the mission of Nightboat Books.

This book is supported, in part, by grants from iF, A Foundation for Radical Possibility, the New York City Department of Cultural Affairs in partnership with the City Council, and the New York State Council on the Arts with the support of the Office of the Governor and the New York State Legislature.

WASHINGTON D.C.
TEN

For:

Family, Friends & Poets